. . . why did you leave in the first place?
The answer to that is in the code,
The code name for America was "Our Mother"
You fight for what you love.
You fight for what is yours.

—TOM HUNTER,
NAVAJO CODE TALKER

Nihizaad bee nidasiibaa'

Code Talker
Stories

Laura Tohe
Photographs by Deborah O'Grady

RIO NUEVO
PUBLISHERS

Rio Nuevo Publishers®
P.O. Box 5250
Tucson, AZ 85703-0250
(520) 623-9558, www.rionuevo.com

Navajo transcription and translation by Dr. Jennifer Wheeler.
English transcription by Deswood Tillman.
Map © 2012 by Tom Jonas.

Navajo title on cover and on title page translates to
"Armed with our language we went to war."

On the front cover: Jack Jones.
On the back cover: King Mike.
On page ii: Tom Jones (right) with fellow marines.

Book design: Rudy Ramos Design
Printed in United States of America

10 9 8 7 6 5 4 3 2 1

Library of Congress Cataloging-in-Publication Data

Tohe, Laura.
Code talker stories / by Laura Tohe ; photographs by Deborah O'Grady.
   p. cm.
Includes index.
ISBN 978-1-933855-74-5 (pbk. : alk. paper) -- ISBN 1-933855-74-6 (pbk. : alk. paper)
1. Navajo code talkers--Biography. 2. Navajo code talkers--Interviews. 3. World War, 1939-1945--Cryptography. 4. World War, 1939-1945--Personal narratives, American. 5. World War, 1939-1945--Participation, Indian. 6. United States. Marine Corps--Biography. 7. Marines--United States--Biography. 8. Navajo Indians--Biography. I. Title.
D810.C88T64 2012
940.54'8673--dc23
                          2012026388

To the memories of my father, Benson Tohe, Code Talker, and to my brother, David Tohe, Green Beret.

Also in honor of and with utmost gratitude to the Navajo Code Talkers armed with Diné Bizaad, The People's Language, who served America for love of family, community, nation, and homeland. In honor of Robert, Ben, Marc, Patricia, and my sons, Jerame and Dez. To the families and descendants of the Code Talkers, and the Navajo Nation.

In Memoriam
Jimmy Begay, Keith Little, Samuel Tso, Frank Chee Willeto

Benson Tohe, shortly after he enlisted in 1943.

Table of Contents

Introduction, 1

The Code Talkers Speak, 11

Dan Akee, 13

Edward Anderson, 17

Jimmy Begay, 21

Wilfred E. Billey, 29

Teddy Draper, Sr., 35

Kee Etsicitty, 45

Samuel Holiday, 49

George James, Sr., 65

Jack Jones, 73

Tom Jones, 85

Joe Kellwood, 93

John Kinsel, 101

Keith Little, 109

Alfred Peaches, 125

Albert Smith, 131

George Smith, 141

Samuel Jesse Smith, 147

Bill Toledo, 153

Samuel Tso, 159

Frank Chee Willeto, 177

The Descendants Speak, 185

Frank and Francine Brown, 187

Larry P. Foster, 197

Herb, Clara, and
Joanne Goodluck, 211

Richard Mike, 223

Michael Smith, 231

Laura Tohe, 239

Diné Bizaad bee Nidasiibaa
(With the Navajo Language
We Fought a War), 249

Acknowledgments, 252

Index, 253

About the Author / About
the Photographer, 256

Seeker returns
Earth circling, stars revolving
He steps into his place
A warrior for his nation
A warrior for the future
He signed away his life
with gratitude, with honor, with love

Naabaahii nádzá
Nahasdzáán nááyis, sǫ' naaǫńdeíjeeh
Bikék'ehgi yiizį́'
Bidine'é binaabaahii
Yideeską́ą́góó binaabaahii
Be'iina' niidiní'ą́
ahééh hasin yee, áhí hwiinidzin yee, ayóó'ó'ni' yee

     —LAURA TOHE, from *Enemy Slayer:*
      A Navajo Oratorio

Introduction

I LEFT PHOENIX BEHIND in the hot desert and headed north toward a summer ceremony. My paternal grandson was going to carry the Prayer Stick in the Enemy Way Ceremony that was taking place at Rough Rock, Arizona. When I arrived at Ganado, dark gray monsoon clouds covered the sky. As I drove parallel to Beautiful Valley, the clouds emptied their contents. Welcome drops of water fell on the windshield of the rental car I was driving. Soon, the splashing sounds of water surrounded me. I was glad for the rain. It was a good sign. Rain fell as I passed the Piñon exit. It stopped as I descended into the Chinle Valley, where the wind took over.

In 2007 Rio Nuevo Publishers asked me to write a book on the Navajo Code Talkers. It was an invitation that I could not pass up because my late father, Benson Tohe, was a Navajo Code Talker during World War II. He never spoke about his military service to my mother or my brothers when we were growing up, preferring to leave the war behind him. There were other reasons for his silence. Once he caught my brothers imitating Hollywood movies, "playing army." He scolded them with, "War is nothing to play with." In 1994 he passed on at the age of sixty-eight without getting the recognition the Navajo Code Talkers now enjoy.

In 1983 I visited him at his hogan (traditional Navajo home) near Coyote Canyon, New Mexico, and he showed me a medal and some photos of his recent trip to Washington, D.C. President Ronald Reagan had recently signed the proclamation to make August 14, 1982, National Navajo Code Talkers Day. My father brought out the shiny medal and said he had been in a parade with Johnson Benally, a relative and Code Talker who went with him to Washington.

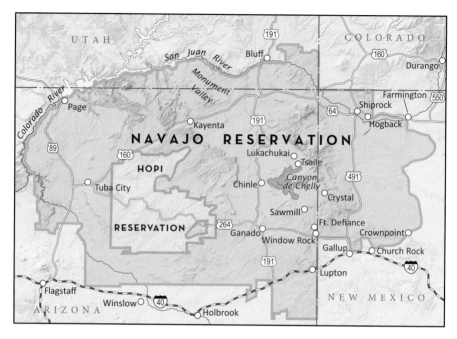

*Navajo Reservation and Four Corners area of
Arizona, New Mexico, Utah, and Colorado.*

I knew he had been in the marines and had traveled to the South Pacific. In college, I collected some of his military benefits for my education. After my visit, I still did not know how important the Code Talkers were or what they did in World War II. During the process of interviewing the descendants of the Code Talkers, I found the same story among them—that they did not know their father or grandfather had been a Code Talker. Upon their discharge, the Code Talkers had been sworn not to reveal what they did as radiomen, as they were called then, to anyone in their family or to friends, because the code might be needed again in the event of another war. Several years later, a student in my class gave a passionate report on the Navajo Code Talkers, how they developed the code words, and their pivotal role in World War II. From then on, I began to learn more about my father's military service.

In 2007 my collaborator and photographer Deborah O'Grady and I set out to begin the work that would take us nearly four years to complete. We attended the Navajo Code Talker Association meetings in Gallup, New Mexico, to introduce ourselves and our project and later to given updates of our progress. Initially, our project was met with unanimous support, but as someone once said, great ideas are also met with detractors. In doing this type of oral history project with elder Navajos, one must take a cultural approach. Fortunately, my extended family had taught me the Navajo language and my clan identity, and I was raised on the Navajo reservation. These were the tools I needed to approach the elder Code Talkers for this project. I began by introducing my clan identity in the Navajo language and explained that my late father had also been a Code Talker. In this way, they would know that my father served with them and that I spoke *Diné bizaad* (Navajo language). I found several clan grandfathers and clan fathers among the twenty Code Talkers who told me moving stories of their lives and military service.

Oral stories are considered a type of cultural wealth, a valuable resource among the *Diné*. Such stories enrich the lives of the *Diné* and are to be passed on to the next generation. "Without stories you are an empty person," my mother once said. Some of the Code Talkers told their stories entirely in English or Navajo, while many code-switched, a mixture of both languages. In exchange for a story, it is a Navajo custom to pay for it or give something of equal value. I could pay only a nominal amount in a gift card. I wish it could have been more for the wealth of stories I received.

We began our project by getting phone numbers and addresses of individual Code Talkers who volunteered to be interviewed. Since there are no street names in the rural areas of the reservation and phone numbers can change like the weather, we were challenged to find as many of the Code Talkers as possible. Of the estimated 432 Navajo Code Talkers, no one knows how many are still living or where they live. Growing up on the reservation, I knew it would be difficult to find them. One has to have patience, perseverance, and a sturdy vehicle that can travel the reservation dirt roads. Traveling to the Code Talkers' homes is a story in itself as we encountered snow, rain, and muddy roads that prevented us from interviews, family members who discouraged their Code Talker from meeting with us, interviewees who left us at the last minute, and even support staff for the Navajo Code Talker Association who tried to block our project. Nevertheless, there were family members of Code Talkers and supporters who fed us, gave me names, and drew maps on napkins and scrap paper to the Code Talkers' homes. In this way, I found several of the Code Talkers, including Teddy Draper, at a local restaurant in Chinle, Arizona. The reasons for their guardedness are understandable.

Since 1968, when the code was declassified, the Code Talkers have been interviewed and photographed many times, sometimes, The Code Talkers say, without compensation for their stories or images. At least eight books exist on the Code Talkers, as well as films, a Code Talker doll, a jigsaw puzzle, t-shirts, and other items. To deter opportunists from taking advantage of the Navajo Code Talker name, they recently trademarked it. But guarding the Navajo Code Talker name and images goes deeper than protecting the commercialization of the Code Talker name.

The tribal history of the *Diné* goes back centuries to a time when the *Diné* women and children were kidnapped by other tribes, Mexicans, and the Spanish. In 1864, under government orders, U.S. Army Colonel Kit Carson forcibly removed the *Diné* from their homeland in what is now Arizona and New Mexico to Fort Sumner, an internment camp in east-central New Mexico. At this place where The Long Walk ended, the *Diné* were treated with disdain and nearly starved because the food, when given, was often spoiled or inedible, and though they tried to cultivate the land, it could not sustain human habitation. They were imprisoned from 1864 to 1868, and many died from diseases and homesickness. Others barely survived the years of hardship. In 1868 the Navajo leaders signed a treaty with the U.S. government that allowed them to return to their land within the four sacred mountains that serve as the boundaries of the *Diné* homeland. It is said that upon their return, the *Diné* leaders spoke of changes for The People. One of those changes was an education for the younger generation, because the Navajo world would henceforth be intertwined with the white man's world.

As the western world encroached upon the *Diné*, they made changes, albeit slow changes. One of those changes came during World War I (1914–1918) when Navajo men enlisted in the military, even though they were not considered U.S. citizens. My grandfather Benny Tohe was among those who fought in Europe and was wounded, and when he was discharged, he was not yet considered a citizen. While some Indigenous Americans were granted citizenship in 1919 based on their military service, it was not until 1924 that all American Indians were granted U.S. citizenship, but they still had no voting rights. Such was the case when Navajo men enlisted in all branches of the military during World War II. Arizona did not grant voting rights to Indigenous Americans, including the Navajo Code Talkers, until 1948. This move came after World War II ended and they were discharged.

Another change took place during the era of assimilation when Indigenous identity, culture, and language were in the process of being wiped out in the government boarding and mission schools on the reservations in the early 1940s. Students were not encouraged to speak their native languages. Keith Little said the schools "had a real strong disciplinary rule that we don't talk our native language and . . . we will be converted to Christianity and take us away from our cultural religions. . . ." Jack Jones spoke of a similar situation, "We have to sneak around to talk to someone, a friend, or whoever we were with." The language they were supposed to leave behind became the language that would help secure strategic islands in the South Pacific for the U.S. and her allies. It was The People's language, the Navajo language, which finally became a secret weapon that the Japanese military could not decipher and gave the U.S. military covert advantage in the South Pacific islands. My impressions of the Code Talkers is how tremendously humble they are, considering their role as radiomen and the sacrifices they made to a country that worked to stamp out the Navajo language, a policy that continued into the early 1960s at government boarding schools.

The Code Talkers' cultural upbringing uniquely prepared them for the task they were asked to do. They grew up steeped in the Navajo language and traditional Navajo upbringing. Most of the parents and grandparents of the Code Talkers had little or no western schooling and spoke only Navajo. Boys were expected to be physically strong and not be lazy. Navajo homes needed water and fuel for cooking and heating, which required laborious work on a daily basis. The *Diné* owned few vehicles in those days. Water, wood, and coal had to be hauled over miles, sometimes from great distances, by mule or horse. People walked, rode horses, or traveled by covered wagon. It was necessary to have strong physical health to do the hard work, and the young were taught to be strong. John Kinsel wrote that one of the teachings was to roll "in the second snow to endure disease, poverty, and health problems." By the time the young Navajo men enlisted, they were already seasoned and accustomed to hard work. Passing the rigorous military training was not a big stretch for them. They were already accustomed to marching at the BIA boarding schools, going without much food, carrying heavy loads, and running or walking long distances. Military commanders commented favorably on the physical abilities of the young Navajo marines who enlisted as early as fifteen or sixteen years old, below the legal age for enlistment. My father was one who got his parents' consent to join at age sixteen. While poverty, lack of financial opportunity on the reservation, and patriotism were reasons the Code Talkers enlisted, others admitted they enlisted because they admired the sharp look of the military uniform the recruiters wore to their schools.

As each new code was being broken by the Japanese, Philip Johnston, a veteran of World War I who had grown up on the Navajo reservation, first brought to the Marine Corps' attention the possibility of using the Navajo language. The Comanche, Hopi, Choctaw, Cherokee, Chippewa, Creek, Sioux, and Meskwaki Code Talkers had also used their native languages during the wars. The military was desperate to find a communication system that was quick, accurate, and secure, one that the Japanese could not decipher. After several tests, it was determined that using the Navajo language could satisfy all requirements. Thirty young Navajo men were selected to develop the code that would be used in the South Pacific islands. The original thirty radiomen, as they were called then, became twenty-nine, as one dropped out.

They used the 26 letters in the English alphabet to devise a list of Navajo words that were translated from English to identify people, artillery, machinery, and places. The words were phonetically spelled without the diacritical marks. They recalled names of familiar insects, minerals, human objects, food, and animal characteristics to devise the code. New words had to be invented because there were no Navajo words for bomber planes, tanks, and other military equipment or for military personnel. The word for "grenade" was "potato" because it could be held and thrown. The tank was named after the tortoise because it moved slowly on land. The Navajo language became the secret, new military weapon. All of the more than 450 words had to be committed to memory and updated periodically. Again, this was not a difficult feat because of the oral tradition. The *Diné* were already accustomed to memorizing stories, prayers, and songs that took days to tell or sing.

After the code was devised and memorized, the Navajo marines shipped out to the South Pacific, while a few stayed behind at Camp Elliott in southern California to teach the code to the next group of recruits. The Navajo Code Talkers eventually numbered 432. The greatest number came from Arizona, followed by New Mexico. Fifty-six years after World War II ended, the first group of radiomen who developed the code were awarded the Gold Congressional Medal of Honor, on July 26, 2001, in Washington, D.C., by President George W. Bush. By then only five were alive and only four were able to attend. Later that year, on November 24, 2001, the Navajo Nation formally recognized all of the Navajo Code Talkers at the Congressional Silver Medal Award Ceremony in Window Rock, Arizona, the capital of the Navajo Nation. The original twenty-nine were designated as gold medal recipients and the rest were designated silver medal recipients. My father was among those posthumously awarded the silver medal.

When I began the interview sessions, I started with a list of questions that would be asked in a traditional interview. The responses were disjointed and my questions seemed superficial, so I returned to Navajo storytelling. When I cued them with "tell me a story about being a Code Talker," their stories had depth and they had much to tell. I did not want to ask too many questions about their military experience in the war, for fear that I might be treading on personal territory. I was reminded of my father's reluctance to speak of his war experience. Mr. Little said that perhaps my father felt that I was not ready to understand. "Maybe he was saving it for when you could," he says. Perhaps he is right.

One of the most fascinating storytellers was Samuel Tso, whose stories were poignant, tragic, and inspiring. I spent two afternoons in his orchard listening to his stories grow as if they were branches on a tree, each branch another story of his life.

He wasn't told until after his discharge that his parents and sister had passed, "Here I went to war for them," he said. One of the reasons he joined was to help his family financially. Sadly and ironically, while he was defending the United States, he lost his own *keyah,* homeland, and his place of birth under a tree near his home. Another family had moved onto his parents' land and there was nothing he could do about it. "There's nothing left for me," he said and left to look for his sister who lived in San Francisco. Mr. Tso is a natural storyteller whose stories have all the right ingredients—details, imagery, imagination, emotion, tension, the ability to create connections with all the branches of his story, and to tell it in a fascinating way. Eventually he returned to his community with a college degree in education and worked for many years as an educator.

The Code Talkers' stories brought out the complex costs of war—spiritual anguish, physical wounds, and mental distress for the veteran and his family. Current statistics reveal the high rate of suicides among the veterans who are returning from the wars in the Middle East. From the stories of time immemorial, the *Diné* have known of war trauma and how to help restore one damaged by warfare. In the mythic stories, twin brothers ask their father, the sun, for weapons that they can use to fight the enemies to make the world safe. They are given special weapons to destroy the "monsters." In modern times, the Navajo marines create a code from the Navajo language to use as a secret weapon. When the twin brothers returned from war, they suffered from what was once labeled "battle fatigue," and "shell-shock" and is now called post-traumatic stress disorder (PTSD). To heal from the pain and damages of war, they underwent a healing ceremony that enabled their restoration to spiritual and emotional balance. This ceremony is still performed to heal veterans who return from war. Some of the Code Talkers spoke of having a ceremony before leaving home that would protect them as they journeyed into dangerous lands among strangers and enemies.

Upon their return, some received blessing ceremonies, which enabled them to leave the war behind and prevented PTSD. Tom Jones recalled the medicine man who told him to remove his uniform. "You're home . . . You will walk this path . . . That's how he did the Blessing Way for me again. That's what I am living on today." For some, it was a more difficult path fraught with alcoholism and aimlessness. For those who moved forward, they became educators, ranchers, law enforcement officers, artists, technicians, carpenters, and served in public office as council delegates. One was elected as Chairman of the Navajo Nation. Jack Jones became an activist and at age ninety continues to fight the good fight for his community in Aneth, Utah, to regain lands lost during the Long Walk era.

Some found work wherever they could, such as in the dangerous uranium mines. My father enrolled in college after his discharge until his father called him home to help with the family coal-mine business. The Code Talkers are now in their eighties and nineties and in fragile health; nevertheless, they travel throughout the country giving talks at schools, universities, military establishments, and they appear in parades and honoring ceremonies. Michael Smith, son of Samuel Smith, founded the annual Navajo Code Talker Day on August 14, celebrated with a parade, barbeque, and speakers in Window Rock. A former marine, he realized that his time with his father was precious and no one else was "putting on a party for the Code Talkers."

In addition to their many speaking engagements, the Navajo Code Talkers are committed to raising funds for the National Navajo Code Talkers Museum and Veterans Center, to be located near Window Rock. The museum will be dedicated to preserving the legacy of the Code Talkers and will serve as an archival repository and as a veterans center.

Approximately eighteen years before President John F. Kennedy gave his famous 1961 inaugural address, "And so, my fellow Americans, ask not what your country can do for you; ask what you can do for your country," the Navajo Code Talkers had already answered the call of duty for their country and community. They devised a secret weapon when no one else could and based it on the Navajo language that was quick, accurate, and, most importantly, never deciphered by the Japanese cryptographers. Any mistakes in communicating messages could have cost precious lives. Major Howard Connor of the Fifth Marine Division declared, "Were it not for the Navajos, the marines would never have taken Iwo Jima." One of my colleagues thanked me because he said if it hadn't been for my father and the Code Talkers, his father, who was stationed in the South Pacific, might not have survived and he would not have been born. The Code Talkers were sent into some of the fiercest battles at Iwo Jima, Guadalcanal, Saipan, and Okinawa. They have earned the profound respect for the service they gave as warriors and marines sent into war. It is said a true warrior does not hesitate to take the right action. "I encourage all members of our country to learn all they can about Mother Earth so they can protect her; they can help her whenever she needs assistance," said Albert Smith.

The *Diné* and the families of the Navajo Code Talkers are tremendously proud of them. They are honored as heroes everywhere they appear, and rightfully so, in parades, schools, and at the many ceremonies where they are invited. After every interview, I gained a more profound respect for what my father and the Navajo Code Talkers did for this country and for their courage to enter a war for a country that had assaulted their ancestors and attempted to wipe out the Navajo language in the schools. Despite it all, it was The People's language that was called for in the United States' time of need. I feel tremendously honored that the Navajo Code Talkers gave me their stories and allowed us to take their photos. Each one deserves a book beyond this humble book. Their stories are tremendously important and are part of the rich legacy they leave as warriors, soldiers, grandfathers, fathers, sons, and brothers.

Note on Navajo Language

Navajo language phrases, sentences, and sections in the interviews are immediately followed by the English translation.

Note on the Photography

In my initial conception of how this work would proceed, I imagined very formal portraits, with each man dressed in full Code Talker uniform, and posed in a serious and ceremonial manner. But as I began listening to the firsthand accounts of the war and, especially, accounts of their lives after the war, I saw so much emotion in the faces and gestures of these men, that photographing steadily during the course of the interview seemed the most appropriate way to evoke visually the drama of the Code Talker stories. In this way, the images also would more genuinely represent the presence of the men, as they are documents of the actual interviews rather than separately created portraits.

At the beginning of each interview, I would explain my role and how I would work. At this time, I would advise each interviewee that if he found my picture taking to be distracting or bothersome, to please tell me and I would stop. To my surprise, not one person ever took me up on this offer.

The gift of meeting these men and hearing their stories is like no other experience I've enjoyed in the process of making photographs. I thank each one of them for their service to our country and for allowing me into their lives for a brief moment to record their images for this book.

—Deborah O'Grady, 2012

The Code Talkers Speak

I wish for sleep, a deep sleep not
hammered with gunfire and the
click of my nerves
nor the sight of bodies and bloody rags scattered like
trash cast to the wolves in the deserted streets
When I'm not looking, they call me a hero

Bił laanaa nisin, bił ntsaágíí doo
éí da'dildongóó dóó
shits'íís doo naha'náágóó
doo at'síís dóó dił bee ádít'oodí nikédél'áágóó
ts'iilzéí mą'ii tsoh atiingóó bich'į' aheeltł 'ííd nahalingo
Doo dínísh'į́į́'góó, naat'áánii dashiłní

—LAURA TOHE
from *Enemy Slayer: A Navajo Oratorio*

Dan Akee

July 15, 2009, Tuba City, Arizona

DAN AKEE IS ORIGINALLY FROM COAL MINE, ARIZONA, and now lives with his wife in Tuba City, Arizona. His grandson was visiting him and helping take care of his grandparents. Mr. Akee is hard of hearing now, and didn't tell long stories like some of the other Code Talkers. Nevertheless, his life growing up on the reservation prepared him for the rigors of being in the marines. Like many veterans who endured military combat, he had difficulties adjusting to civilian life because of the terrifying events and deaths he had witnessed up close. PTSD plagued him for years until he found a way to put his life back together. At the time of my visit, he said he had 113 grandchildren. He had been a teacher for a time. He showed me a book of Navajo terminology that he wrote and used when he taught. He was eighty-seven at the time of this visit.

■ ■ ■

I am *Kiyaa'áanii*, Towering House People clan, born for the *'Áshįįhí*, Salt People clan. My maternal grandfather clan is the *Tł'ízí łání*, Many Goats People clan, and my paternal grandfather clan is the *Tódích'ii'nii*, Bitter Water People clan.

We have been blessed. Our language is very sacred and it represents the part of life that is true; it saved a lot of people. So I usually say to The People that you should be proud of your language because it was used to make the code and history. This is my own book; I wrote it. I don't think I will teach anymore. I'm kind of crippled now. I'm eighty-seven right now, an old man.

I joined in 1943 and was discharged in 1945. I have been to Roi-Namur Marshall Islands, Saipan, Tinian, and Iwo Jima. I went in the second wave. After the first wave went in, I saw young men lying all over the beach and I had to step over them. I delivered my messages. One time we were pinned down; we were

blocked. The machine guns were shooting at us and we just lay flat. Then they told me to send the message. If there was a mistake made, it might cost someone's life. "Don't ever make a mistake." That's what we were told by the instructors.

I was eighteen when I joined. See, at seventeen I wanted to and they turned me down at Fort Wingate. Then I went back to school and then right after school, I went down and signed up again. I was a foolish guy. I chose the [outfit] doing more of the fighting than any other division. I enlisted because I liked the uniform. Yeah, they looked sharp. Hey, I want to be like that. That was the cause of it. I didn't know what I was doing. Heck, I just went in. Someone said, "You'll be sorry." I didn't know what they meant until later on. I was sorry too.

I grew up herding sheep. My mom didn't want us to go to school. I was only six years old when I went to school. They found out that I had TB [tuberculosis] and sent me to Kayenta. For two years I was over there. Then I started learning English in school. I didn't have a name. I said, "*Kelchíí'í*, Red Moccasins, that's my Navajo name." I had two brothers who were in the service. One was in the army. He got wounded and died. The other one died from cancer. They asked my older brother, "What's your name?" He said, "*Ashkii, Ashkii*, boy, boy." That's how we got our name. They said, "Your name is Lee Akee and you're Dan Akee." They just gave us a name. When I was very small, I noticed that when you talk Navajo, they use brown soap [to wash your mouth] in the boarding school. It's awful, it's bitter. They use it to punish you.

My mother herded sheep all the time. When I was very small, my father liked to gamble and then he just left. So my mother and I and my brother were the only ones living together. After I came out of the service, I went back to school down at the Sherman Institute and I started getting sick, getting nightmares. So I wanted to continue education, but I couldn't. So they gave me a Navajo singing, a *Nidáá'*, Enemy Way Ceremony. The doctor wouldn't help me. I had nightmares. So I started drinking in Flagstaff. I went down and started drinking until I started spitting blood. That's how bad it was.

Then when I went to the doctor, he asked, "Do you drink a little bit?" I said, "Yes." "Well, I can't help you." "Okay, thank you." I started walking out. When I got to the door, he called me back. "Come here, sit down." He told me. "Did you ever go to these?" He was a Christian man. Then he started talking about God and all of that. This is a miracle. I tell you the truth. I changed. By the time he got through with me I was a different person. Then when I got home, I used to hide liquor, I took it all out and cigarettes, no more. For fifty-three years now I haven't had any smoke. I became a Christian. That's what changed me. I could feel it. From then on, no more nightmares. I got into an accident last year and they cut right here on my brain. That's why I don't talk very good, and I forget a lot of things. I'm getting better anyway. I am an ordained minister too. I used to teach a lot but not any more. I'm glad I did. Some times I cry about it.

What I used to be as a Code Talker, it was for the love of people. Every time when I go around, people come around and ask me, "Are you a Code Talker?" "Yes." "Well, shake hands with me. Thank you for your service and all of that." That's the way I like it. I said, "God, keep me until I'm one hundred years old. I want to be one hundred," I said.

Edward Anderson

November 2010, Phoenix, Arizona

I FOUND EDWARD ANDERSON WEARING A RED BALL CAP with a marine emblem and sitting in a wheelchair in his room at the Phoenix Veterans Hospital. The VA hospital had recently honored him for his service in commemoration of Veterans Day. His daughter and granddaughter were visiting him when we arrived. His living area was a hospital room with a cloth curtain separating his roommate's half. He had only a few personal items on display—photographs and a Code Talker poster. He looked fragile, like many of the Code Talkers. Though he wore a hearing aid, it was difficult to communicate with him in Navajo and English. While I preferred that the Code Talkers tell their stories in their way, it appeared that Mr. Anderson might have some difficulty and I didn't want to wear him out asking questions. He did not give his clan affiliation and mentioned several times that his memory was not so good. His story was peppered with code-switched nouns and verbs that worked as a shorthand way of communicating terms not readily used in the Navajo language. He spoke for a short time until it appeared he was tired, and the session ended. As we gathered our equipment, his room reminded me of the institutional living quarters of the boarding school. I wondered if living in the VA hospital reminded him of the time he spent in the hospital to recover from his war injuries. We left him to continue visiting with his family. We closed the door and made our way down the fluorescent-lit hallway.

■ ■ ■

Kwe'é Phoenixgi danihi'diisgį́ tániilt'áo. Ła' éí Peter Nakai wolyé ńt'ę́ę́'. St. Michaeljį' ayééh ńt'ę́ę́'. Ła' éí Ganadodi bił da'íínishta' ńt'ę́ę́'; Leo wolyé ńt'ę́ę́' éí Kayentadę́ę́' naaghá ńt'ę́ę́'. Nihits'ą́ą́' fail áyiilaa Phoenixdi. T'áá nihí t'éí ch'íniit'áázh naakidiniil'táo. Nakai éí háágóóshį́į́ anáánáádzá. Ła' éí Tom

17

Senior wolyé ńt'ę́ę́'. Separate ánihi'diilyaa. Háágóóshį́į́ íiyá. Yéego hodíína'go
índa doo Code Talker niidlį́ da áko. T'áádoo le'é biniiyé sign up áshlaa ńt'ę́ę́',
attacker. Ńt'ę́ę́' doo shaa hwiinít'į̇i da. T'óó sédá. T'óó sédá. Hodíína' ńtę́ę́'
biiskání daats'í Bilagáana léí' yah íiyá. "Niísh Diné nílį́?" shiłníi lá. "Ao',"
bidishní. "Áko lá, hágo," shiłníigo bił dah dii'áázh. Ńt'ę́ę́' ńléí ólta'di léí' bił
ní'áázh. Ńt'ę́ę́' áádi Code Talker t'óó ahayói. Da'ółta' lá. Áádi ídahwiil'aahgo
díkwíishį́į́ two months daats'í azlį́į́'. Áádóó rifle rangegóó da tádíiyá. Yá'át'ééh.
Áko ndi doo hąh bóhooł'ą́ą' da. Áko nizhóní yee' ńt'ę́ę́'.

I was at Guadalcanal. Áádóó straightgo nániikai. Díkwíí months shį́į́ nihee
náá'da'asdlį́į́'. Áadoo December or November New Guinea holyéegóó niikai. T'áá
ni'. Shábííghah. Áádi train ánáádeel'į̇i ńt'ę́ę́' áádóó inda ńléí New Britaingóó.
Áádi December 23rdgo áádi land áda'iilyaa. Hayíítkąo. Land áda'iilyaadóó land
biihiijéé' diné da'ahihgą́a léí'. Abinígo. Doo áhoot'éhí da. T'áádóó hodíí'na'go
ałk'ijiijéé'. Ei tł'éé' bíighah t'óó ndaháátą́ dóó biiskání. T'áádóó náádanihiiská.
Hos'ị̇įdgo ńléí haa'íshį́į́ airportdi yii'néélgo áájį' áko December 29. Áádi
atíshi'diilyaa. Áádóó doo ééhoozin da. Tábą̨ą̨hgi shiijéé'go naaki daats'í danihiiská
ákǫ́ǫ́, gi át'é, doo shił bééhózin da. Áádóó ńléígóó háágóó shį́į́ náánihi'deesgí
ha'nóo. Hospital ship sizį́ jiní. Yich'į̇' shi'dooltéélgo ałk'ináájiijéé' jiní. Japanese
plane áádę́ę́' níjéé'. T'óó diné adashiisxan dóó yóó'íijéé' háágóóshį́į́. Áádi t'óó
tátkáá' nihił dah nida'a'eelgo. Hóla hahgoshį́į́ ałtso. Hajoobáá'ígo ńléí hospital
shipgi niikai. Bii' nidanihi'diizhjaa'. Éí áádóó New Guinea hodoo'niid. Áádi
army hospital léí'gi danihi'diisgí. Díkwíishį́į́ áádi náánihiiská. Hospital góne'
t'óó ahayói. Doo ééhózin da. T'óó nihee nidahonigaah. Áádóó hospital ship
bii' nináádanihi'diishjaa'. Nihił dah náá'dii'éél. Haa'ígishį́į́ bridge daats'í t'áá
straight nihił ninááda'iiz'éél. Navy hospital léí'gi yah anáádanihi'diishjaa'.
Áádóó nááná łahgo díkwíishį́į́ náánééská. Doo shił bééhózin da. A month daats'í
náá'asdlį́į́' hóla. Áádóó k'ad Stategóó nikééníyá shidoo'niid. Áádóó inda nihił
dah nááda'dii'éél. Háágóóshii t'óó, Hawaiigi stop ádeiilyaa, jiní t'óó. Áádóó
inda haashį́į́ nízah Oakland, California hospitalgi áádi nihił ninááda'iiz'éél.
Oakland hospital ha'nǫo. Áádi t'áá yá'át'ééh nísísdlį́į́'. Áádóó Yosemite National
Parkgóó náánísdzá. Áádi náásésdáh ńt'ę́ę́'. Áádóó nát'ą́ą' ńléí Oaklandjį'. T'áá
yá'át'ééh nísísdlį́į́' sha'shin áyą̨ą̨ nikéédiisdzá áłts'íisígo.

■ ■ ■

We were brought here at Phoenix, three of us. One's name was Peter Nakai. He was
married into a family at St. Michaels. The other one I was going to school with at

Ganado; Leo was his name from Kayenta. He failed [the test] in Phoenix. Just the two of us remained. I'm not sure where Nakai went again. The other's name was Tom Senior. We were separated. I'm not sure which way he went. Finally, we were not Code Talkers. I had signed up for something else, to be an attacker. Then they ignored me. I just sat and sat. Then, perhaps the next day, a white man came in. "Are you a Navajo?" he asked me. I replied, "Yes." "Well, then come with me," he said and took me to a place where learning was going on. There were many Code Talkers there. They were apparently learning. We were there about two months learning. And then I even went to the rifle range. It was good. But I didn't learn it quickly.

I was at Guadalcanal. And then we all came straight back. I'm not sure how many months we spent again. And then in December or November we went to a place called New Guinea. On foot, ceaselessly. We trained there again then on to New Britain. We landed there on December 23 at sunrise. When we landed, we got onto the land where people were fighting. In the morning, stillness. Then suddenly fighting began. We sat all night and the next day. Then the night passed again. In the morning, as we progressed, there was an airport somewhere, and it was December 29. There I was injured. Things became unclear. We spent about two nights on the water's edge there, I think; I don't remember.

And then they told us they were transporting us somewhere again. It was said that there was a hospital ship. It is said that when I was being carried there, fighting began again. The Japanese planes arrived from there. The people just threw me down and ran off somewhere. We were just floating on the water. I don't know when it was over. We finally arrived at the hospital ship. We were carried onto it. And then they said [we were in] New Guinea.

We were taken there to an army hospital. I'm not sure how many days we spent there again. There were many in the hospital. It was chaotic. We were just hot. And then we were carried onto the hospital ship again. We sailed off again. There must have been a bridge somewhere. We went straight again. We were transported to a navy hospital again. I'm not sure how many more nights we spent again. I don't know. Perhaps a month passed again; I'm not sure. And then I was told that I was going back to the States. And then we sailed off again. I'm not sure where, but I was told we made a stop at Hawaii. And then I'm not sure how far, but we arrived at a hospital at Oakland, California. They said it was Oakland Hospital. And then I got well. Then I went to Yosemite National Park. I stayed there again. Then back to Oakland. I guess I got well because I started walking slowly again.

Jimmy Begay

July 6, 2009, Sawmill, Arizona

JIMMY BEGAY LOOKED QUITE DIGNIFIED in his yellow Code Talker shirt and silver and turquoise bolo tie. His wife and son, Perry, were nearby. Perry is his father's escort, driver, and guide; it is often customary among the *Diné* to have a child or grandchild take this responsibility when the parents become elderly and need help. Mr. Begay didn't say how many children he had, only that one son lives in Crownpoint and the others live in Albuquerque. He enlisted when he was almost seventeen years old. He spoke of the harsh existence herding sheep, but it did not compare to the cruel treatment he received at school, where he wasn't allowed to speak the Navajo language. Nevertheless, he participated in sporting events, including boxing, while at the school. After returning from the war, he worked as a security guard at the Bellemont Depot, an ammunition camp in Flagstaff. Ironically, he met some Japanese people there that he said were "pretty nice" to him. After the plant closed, he became a lumberjack and eventually learned how to operate a power saw for a lumber company. When word got out that he knew everything about fixing and operating power saws, he was offered training in chainsaw operation and was promoted to chainsaw dealer. In 1950 he put his carpentry skills to work and built the home for his family that he was currently living in. Without any help from the military, he built it little by little. "Still in it," he says.

In preparation for his departure to the war, his grandfather gave him a protection blessing and another blessing when he returned. Like many veterans, he suffered from traumatic dreams of the war. Mr. Begay knows firsthand the perils of entering a war and, like his grandfather who blessed him, he offers prayers for the younger generation of men and women headed for military service.

Naaneesht'ézhí Táchii'nii. Kinyaa'áanii éí báshíshchíín. Honághááhnii dóó Tótsohnii éí dashicheii ádaat'é. I am Charcoal Streak People of the Red Running into Water clan. I am born for Towering House. One Who Walks Around clan and the Big Water are my maternal grandfathers.

■ ■ ■

Well, my folks came from the other side of Sanders near Holbrook there, up this way. That's where they used to have a cattle ranch. That's where my dad's from, over there. Shimá éí naghái Tsézhiní dahojiní níléí Tóhaach'i níwohdi níléí halgaidi. Áádęę' shimá ndaakai shimá yázhí da danilǫo. Haashį́į́t'áo ahidahidiikai sha'shin. Áko kéyah ńdahodii'ąa lá naghái Ch'óshgai Mountain bikáá'gi. Ákwe'é éí nda'niilkaad ńt'ę́ę́'. Dóó béégashii da łį́į' da holǫo. Kot'áo éí bee nihiyaa dahoo'a'.

Shighan éí Red Lakegóó atiin old road dził bitsį́įgóó atiin ńt'ę́ę́'. About six miles daats'í Fort Defiancejį'. Ákwe'é tó háálį. Éí ákwe'é shighan kéyah ałdó'. Two acres nihikéyah ńt'ę́ę́'. T'ahdii ákwe'é kééhwiit'į. Kin bighą́ą́'di éí shį́įgo kééhwiit'į. Sometime we move down to Lukachukai at winter. Kojigo dó' Crownpoint áájigo ałdó' ńdadii'nééh ńt'ę́ę́' with the sheep. That's just the way we were raised. Deesk'aazgo éí deesk'aaz. Sheep bikági danihi'éé' ńt'ę́ę́'. Násdǫ́ǫ́zgo biyi'déé' ditł'ogo. Nihiké'achogii ałdó' t'áá éí bee nda'niilkaad ńt'ę́ę́'. Shínaaí éí táá' ńt'ę́ę́'. Ła' éí bił daneedzá dóó bił da'íiníílta'.

Áádóó ólta' éí Fort Defiance Indian School ákwe'é éí ndanihidziznil shí dóó shitsilí. Ániilts'isí sha'shin áyąą doo hózhǫ́ bénáshniih da éí. Shí daats'í seven daats'í shinááhaigo. Shitsilí éí five daats'í bináahaigo ákwe'é ndanihidziznil. Ákwe'é da'íiníílta' ńt'ę́ę́'. Áko t'áá íyisíí, at that time they were kind of siláo k'ehjí nahalǫo da'jółta' lá áko. You march to school, you march to where we eat, to where they train us at boarding school. The Board Advisor's name was Mr. Caro joolyéo. He was First World War I. Éí siláo jíłįi ńt'ę́ę́'. Ákot'áo éí ákwe'é nihiyaa dahoo'a' da'íiníílta'go. We march to school, everywhere we go, dining, moviegóó da ałnáádeiikahgo. Ákót'áo nihiyaa dahoo'a' ákwe'é Indian Schoolgi march ádeel'ǫo ákót'áo t'éíyá. Áádóó t'áále'égóó naanish ádaałts'ísígíí éí da bídahwiil'aah like, carpenter, shoes maker, and all that. T'áá nihí nihikee' ádeiil'įi ńt'ę́ę́' nihikee' bigházhashgo. Ńdeiilkadgo da. That's how they raised us. It was pretty strict. T'áá íyisíí t'áá yéégo bee atsxis da nihídahidéélnáá'. T'áádoo le'é ajiisihgo, they treat you that way. T'áádóó ńléí schooldi dó', when we go to school and we talk Navajo over there they

punish you. Ákót'áo tídanihijił'įi ńt'ę́ę́'. They whip us sometime. Sometime nihílátł'ááhdéé' ńdeenitłał ńt'ę́ę́', teachers. Kót'áo nihiyaa dahooł'a'.

Áádóó jooł da bee ndeii'né éí football dóó baseball da. Áádóó boxing team da atah nishłįi ńt'ę́ę́'. Wrestle da. I was playing football too. Baseball. Ákót'áo nihiyaa dahooł'a'. Those advisors, Mr. Caro joolyé. Ha'át'íí shį́į́ át'ée sha'shin, naakaii daats'í át'é. Ałníí'dóó łahjį' éíyá t'áá bilagáana sha'shin. Éí nishłį́ éí doo níi da. T'óó ákót'é. Ákó teachers dó' t'áá ákót'é mistreat us. Ń danihinłtsxisgo da. Ako Diné k'ehjí éí doo yádeiilti' da bilagáana k'ehjí t'éíyá. Ákót'áo éí yá da'ííníílta' ńt'ę́ę́', ao'. Kind of hard, áko. Áko boxing team atah nishłį́igo éí nízaadgóó tándiikah like, Phoenix, Albuquerque, Santa Fe.

Shádí dó' hółǫo ńt'ę́ę́'. Táá'. Naaki éí íílta' Wingatedi. Éí dó' biyaa dahoo'a' áájí ólta'jí. Nihí éí akéé'di índa ndanihijiznil. Ákót'áo łą́ą́ kééhwiit'ǫo ndahashzhiizh. Dibé éí lą'í da ńt'éé'. Áyǫǫ dį́į́'go ał'ąą shijéé' ńt'ę́ę́'. Éí télii yikéé' nda'ałjidgo nda'niilkaad ńt'ę́ę́'. T'áá e'e'ááhí da ńdanihiilkááhgo. Ákót'áo éí nihiyaa dahoo'a't'áá hooghangi. Dóó ako 1942jį' ahoolzhiizh. December seven daashin éí Japanese shį́į́ ashjǫǫ náádayiidlaa Hawaii ákódayiilaa. T'óó ákódzaa. Áádóó ashiiké bił ahéédahoszinígíí boxing team bił atah danishłį́ yę́ę́ da. Sports da'niitahą́ą́. Dikwíí shį́į́ tániilt'áo éí íyisíí join the marines dadii'nǫo áádóó t'óó ádadii'níi ńt'ę́ę́' t'áá ákódzaa. We joined the marines. K'adę́ę́' seventeen shinááhááhgo ákót'áo enlist áshlaa one month hadziihgo.

■ ■ ■

Well, my folks come from the other side of Sanders near Holbrook there. That's where they used to have a cattle ranch. That's where my dad's from, over there. My mom is from Black Rock they call it, past Tohatchi at the valley. That's where my mother comes from, my aunts and them. I'm not sure how they all got together. They chose land on top of Chuska Mountain. That's where we used to herd sheep. And there were cows and horses. That's what we were raised with.

My home was on the way to Red Lake on the old road near the mountain. It is about six miles to Fort Defiance. There's a spring there. That's where my home is plus land. We used to have two acres of land. We still live there. In the summertime, we live just above our home. Sometime we move down to Lukachukai in winter. This way too, toward Crownpoint, we used to move with the sheep. That's just the way we were raised. When it was cold, it was cold. Sheepskins were our clothes with the wool inside out. We used it as our loafers, too, when we herded sheep. I was raised with three older brothers. I went to school with one of them.

As for school, they put us at Fort Defiance Indian School, me and my younger brother. I must have been small because I don't remember it well. I must have been seven years old. My brother must have been five years old when they put us there. That's where we attended school. At that time they were very strict, using military means, at school. You march to school; you march to where we eat, to where they train us at boarding school. The Board Advisor's name was Mr. Caro. He was in World War I. He was a veteran. That's how we were raised while we were going to school there. We march to school, everywhere we go, dining, even to the movies. That's how we were raised there at the Indian School, having to march everywhere. And then we learned minor jobs like carpentry, shoemaker, and all that. We used to make our own shoes when our shoes got worn out, even sewing them. That's how they raised us. It was pretty strict. We were even severely punished with whips. When you made a mistake, they treat you that way. Also, when we go to school and we talk Navajo over there, they punish you. That's how they abused us. They whipped us sometime. Sometimes teachers whipped the palm of our hands. This is how we were raised.

And then we played sports like football and baseball. And I used to be part of the boxing team, even wrestling. I was playing football too, and baseball. That's how we were raised by our advisors. Mr. Caro is what he was called. I'm not sure what he is, perhaps half-Mexican, the other half must have been white. He never identified himself that way. That's just how it is. So the teachers were like that, mistreating us by whipping us and such. So we did not speak Navajo, just English. That's how we were going to school, yes. So it was kind of hard. When

I was on the boxing team, we used to travel far, like to Phoenix, Albuquerque, and Santa Fe.

I used to have older sisters too. Three. Two of them attended school at Wingate. They were raised at school also. We were placed last. That's how we lived through those times. There was a lot of sheep. I know because they were divided into four herds. We used to herd them with donkeys. We used to sleep anywhere when the sun set. That's how we were raised at home. And then 1942 came. I think it was December 7th when the Japanese attacked Hawaii. That's what happened. And then the boys that I knew, those who were on the boxing team with me, those of us in sports, and I wanted to join the marines, especially three of us. We were sort of just kidding, but it happened. We joined the marines. I was almost seventeen years old when I enlisted, about a month away.

■ ■ ■

They taught us how to fight with rifle and knife, man to man. That's how they trained us. Pretty rough. The only thing happened just before we finished boot camp. They put us in the water to swim. Nobody knew how to swim. One sergeant said, "What's wrong with you guys? Never seen the water?" We said, "We don't have no water on the reservation." So they taught us how to swim.

Sometimes I received a message; sometimes I sent the message. [If your radio was busted] you had to run over there, sneak around. Some of them, they give you a .45, then another gives you a small rifle. The rifle was kind of heavy. Sometimes you had to crawl, sometimes you had to run in the brush, high-tail it in there. I guess some of them didn't make it. I don't know. That's how they did this, some of them. So you just have to send that message.

My grandfather gave me a one-night ceremony. That's how I went in. We did all right. Some of them, I guess they kind of had a hard time, you know. A lot of them were lucky. But if you had a ceremony like that, my grandfather said, "This shield, you're going to put it on you. No matter how good of a shooter he is, if he decides to shoot you, this bullet won't go through; it'll come out all right, but it won't go through," he told me. He showed me. I remember this. He gave me a small stone. It was an arrowhead. I carried that one around. I don't know where I put it. I still had it. Some time ago, all of a sudden, I missed it. That's what he told me. Keep that one on your body all the time. So, yeah, I had a lot of close calls. They threw the dust on you. It rains. Sometimes you go to sleep in the foxhole, sometimes you wake up and you're sitting in the water, laying in the water, when it rained. Because the rains came down when it's warm; it's hot over there. I guess you might call it lucky. You'll survive.

I guess the prayers had a lot to do with it. So I respect a lot of it that way. After I came back, my grandfather did the same thing. Overnight he took me out, outside in the morning, maybe four or five o'clock in the morning. Took the water out, then they washed you out and then they put on white corn pollen. They dry you with that one out by where they throw the ash. That's what they do, some more prayers, more singing. And then they say, "Don't bother you," like imagination. Sometime you start dreaming about it. They say, "Don't come to you." It didn't to me. It was pretty good until I got sick over there in Albuquerque. I don't know. Drove me nuts almost. Dreamed a little bit about those things.

Why in the heck didn't they let us talk Navajo over here and now we use it over there? Some things don't go together. You know, I didn't even think about those things when I was over there until I came back. I was puzzled about why. And then I kept thinking about it. And then I learned how to pray a little bit, not a whole lot. I prayed for a lot of Vietnam veterans when they were leaving, like when my grandpa used to do it. So I put that thing together with the prayers. See, the animals, the insects, they were made by the Almighty. So they're just like us, like humans. A life on Mother Earth, birds, eagles, and all those. Then I think about it. Then finally put it together. So no worry about it—the animals, insects, all that, I guess. The Indians, these old people, they say, "You are just the same as Christ, Jesus." Jesus went to the mountain and prayed. And Navajos did the same thing. During the Civil War around here, they go to the mountain, like the sacred mountain, the four sacred mountains. So I figured we got help from the Almighty. Because the other people they were killing people. Then I felt all right. I prayed a lot [for those in the] service after I came back.

Sometimes I tell the kids, "Don't lose your language. Hang on to it! It's a wonderful thing. It's something that nobody can believe. It never happened in the nation. Used the language as a code and nobody break it. So that's something that's sacred. So hang on to it. Some day you might use it when they have Civil War over here, like at Chinle, in the canyon, the way those soldiers treat the Navajo." Now when we go some place, like different states, those white kids they want to learn Navajo. I went down to Texas a few months ago, and there were two teachers down there, Navajos. They said they're going to build an

Indian school down there and teach all the white kids Navajo. They told me, "What do you think about that?" "Go ahead," I told them. "It'll be something, never been done before, Indian school down there."

We didn't know [if we had bodyguards]. They didn't tell us. If the Code Talker [is caught] by Japanese, he had to shoot the Code Talker. That's the way it's set, I guess, so I don't know what you want to call it, bodyguard or whatever. One guy told a Code Talker over there that when they visited he said he was a good buddy of his, always by him. [He said,] "You know what I was doing? I was going to shoot you. You didn't even know." He's the one who told him finally, and from there we found out at the time it was like that. It happened. I guess one of the Code Talkers went to the restroom, and he came out from the foxhole, and this navy man shoot him right there. Can't say nothing, I guess. We're already warned. Don't make noise or anything because you let your enemy know where you are. We went out one time looking, two of us together, Code Talkers. There were a lot of trees in the woods. He went around the other way, and I heard the noise over on the other side. I ran back over there and my buddy was fighting with Japanese. He used the knife. He cut the throat, four of them. When he came back, he started seeing those people, imagination and all that. He said, "They're trying to kill me." He told me that one time. I guess that's what got him too. *Hwił niiltłi' daats'í wolyé.* It traumatizes you, perhaps it is called.

Wilfred E. Billey

November 2009, Farmington, New Mexico

THE COTTONWOOD TREES ALONG THE SAN JUAN RIVER burst with yellow leaves. You could almost hear the leaves rustling. The autumn light would soon filter into winter. On a crisp November morning, we arrived at Wilfred Billey's home in Farmington, New Mexico. Mrs. Billey and her daughters welcomed us warmly with fresh coffee and doughnuts. We were traveling with my friend, Juanita Lowe, who was the niece of Mr. Billey and had helped set up this interview. While the women visited at the kitchen table, Mr. Billey told me stories of how the code was created and of the battles he had fought in. Barbara, one of the daughters, sat with her father and brought out photo albums. Mr. Billey spoke of the horrific scenes of the dead bodies of marines and Japanese on the beach and in the water. He met several Code Talkers at several battle sites, including Frank Pete and David Tsosie. He had been in New Zealand and to the islands of Tinian, Saipan, and Japan. As he told his stories, some in great detail, it made me realize that even though it had been more than sixty years since the war ended, the men who had served this country did not forget, could not forget the casualties and cost of a war that took thousands of American and Japanese lives in the South Pacific. Mr. Billey wore a red garrison cap. "Life" was stitched in gold letters on one side. It was ironic and yet a fitting word for what he must have clung to amid the death and destruction and what he embraced when he returned. After his discharge, he continued his education and earned his masters degree, had a successful career as an educator, and now retired, was surrounded by his loving family. When we left, it felt like we had visited family.

■ ■ ■

I am *Táchii'nii,* Red Running Into the Water People clan, and born for the *Bitła dahjilchíí',* Red Cheek on Side of Face People clan.

We got back one night. I guess it was close to summer in May. When we got back to Camp Tarawa, there was nobody there. They put us on the little ship, a destroyer escort. The whole battalion was there on the destroyer escort and we took off. They told us we were headed to Japan. They didn't tell us that we were headed to Saipan. On the second day, we caught up with the convoy. There were hundreds and hundreds of ships going in formation: aircraft carriers, battleships, cruisers, destroyers, and transport ships. We were supposed to make a special landing but for some reason they called it off. We got there in the afternoon and we got off the ship. We got on the beach and the guys were getting off the ship and then they start shelling us from the jungle with the big guns. Then that's when I ran into another Navajo guy, his name was David Tsosie. On the island he was carrying his stuff off the ship. The last time I talked to him he was joining with the Eighth Marines. I didn't see him again afterwards.

I guess really I joined because all of my friends were going in, like that group that I showed you, that group picture from school. They said we are going to be in communication and for that reason we are going to look real sharp. That was some of the reason. Actually what happened was we didn't know that we were going to be Code Talkers. The Marine Corps, from 1942 to the end of the war in 1945, didn't call us Code Talkers. They called us radiomen. The word Code Talker didn't come about until 1972 when the Code Talker Association was organized in Window Rock, Arizona. But during the war, we were called radiomen, not Code Talkers. There was a guy, a white man; his name was Philip Johnston. When he was just a little boy, his dad and mom were missionaries over in the Arizona portion of the Navajo reservation. When he was a little boy, he played with the Navajo kids and he learned some words in Navajo, but he wasn't really fluent. To make a long story short, his family moved back to California. He graduated from college and became an engineer. In the early part of 1942, he was working for the city of Los Angeles as an engineer. The Japanese were in the news all the time and he read in the paper or heard over the radio that the Japanese were breaking codes and that brought the idea [to use the Navajo language as a code]. That was his idea.

The first group of twenty-nine was trained in 1942. They developed the code. But they kept about three or four as instructors and the rest of them went

overseas. So the Code Talkers were on Guadalcanal in August of 1942 from that twenty-nine. When we arrived in Camp Elliott they told us we had to learn communication in Navajo. The Marine Corps demanded that if a message is sent from this point to this point, it must come out exactly the same. They don't want interpreting. They want the message to be [written exactly as it was sent]. From the twenty-nine I remember John Benally. Another one was John Manuelito and some of the others. John Benally had some college experience. He graduated from Santa Fe Indian School. He said the first thing we need to do is develop an alphabet from A all the way to Z. He said, "A . . . let's call it *wolachii'* . . . ant. It starts with an A, see. And then B, let's call it . . . *shush* . . . bear." Like that all the way down to Z. And Z was *béésh dootłizh* . . . zinc. In the process of this, they learned that there were many military words that they didn't have in Navajo. There were no names for aircraft carrier. No names for different types of fighter planes, different types of weapons like machine gun. So they developed a code and gave a name for each one. And these guys had to memorize it. It wasn't easy and that is the reason why some couldn't make it. They were reassigned to another outfit.

During the war I was in Tarawa, Saipan, Okinawa, and then in the occupation of Japan. On the island of Tarawa, the first battle that I was in, I didn't use any Navajo. All I did was radio watch. They had three battalions that gave orders. So that's where I used the Navajo language. Howard Billiman sent me a message and I wrote it down. The [message] came in Navajo, but you wrote it in English and gave it to whoever needed it, like the battalion commander. So that's the way it was done. When I joined my communication section in New Zealand,

Camp Elliott, San Diego, CA, 1943. Left to right: Sam Billy,
George Kirk, Rex Kontz, Sandy Burr, and Wilfred Billey.

I met a guy in the radio section. He was an Indian guy but was not a trained Code Talker. He was a member of the Mission Indians. But he was a really well trained radioman. The guy's name was Levi. He was on the second or third raid on Saipan and got shot and died. The radio chief, the guy that was in charge of the communication section, asked me, "Would you like to take Levi's place?" So that's what I did. I was with A Company for the rest of the operation of the island when we took the island. We invaded in Tinian in 1944. If there was a Navajo message coming in, they called me back or sent a message back to the rear, because that's the way we operated. Usually the company commander wrote out the message and you translated into Navajo. And on the other end, the guy receiving it was writing it in English. That's the way it was.

When we got to Okinawa, we made a fake landing toward the island and then turned around and came back to the ship. We got orders from the higher up that said you guys can go back to Saipan. We got back on the ship and took off. There were a lot of Kamikaze, the planes that dive onto the ships. We got back to Saipan and after about two weeks, the war ended. That's when they dropped the bombs on Hiroshima and Nagasaki. Then we got orders to go to Japan. We went to Nagasaki. Nobody said anything about radiation. We walked all over where they dropped the atomic bomb. The railroad ties were all twisted up, you know, and it was flat. Later they told us to go back to the United States. So we went back to San Diego.

When I was in Japan, I had very good people in my communications section and they told us about how civilian life was going to be when you got discharged. I didn't graduate from high school and I wanted to graduate and go to college on the G.I. Bill—that was on my mind. So I came back to my old school and I talked to the superintendent. He said, "You guys can come back." There was seven of the group that didn't graduate, but [after] we got back, we graduated from high school. Then in 1946, after I was discharged in January, I really zeroed in on going to school. In the summer of 1946 I was in Wheaton College, about fifteen miles from Chicago. That's where Billy Graham went. I was there three summers. I got my high school credits out of the way. I came home and then I wanted to go to school again.

I went to Highlands University in Las Vegas, New Mexico, and graduated from there. I also went to the University of New Mexico and New Mexico State. I did my masters in education at the University of Wyoming in Laramie, Wyoming. I went back to my old school. I spent about thirteen years there. I was in charge of the boys' dormitory and I also taught shop and was a guidance counselor. Then I was a principal for Shiprock High School for about fifteen years. I finally decided to quit the high school and went to another part of administration. I was in charge of a federal program for ten more years and then I retired. I did a lot of graduate work. In fact, I was getting into my doctorate degree, but I didn't finish. The College of Santa Fe contacted me, and they wanted me to be a commencement speaker in Albuquerque. So I was a commencement speaker for about three hundred people. They gave me an honorary doctorate degree. That was the easy way.

One of the things that I can remember is that I have great respect for Navajo language. I have a great respect and when I was working at the high school, I told my kids to learn the Navajo language. The English is okay but learn the Navajo too! So I hope that they don't forget their own language. I think that it is very important to know because of the history behind it. After I retired, I traveled all over the place in the United States—Ohio, New York, and I went to Niagara Falls to speak to the people about the Navajo Code Talkers. I was invited to the Military Institute at West Point, but I couldn't do it. I told one of the guys, his name was Billison. He went there in my place. So I have been all over the place. I was invited to go to England too, but I didn't go over there.

Dinéjígo be'iina 'éí t'áá 'át'é bee hadíínísht'é.
Sa'ąhnaaghái ba'álchíní nishłį́.
I am fully dressed with Navajo tradition.
I am Child of Long Life.

—TEDDY DRAPER

Teddy Draper, Sr.
July 18, 2010, Chinle, Arizona

THERE WERE NO CURRENT PHONE NUMBERS or email addresses for Teddy Draper, Sr. But I had seen him dining in one of the restaurants in Chinle, Arizona. One morning I dropped in to have breakfast, hoping he would come in. He didn't show. That afternoon I returned to the restaurant on the chance that he might appear. Fortunately, he came for lunch wearing his red Code Talker baseball cap. After he settled in, I introduced myself. He graciously accepted my invitation to tell me his story.

Mr. Draper told a fascinating story about the battle of Iwo Jima, sometimes using metaphors to talk about war and himself. Among his medals, he holds the distinction of Sharp Shooter and the Silver Medal from the Navajo Nation. William Tecumseh Sherman said, "War is hell." The horrendous description of death and violence on the beach expresses what Mr. Draper and all those who fought that day endured. War is cruelty. It leaves its mark; it scars the soldier. The ghosts of war are often confronted in another war on the home front when the veteran returns. For some, it is confronted with self-destruction. For others, like Mr. Draper, it is fought with a sacred ceremony that "kills the enemy." In taking this path he affirmed his belief in the Navajo Beautyway philosophy that teaches that one should strive to live to old age "adorned" with traditional Navajo beliefs. He received the Purple Heart for wounds received at Iwo Jima but had to hire a lawyer to obtain his disability compensation because his records were not kept or they were lost. Several of the Code Talkers mentioned a similar experience or are still in the process of claiming their benefits.

■ ■ ■

I am Teddy Draper. It's a given name from the BIA, Bureau of Indian Affairs, but my real name was *Asdzą́ą́ Áshįįhí Yę́ę́ Bich'é'é Bitsói,* Grandchild of the Late Salt Clan Woman's Daughter. My mother was *Áshįįhí,* Salt People clan, therefore I am Salt People clan and on my father's side, *Naakaii Dine'é,* Mexican People clan. *My nálí, éí Tódích'íí'nii.* My paternal grandmother is the Bitter Water People clan. My family is now in the fourth generation.

1923 yéédą́ą́' shi'dizhchį, jiní. It is said that I was born in 1923. That's what my father says, but my mother said I was born in 1921. I took 1923, so I'm eighty-six years old. I was drafted by the U.S. Marine Corps in 1943 and was discharged May 20, 1946. I was still in high school, just starting tenth grade and eighteen years old at the time. They had a form with four choices: number one Air Force, number two Merchant Marines, and number three [Army] and number four Marine Corps. They told me, "Teddy, you're going to the United States Marine Corps." I said, "How come? I wanted to go to air force." That's the way they set it. That's how I could fight.

I didn't know I was selected for the Code Talkers. They gave me orders to go to Camp Pendleton. So I got on the bus and they told me to wait at the big gate, the United States Marine Corps entrance. There were two MPs [military police] coming. One of them said, "Are you Private Teddy Draper?" I said, "Yes, sir." "We will take you to the headquarters. Get all your gear." They marched me, one on this side, one on that side, to the next building. The sign said, "The United States Marine Corps Communication." At first I was scared; I thought something was wrong. One of them says, "I'm going to ask you a few questions. Are you Private Teddy Draper? Are you a Navajo? Do you speak Navajo language?" I answered, "Yes, sir," each time. "We have Navajos here in special duty." They selected me for a Code Talker. They said, "Today there are twenty-seven Navajo Code Talkers in the marines out in Guadalcanal. And you are one of them going down, and we have almost two hundred Navajo Code Talkers heading for the South Pacific. They are all on the ship, all in training. You will do the same thing. You will be trained to be a communicator and learn secret Navajo code talk." Using Navajo language in the United States Marine Corps? I wondered. "You have to send messages in the code and rewrite the code in English on paper." That was going to be my job. My equipment was the radio. I have to work in the battlefield and also repair the radios. "If there's a dead battery or something's wrong, nobody's coming to pick it up. Then you have to take it to the front or send the message to the front line." These are the types of information they gave me. But I had to go to code school. They said, "You will have a dining room, exercise room, training place, and classroom." They said not to talk about it anywhere. It's restricted and if I do, I might go to the penitentiary. So I learned all the vocabularies.

There were two or three classes every day. I think about all the things that I did that I shouldn't have done in my life, and then I got into the marines. I got out from code school with honor. Then I had to go to school again. It was almost like basic training. I started climbing trees because we're wire men. If there's a tree, we have to put that wire there. It was called survivor training. The boys were out there fighting too; more boys come in, more boys go to war.

They sent us to the big island, Hilo, where I took training again. We had to climb and practice night and day and on the battleship carrying my radio and my axe. We did night fighting too. You get a knife and go for the throat; that's your target. Sometimes for two or three days we didn't have water. It was survival training. Then they sent me out with my own group. We went to Marshall Islands. From there, we were sent back to the Hawaiian Islands again. This time it would be an invasion with the whole divisions—First, Second, Third, and Fourth Marine Divisions. I was with the Fifth Marine Division this time. They talked about Saipan and Guam. In Guam they took all the civilians out of those islands. That's where the Navajos [soldiers] were. We started getting ready for another invasion. But they don't tell us where. It's a secret island that we're going to invade. We went back to Guam to get ready. The two divisions, Third and Fourth Divisions, joined us. I got to see beautiful sailors' ships all over the ocean. *Ts'idá t'óó ahayóí.* There were many. We had that many ships. That's enough to go to Japan and kill all the Japanese, is what I thought.

Then I'm ready, fully dressed for combat. We started from Guam, but they told us we were going to Iwo Jima. No wonder we were practicing in caves, climbing mountains, and running in wet sand. We were going to Iwo Jima's volcano island where they have a lot of sand. But it's not really sand. We started moving on the thirteenth of February, 1945. Then we learned that they took all the civilians back to Japan. No ladies. The Japanese had built the fortification for

two years, some said twenty years. We called it a direct invasion; in other words, it's a suicide mission. On February 19, we got to Iwo Jima early in the morning. We can hear *Boom! Boom! Boom! Bang! Bang! Bang!* I got on top of our ship and looked to the north and straight ahead. Then turned a little bit to the east, and I could see the outline of the island. It's kind of small. And then I thought, we're going to win it. Daylight came and we were close, about five miles from it. Then we started getting ready. Our leaders checked us for everything—what we need, and what we have to carry. At 9 o'clock, we began the invasion of Iwo Jima. There was the mountain, something like six hundred feet high. This was the Code Talkers' war. We were already receiving messages in the Navajo language. At 9 o'clock the first, second, and third waves came. They were big groups. They called it by number—Twenty-sixth Marine, Twenty-seventh Marine, and Twenty-eighth Marine. I was with the Twenty-eighth Marines. We were under Mount Suribachi, under Japanese territory. There were lots of caves there. Airplanes came in straight and battleships were lined up, so were the shells.

When we landed our troop was kind of far away. Radioman Frank Toledo from Cuba [New Mexico] was the one working right there at the beach with them. When we got to the beach, we found out the Japanese had buried land mines in the ground. The marines got close to the Japanese who were in tunnels. I wondered why they blew up the caves when more Japanese were coming out. And after we finished with Iwo, the whole mountain was full of tunnels from the other end and across the inside to the little top. It looked like a checkerboard inside, the way they designed it. They had room for thousands of men in those tunnels. They came out of the hole again and more shooting. Next to the beach, they designed the sand like a stairway. If you climb, the Japanese will fire at you from the mountain. We had the platoon go out first before we made a move. And then they stopped. Somebody was crawling around looking for something. I don't know what he found or what he lost. It was Ira Hayes. I was wondering what he lost, but after the war somebody told me. Hayes slowed us and for that we almost failed. He was looking for a homemade tweezer that he made out of wire and had dropped.

We had to crawl, but we couldn't crawl in the black sand. It's shiny like glass. When you put your foot in and take it out, the sand went back into the hole. And then there were booby-trap land mines. I put my hand on something really cool, and it was a land mine, this big [gestures]. And right next to my finger was the starter button. If you touched it, it would blow up. I put the flag on it so the man crawling behind me would know. We were almost together, but we were supposed to be staying apart, *nihita' nahaz'ǫǫ, tániilt'áo,* with space in between the three of us. We still carried what we needed and the *Bilagáanas,* Anglos, they carried part of our equipment too. Where I was shooting, there was a gate, a machine gun coming down. The bullets were hailing down. A lot of marines died. Their positions were—sitting down, looking that way, two of them together, and some of them laying with no head. Many of them had their brains exposed. They were really white. And then the bleeding. Most of the crew were on the sand and bloody. And the coroner was supposed to pick up those wounded people, but they couldn't. But we made it to another seventy-five yards, I guess. And then we got in the foxhole. Then we started again. Something hit me somewhere down here [gestures to his leg]. I told James, "I think I got hit somewhere." "It's in your shin," he said. It made a big bump. He said, "It's smoking!" I looked at it, and it's almost gone. I rubbed it. It hurt and burned a little bit on my shin. Then I said crazy words in Navajo. I told the Japanese, "You had the opportunity to kill me, but you failed! Now you can't kill me anymore! In three days I'm going home." So, that's a Navajo kind of prayer.

I was carrying my bags and the radio. It's heavy. Then we get on top of the sand hill. We're going to set up our radios and the telephone. We're setting up the radios and the cable for the telephone, but we had no battery wire. We missed bringing it. My sergeant who helped me all the time got wounded and a few others. He said, "Go back to the beach, Teddy." I had just come from there. I started to hesitate. Then I took off my shoes, socks, pants, and my pack.

I thought about running. No matter how hard it is, I'm going to run. In high school at Fort Wingate the year I left, I was a state champion for New Mexico. I know I can do it. *Áádóó dahiishte'*. I took off running. I dropped some of my stuff behind the wounded marines. I made it. There was a supply on the beach. I was lucky. I got the wire and two of the boys. This time it was uphill. *T'áá ákót'áó nináánishwod.* I ran back in the same manner. "Did you get the wires?" asked the sergeant. I said, "Yes." Then they fixed the telephone. The Sargeant picked up the book. "Teddy, we were in the hole. You earned a medal." He started writing. I asked him, "What kind of medal?" He just said, "You earned a medal." And I said, "Medal?" "Well, what the hell do you want?" *shiłníi lá,* he said to me. I said, "I want to go home. I need a promotion." With a promotion you get a little bit more money, but a medal is nothing. He put it in writing. My rank was corporal in combat. From there I earned my rank and had to take care of the PFCs [private first class].

We were set up for the night. We had moved back about a hundred yards. They came right away, the Japanese. We went all night long. We got on Mount Suribachi from the north. There was a boy telling a Navajo on the radio to send a message. The Navajo didn't get heard. "What's going on?" they asked me. It was early in the morning. There was a platoon coming from the ocean. We were losing our ground. But the airplanes and the ships were still fighting at Mount Suribachi. We tried to fix the wires to take the telephone out to the front line. We couldn't do it, just too many Japanese.

There were tunnels in the ground. The Japanese came up from those tunnels at night. The doors were round. They camouflaged it so they could see you. We needed reinforcements. The Fourth Marine Division knew. The Third Marine Division had landed right next to us. We set up. Two Navajos in my division got killed. One was Paul Todachine[1] and the other one was Peter Johnson. Another one was wounded. That's the first time it happened. One was from Shiprock. Another one was Tsosie; I think he was from Sawmill.

You fight with Japanese, hand to hand. I was wounded out here. I got cut right here and right here and up here [gestures to his shoulder] from artillery shell. I guess they are still looking for me out there. It was on my shoulder. I had two operations on this one and now there's just a hole in there. My goal was to stay alive and to try to get my boys to stay alive and to save lives. The first day all

[1] He may have meant Paul Kinlahcheeny who was KIA (Killed in Action) in Iwo Jima.

the platoons *jó nizhónóo daarank.* They were ranked well. When they landed, there were corporals and sergeants. Then the lieutenants, sergeants, majors, and privates were killed. Many privates were now in command of the company. I was a corporal and I was wounded. It was hard for me. But I stayed in even when I couldn't see, even when I couldn't hear. When I came back to the reservation, I wore a hearing aid. I'm using two hearing aids now. *Áko éí soundígíí éí bee yá'át'ééhgo diits'a'.* They improve sound.

I told my father I was going to the military because there was a law. If I didn't go when I was called for the duty, I would be sent to jail. *Ałts'ą́ą́hdéé' hótą' nahalin.* It seemed like each side was holding me. He understood, but he didn't sign, so he prayed for me. *Shá tsodizin áyiilaa tomorrow daddiishááhgo. Éí shį́į́ it helped me on the mountain.* He performed a prayer for me the day before I was scheduled to leave. That's probably what helped me on the mountain. See, I'm a traditional Navajo. I was raised that way. *Dinéjígo be'iina 'éí t'áá 'át'é bee hadíínisht'é. 'Éí nishłį́. Są'ąhnaaghái ba'áłchíní nishłį́. Dóó índa 'éí hatááł lą'í da shá 'ályaa ńt'ę́ę́'.* I am fully dressed with Navajo tradition. That's what I am. I am Child of Long Life. I had many ceremonies performed for me. When I came back from war, I lost all those prayers and songs. *Shiłts'ąą silį́į́'.* I lost them all.

I was wounded, so when I came back, I reported as wounded. They denied my combat wound. They say, "You don't have any documents." It's probably still in the sand where we fought. I start walking to the west, to north, to east, then came back from the south looking for my boys, for my witnesses. I had friends still living at the time, only one living right now. They made a statement for me. Then they took me to Phoenix Veterans Administration office. They look at it. "I don't think this is a good document," they said. I said, "I looked into your book. Somebody must act as a witness to a wounded man. That's the rule." I showed my wounds, but they don't believe me. I held the Purple Heart. They still denied me. And then I got a good attorney from Texas; he's the one that secured the Purple Heart for me. Right there those doctors consented to the wound. My Purple Heart is a federal level Purple Heart. *Kodóó t'áá 'át'é Washingtondóó sign ádayiilaa.* From here, they all signed it from Washington. So I got all the benefits about eight years ago. So that young man is really good.

When I came back, they called it post-traumatic. I guess it's a disease, *ndaaldoógíí, Bináá' Adaałts'ózí bich'į́įdii shį́į́,* those that float around, the

Narrow Eyes' spirits probably. It almost killed me. I had trouble and I drank to feel all right. Then later on, I see *adláanii,* drunk person, together; it's bad. I came out of it. I was glad my daddy performed [a ceremony] one night. I couldn't go see my family and I couldn't go see my brothers and sisters. He was right. He's the medicine man. I'm happy now. That's the reason I lost my first wife. I have six children, and I lost one. I have five still living. And the last one got a good education. He stays here with me now. My other son, Teddy Draper, Jr., is a silversmith.

I used the Navajo language to save myself. It is a strong language. I was born with it; it's in my blood; it's in my flesh. I used it against the Japanese, the enemy. The way I think of the language—it brought confidence, power, and also it blocked the killing. *Nihizaad t'éí bee yéélti'go. Áko Bilagáanaji ánii łeh, "It's a hundred percent." Bíighahgo nihíká eelwod in the war.* When we used only our language the Anglos say, "It's a hundred percent." That's what it's equivalent to as it helped us in the war. When I used it, my friends, my white boys, were talking about it. Later somebody explained, "You saved all the marines in your group. And you saved the rest of them." So it's a language that's strong. The Japanese got weak in Saipan. The Navajo language blocked the vision of the Japanese and their feeling. *Yik'ee doo bitah dahoyiina' da, jiní.* They become weak because of it, they said. *Áko éídí sélhxį.* So I killed it. Never talked about it. *Bizádíígizh. Áko éí nahí hóshlaa t'óó bá naanishígíí át'é. Yáshti'ígíí, a lot of leaders in Marine Corps ákó daaní, "Diné bizaad doo chooz'įįdgóó 'éíyá doo kǫǫ síndáa da ńt'éę' k'ad, shiyázhí." Diné bizaad chooz'įįdígíí bee honeezná.* I cut his throat. I put it away, for it was our job. I talked to a lot of leaders in Marine Corps, who said that if the "Navajo language was not used, you would not be sitting here now, my child." The war was won because of the Navajo language.

Not only that, but they say lot of soldiers while they were fighting, *éídígíí yee yéédaalnįįh łeh. T'óó ahayói.* They remember it. Many of them. They write to me. We appreciate that. I go to places in the United States, many of them know about the Navajo language code, and some ladies have tears. I don't know them, they don't know me, but I'm the Code Talker. *Baa nisiikaígíí, Diné bizaadígíí,* what we did, the Navajo language, it helped the United States a hundred percent. Yet we lost it too. The Japanese came to Flagstaff, to Albuquerque, and Denver to learn the Navajo language. Then they went back. They knew that the United

States would use some of those languages that they thought they learned, but they never decoded it. They tried really hard. One Navajo in the Philippines said he was captured and the Japanese pinched him with the bayonet. "There's Navajo talk on the radio. What is he saying?" The officers are waiting for another Navajo talking. And then the Navajo language came through on the air. They know he's a Navajo. "You're a Navajo. What are they saying?" He says, "I don't know. They're Navajo words, but they don't make sense. I don't understand what they're saying." One time he heard, "Do not eat the prisoners." And he heard Navajo talking again. "Go cut your throat off right now." He said, "I think the Navajo language is kind of twisted and changed into code. What I got now," he says, is, 'Horse and horse ill' and I hear the words 'here.' It sounds like 'the horse ill' or something. And they call for numbering," he says. " 'Horse ill, 3–6–3.' " That's all he understands. And then the Japanese talk about it. They think they have cavalry, 363 are ill. The way the Navajo prisoner heard it was that the horse was ill, *łį́į́' daatsaah,* horse is dying 363. After the Japanese studied it they understand that the cavalry has 363 horses that are ill. They were glad. In the code the h in horse is *łį́į́'.* But they were talking about a hill in the code. Six was the number of the hill. So they put him under the small shade. He was punched all over his body. But he came home to the United States.

These medals are for being honored. This medal is for serving in the [Asiatic] Pacific war. This one is for being a sharpshooter. This is from the people of Guam. They gave me a medal because we saved them.

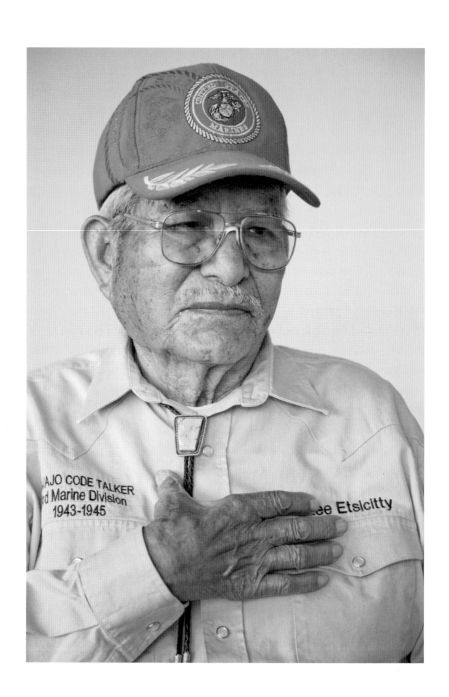

Kee Etsicitty

July 6, 2010, Gallup, New Mexico

THE BRIGHT JULY SUN BORE DOWN while we waited for Kee Etsicitty at the Gallup Veterans' Memorial Plaza in Gallup. The Memorial lists the names of veterans from the local area who have served or were killed in the wars from World War II on. He arrived with his son Curt, who assisted him, as he was unsteady on his feet despite his cane. He looked striking in his yellow Code Talker shirt and red cap that bore the United States Marine Corps emblem. Curt pointed out his father's name among the list of other Code Talkers. As he pointed out his name, a tourist happened to be walking by. She must have heard our conversation and asked if Mr. Etsicitty was a Code Talker. He affirmed and she asked to take his photo.

After some small talk, we moved into the nearby café for his storytelling. Unfortunately, the recording took place in a noise-filled café that blocked out Mr. Etsicitty's voice. I am somewhat leery of technology gadgets that require detailed knowledge to operate, so I took notes while Mr. Edsicitty told his story. My apologies to Mr. Etsicitty for any errors.

Mr. Etsicitty is *Táchii'nii*, Red Running Into the Water People clan and born for *Tábąąhá*, Water's Edge People clan. His paternal grandfather clan are the *Kinyaa'áanii* Towering House People clan, and his paternal grandfather clan are the *Kinłichíi'nii*, Red House People clan.

"The only thing I knew how to do was to ride a horse and take care of the sheep," he said about his home life before he attended Fort Wingate High School where he joined the marines. When asked why he joined the military, he said he liked the uniform, the economic benefits, and the buddy system, which he heard about through word of mouth. He feared that if he failed at getting into

45

the Marine Corps, he would end up in the army instead. His story is similar to the other Navajos who were selected to be radiomen based on the rigorous physical and language skills required at Camp Elliott. He spent eight weeks in communication school memorizing more than four hundred code words that he would eventually use in Guadalcanal and other South Pacific islands. He made some mistakes and was scolded by his superior officers, but he corrected himself and learned not to make them again. Under the threat of being sent to the penitentiary, he was told not to divulge any information to anyone, including family members, about his key role as a Code Talker.

After his training was completed, he boarded the USS *Mount Vernon* one night without knowing which direction he was headed. Before leaving he saluted the ship and settled into his small bed with only the thought that he was going to cross the equator. The ship took him first to New Caledonia and to islands in the South Pacific before landing at Guadalcanal, a strategic island location that would block the advance of the Japanese into the South Pacific. When he landed at the beach, a truck waited to take them to their location. He remembers six Code Talkers were sent to different divisions. One of his most vivid memories of the war is hearing the bombs falling. For a young man growing up on the reservation, living mostly a pastoral life and surrounded by the stillness of his desert homeland, this was surely a terrifying sound.

When I asked how and if he maintained Navajo culture in the marines, he spoke of the power of prayer. "When you want to say something, you go to the highest place," he said. His grandparents taught him how to say the prayers he recited in the morning. The prayers maintained his courage and acted as a shield against the violence and death that constantly surrounded him. "That's what I had in me. That's what helped me. I went in that fashion to the war," he said thoughtfully. "My language helped me," he added. Mr. Etsicitty is one of the Silver Medalists. He earned eight military section ribbons, including six for the Asiatic Pacific theater. His story, like the other Code Talkers' stories, was moving in that he was willing to put his life on the line for the country that only seventy-seven years earlier had captured his ancestors at Fort Wingate and sent them to Fort Sumner.

Samuel Holiday

July 15, 2010, Kayenta, Arizona

WE WERE LED DOWN THE MAZE of HUD (Housing and Urban Development) homes to Samuel Holiday's home in Kayenta and were welcomed by his daughter. While we visited, she brought out many photographs and mementos of her father. Before we left, she made an appointment for me to meet with her father in Las Vegas, as he was with her mother, who was hospitalized in nearby St. George, Utah. Mr. Holiday called me his "daughter," because he is the same clan as my father. Two hours passed quickly while Mr. Holiday told fascinating stories of his youth and military service. His life story represents some important historical eras for the Navajo Nation. Ironically, he grew up afraid of the *Bilagáana,* Anglos, because his ancestors had suffered from PTSD while imprisoned at *Hwéeldi,* or Fort Sumner, as it is also known. His mother was a resilient and independent woman who raised him and his sisters with strong traditional values, taught them about the importance of rising early and the medicinal qualities of plants as they walked to places. It was a time when few vehicles traveled on the reservation; a time when The People lived a harsh existence, but it made them sturdy and self-reliant; and it was a time when the Navajo language was spoken in everyday communication. This background would serve him well in the military from 1942 to 1945 and for the rest of his life. Before he left for boot camp, his father performed a blessing on him to protect him in the war. When he returned, another ceremony restored him to his family.

Forbidden to speak of his service as a Code Talker, it wasn't until his granddaughter began to ask him questions, and told her classmates that her grandfather was a Code Talker, that he broke his silence. Even then, he knew he had to be careful about talking about war to young children, lest he confuse them and cause harm. In the Navajo worldview, language is to be spoken with care and ethical consideration. Mr. Holiday is from the generation that believes in the sacred power of language to heal and its malleability as a weapon.

■ ■ ■

Nishłínígíí éíyá Tódích'íí'nii. Shitsi'shįį́ nílį́. Bit'ahnii báshíshchíín dóó Tł'ízí Łání éí dashinálí. Nááná Tsi'naajinii éí dashicheii. My father éí awéé' nishłǫǫ́ asdzání ła' yaa náánádzá jiní. Áko [nihimá nihineesą́] t'áá sáhí, my sister and me and my younger sister. Áko kót'áo shiyaa hoo'a' níléí Monument Valleydi. All I know is herding sheep and sometime I work on my home. Íídą́ą́' t'óó nihighan t'éí hólǫ́ ndi tó éí ádaadin. Íídą́ą́'nizaad dę́ę́' télii da t'éí bee tóshjeeh bee ndahiigeeh. Áko éí t'éíyá bee ninádahiijááh. Nááná t'áá éí dó' chizh da bee ninádahiijááh. Áko ákót'áo shiyaa hoo'a'. Grew up in Navajo tradition. Haiłkááhdą́ą́' nááníhizhdii'nił. Naadą́ą́' łigaiígíí abínígo t'ahdoo ha'a'aahgo nááníhizhdii'nił. T'óówáhádzoo t'óó jooshłá. "Kǫ́ǫ́" jinǫo ak'áán nihaa jijih. Éí éíyá safety shį́į́ biniiyé dóó yá'át'ééhgo t'áádoo le'é ánáádeiilnééh dooleeł dííję́. Dibé da bá tsozdilzingo. Nááná ch'il danilínígíí dó'. Íídą́ą́' ch'il t'óó ahayói ńt'ę́ę́'. Áłahjį' nahałtin. T'áá éí azee' nilį́i ńt'ę́ę́'. Azee' íił'íní éí ádin. Áko kót'áo shiyaa hoo'a' Monument Valleygóyaa. Áko áádóó ńléí t'áádoo le'é bikéé' joogáálgo éí éíyá t'áádoo le'é bee nihił nááhojilne', ch'il díídi deełni. Nááná ła' jiłt'oí wolyé léí' tó bąąh hólǫ́ jinóo. Ákót'áo naalyéhé bá hooghandéé' t'áádoo le'é ádin, naadą́ą́' ak'áán t'éíyá. Abe' dó' dóó atsį' t'éíyá. Łahgo át'áo ánjoodliiłgo. Áko t'áá hwó t'éíyá naalyéhé bá hooghangóó da ałnáájídááhgo éí áádi da hwił néiikah. The closest one was Ooljéé' Tó, about 25 miles daats'í. Take her one day to get there. K'ad éí áyíídí yee'. Sometime t'áá ni' ndi ákǫ́ǫ́ ałnáájídááh. Only one day.

Bilagáana dó' baa hojilne'. One day t'ah ńt'ę́ę́' Bilagáana léí' hootaaghá, jiní. Áłchíní náyiilááh, jiní jinóo. Kayenta hoolyé, jiní jinóo. "They take children away from their parents, take them to a boarding school." Doo chxoo'óo béésísdzííd áko. Áko the reason why I'm afraid of the white man is that she told us about the Hwéeldi, Fort Sumner. My great-great-grandma dóó my great-grandma Hwéeldigóó jookahgo éí ádin, jiní. T'óó ákódaane'ígíí éí t'óó t'áá ádzaai yóó' ádeele', jiní. Shimá sání éí ákódeelééh ńt'ę́ę́' shį́į́, my grandma baa saahojisłį́į́'. Four years. Áko díí k'ad t'óó ahayói nahaaznii', jiní. Navajo jinóo. Bilagáana bił deeskai, jiní. Nááná naakaii éí sáanii at'ééké da t'áá yá'ádaat'ééhgo dabííyisígíí éí ahandayii'éésh, jiní ałdó'. Áádi shį́į́ nihik'éí dahólǫo át'é, Mexicojí da. Jinóo baa hojilne'ni' áko. Biniinaa t'óówáhádzoo binásdzid ńt'ę́ę́' Bilagáana. Shimá sání éí áádę́ę́' nináhaaskai. "Áko éí éíyá t'áá yéégo hánáháchįįh ńt'ę́ę́', jiní. T'ááyó t'áá yéégo ninádahwiiłxą́ą́h ńt'ę́ę́'," jiní. Áko ninádziiskaigo bik'i néélchííh silį́į́', jiní. Háágóshį́į́ dilwoshgo, jiní. "Aadę́ę́' łį́į́' bił náánáajah! Aadę́ę́' bee ná'níltałí dadiits'a' aadę́ę́'!" jinóo jidilwosh. Jinóo baa hojilne' łe' biniinaa t'óówáhádzoo binéiildzid łeh ńt'ę́ę́'. Ńt'ę́ę́' nínáá'niilkaad ńt'ę́ę́' dzaanééz dahashja'. Dį́į́' daashin éí dahashja'. Áádóó tsinaabą̧ą̧s ałdó' sizį́ ałk'idą́ą́' army bitsinaabą̧ą̧s ńt'ę́ę́'. T'ah ńt'ę́ę́' tł'óó'góó sizį́. Ha'át'íí lá nisǫo. Ńt'ę́ę́' shimá shidááh níyá nahǫo. Hastiin nahgóo sidáhígíí éí k'ad bił nináánásht'aash, nóo shił hoolne' dóó nílóógóne' bił yah ííyá. Áádóó t'óó ch'éénísdzá. Áko t'óó ákǫ́ǫ́ na'nishkaad. My stepfather, he's from Kayenta area haa'íshį́į́. Áadi bik'éí dabighan.

When I was about ten years old daats'í níléí Kayentadi įįdą́ą́' ayóo ndahałtin. Áádi na'nishkaad. Tóówáhádzoo deesdoi. Dibé náákah. Shí yah adeeshniłgo. Nízaad dę́ę́'' tsé deez'áo. Tó t'óó ahayói silį́į́'. Ńt'ę́ę́' níléíjį hanáásh'na' ńt'ę́ę́' hááhgóshį́į́ dił. Hajoobáá'igo áádi nánísdzá. Shijáád nááshoł ńt'ę́ę́' kodéé' my mom came out, ch'iiyáán halchingo. Hastoi ła' hwá ndaalnishgo. Áádę́ę́' shį́į́ ła' bich'į̧' naaswod dóó dah shidiiłtih ńléí Kayentajį'. Áadi shił énáhoosdzin. Three months daats'í shee azlį́į́'. Áłchíní yázhí éí shį́į́ patient danilínígíí ła'[azee' ál'į́į́di] yá'át'ééh daazlį́į́ ndi da'ółta' lá. Ádaałts'íísí yee'. Ńt'ę́ę́' íínííłta' shidoo'niid atah. T'óó shijáád naashtingo. Áłchíní yázhí t'óó shádadoolnihgo. "Dijád aadę́ę́' náánáádááł," daanóo dashótaał łeh hiiłch'įįhgo rest ha'nóo beeldléí nihá ninálka'go. Hááhgóshį́į́ dashótaał łeh. Ákót'áo shiyaa hoo'a'. Three months daats'í shee azlį́į́'. Ńt'ę́ę́' ólta'góó Tónaneesdizígóó áádi íínííłta' doo shidoo'niid. Áko t'įįhdígo bééhosin sélį́į́, "no," "yes," "ABC," "łééchą̧ą̧'í" da wójííʼgóó, t'áá hayói selį́į́. T'ah ńt'ę́ę́' t'óówáhádzoo strict. Áłchíní yaa ádahalyánígíí Gary Jones and another lady áłchíní yaa áhályą́ą́ lá. Boysjí áájí atah yah ashideelt'e'. Áádóó "k'ad t'áádoo Diné k'ehji yánílti'i, Bilagáana k'ehji t'éí yánílti'," shidoo'niid. Áko doo chxohoo'į́įgóó shił nanitł'ah silį́į́. Áko ndi I've been trying my best. Ńt'ę́ę́' [I] made [a] friend. Kitchendi da'iidą̧o cookies ła', I put it in my pocket. Éí baa násh'nił. Ńléígóó nééta'sh. I try my best learning. Dinék'ehjígo I know what you mean, but Englishjí doo shił bééhózin da. Ákót'áo two months daats'í azlį́į́'go náás ashideest'e' second gradejį'. Áádóó índa t'áá hayói. Áádóó nááná ashiiké dó' doo chxoo'íígóó be'édadíílááh. "Nizazdeests'į́į́ł," ha'nóo da t'áádoo le'é naashléo secretively. T'áá éí ałts'áá dayiiznil. First year football yee ndaanéé lá áádóó boxing. Áádóó I joined the boxing. Next year áádi náánísdzá. Boxing anishtah. No more bullies after that. Áko ákót'áo I did four years.

Hooghandi nánísdzá ńt'ę́ę́' naalstoos ííł'íní nihicoder yę́ę t'ah ńt'ę́ę́' nihaa ní'áázh. "Ei díkwíí bináάhai?" nihiłní. "Ániid índa tseebį́įts'áádah honááhai," yił nii lá shimá. Ńt'ę́ę́' áníí lá, "Da'ahijigá. Bináá' ádaałts'ózí éí yił ak'iijéé'" jiní. "Áko "ákǫǫ ashiiké," nóo shimá yił hoolne'. Shimá ch'ééh ájíít'įįd, "Dooda. T'áá ei t'éí na'niłkaad. T'áá ei t'éí choosh'į," jinóo. "Azee'ál'į́įdi sidáá ńt'ę́ę́' dóó ółta' ńt'ę́ę́', t'áádoo át'éhígóó nihaa nádzá." Ákót'áo Bilagáana recruiter nilínígíí nihaa ní'áázh. Provo, Utahdi, school dajinóo trade éí shį́į carpenters da áádóó welders da machines yídahooł'aah áádi atah náánísdzá. Áádi atah díkwíí shį́į ashdla' daats'í shee nídeezid. Ńt'ę́ę́' naaltsoos sheélwod. "Report ánílééh Flagstaffdi," shidoo'niid. Áádóó bus biihishwod. Áádóó ńléí Phoenixdi áádi exam ánáánihi'diilyaa. Áko I passed it. Áádóó San Diegogóó. Áádi atah boot campdi atah t'áádoo le'é bídahwiil'aah ńt'ę́ę́'. Rope dó' bąąh nidaji'na'go. Díkwíígóó shį́į ndanitł'ahgo. Áádi ałtso nááná. Camp Pendletondi nihi'deet'eezh. Da'íiníílta'. Nááná wrestling dó' bínáádahwiil'ą́ą', áádóó bee'aldǫǫh ałdó'. Nááná Bináá' ádaałts'ózí áłts'íísígo bizaad, "Come out with your hands up. Lay down your arms," ha'nóo. T'ah ńt'ę́ę́' naaki daats'í shee ńdeezid.

Tsinaa'eeł biih náánééjéé'. Tł'éé'go. Ńléí Hawaiidi nihił nináάda'iiz'éél. Áádóó nihił dah náá'dii'éél. Saipandi nihidoo'niid. Áájį̇' Japanese dahinéél náánihidoo'niid. Shí éí Second Wave. Áádóó t'áádoo hodina'í áádę́ę' da'diłdon. Machine guns yee. T'óó yísíníts'ą́ą'. Chidí naat'a'í nihik'ijį̇' haazhjéé'. T'áá nízaad. Bilagáana ła' bił da'diildǫǫh. Suicide. Éí t'áá át'é baa nidahołne' ha'nóo. T'óó náás bił hodideeshzhiizh. Hííłch'į'go índa. K'adę́ę e'e'aahgo índa Road Man daats'í wolyé Second Wave yiłní. Áko doo chxoo'íígóó níyol. Ocean wave díígi át'áo náádiidááh. [Yáádiilchi'go halne'.] Tó nihik'iigo'. Shiyéél át'é nahjį̇ ahííłxan ńt'ę́ę́' ndaaz. Gas mask shį́į hashį́įt'áo yishoł ńt'ę́ę́' bits'ą́nísh'na'. Náádiish'na' ńt'ę́ę́' tó shił naanáálk'oł. Tó shizéédéé'á. Beach patrol ła' shá k'íínígizh. Áko ła' nídahaas'na' lá ałdó'. Ahínéékai. Be'eldǫǫh yę́ę da ła' ádaadin. Kodóó diniitł'iizh. Áko biiskání beachdi pack ádeelyaa, be'eldǫǫh da. Ákóyaa bił ní'áázh. Ła' t'áá íídą́ą́' daneeznáa léí' nijizhjéé'. Ła' éí azee'ál'inígóó. T'óó ahééniit'áázh. Hodíłch'ilgo t'áá íídą́ą́' Japanese hada'azgeed lá. Ákoyáá eeshwod. T'áá áyídídę́ę' náádiists'ą́ą'. T'áádo baa ákóniizį́'í t'ááyó doo shił ééhozin da. T'ááyó shił nahonlyil. Áko doo ádaahashne' da. Dinééł'ı́į́'. Áádę́ę́' Red Crossjí t'óó áko anídayiigeeh. T'óó bił ánisht'é. Two days daats'í da'dildon. Áko t'áá nízaad di. Ńt'ę́ę́' airport Japanese, t'ah ńt'ę́ę́' ákǫ́ǫ́ atah shi'doot'ááł. T'áá yéégo t'ahdii haashı́į́nisht'é. Áádi atah da'diildon. Díkwíí shı́į́ nidasiiltseed áádi. Áko nihí HSN Company ńdóhkááh nihidoo'niid. Shí áájí anishtah. Atah nánídsdzá. Doo shitah ákóhoot'éé da. Shił nahonilyil. Łeezh dóó dust łizhin nahalǫo t'óó wáhádzoo deesdoi. Air dijéé' nahalin. T'ah ńt'ę́ę́' nániikai ńt'ę́ę́' Japanese léí' prisoner doo about two or three daats'í MP yił naazı́į́. Éí bííghahdi niikai. Ńt'ę́ę́' nihicompany ła' tá'ádadigis níléídi shell hole there's water. Áádi tá'ádadigis. Bich'į̈' na'ádinishłóo. T'áá shı́į́ yá'át'ééh doo niizı́į́'. Tsxíiłgo tá'ádesgiz. Kósdzaa [Yáádiilchi'go halne'] ńt'ę́ę́' Band-Aid shı́į́łjah t'ah ńt'ę́ę́'. T'áá ádzaagóó yaadahalne' díídi. Shą́ą́' Windtalker deełnínę́ę́? Ła' shił náádahalne' áko. Book ádayiilaágíí doo ákót'éé da. Áádóó ákót'áo t'ah ńt'ę́ę́' shich'į̈' haadzíí'. "I'm a marine," bidishníi lá. "Get out of here, Jap!" Áko "Don't give them a chance. Japanese are really tricky," danihidi'ní áko. T'áá łinishchxíí'go ńléí Japanese áájigo ńdiishwod. Bilagáana ayóo nihaa daaldlohgo bił ahaadeiidloh. Dashinéł'į áko. "Hey, hey, that's our man," dashiłnóo. I said, "I'm a marine." Áko índa shéédoochid. Ákwe'é łahgo át'áo ádayiilaa lá Windtalker biyi'.

Bee adiltąshí ałdó' nídiilá. Áko díkwíí days shı́į́ azlı́į́', eight days daats'í. Áádóó łahgi nináánii'náh. Japanese dabighan ńt'ę́ę́' lá. T'óó ahiih nídahasdááz lá. Bomb deediiłtaa' lá. Áko chicken doo chxoo'ı̨į̈góó nídaaldzid. Áko we were stuck there. Ła' nááná company nagháíjígo chicken ch'ééh bił dazhdideeł. Tł'óó'góó bee adiltązhí naashléhę́ę́ baa ákoniizı́į́. Áko díídí chicken ndasiiltseed áádóó bik'ijį̈' t'áh ńt'ę́ę́' regiment ninááná'ná. Áájí éí Diné ałdó' ła' bééhosin. Áájí atah naaki. I haven't seen them for a long time after all this happened. Tł'oh naazhóód nahalǫo biyaadi hashtł'ishgo át'é. Bich'į̈' dah diishwod ńt'ę́ę́' hastł'ish biih déshtááł. Áko ńléídi nináo kodóó náánii'ná. Ńléíjí da'diłdon. I want to see George, nisǫo. Áádóó shikee' militaryígíí hashtł'ishgo ádaadiish'nilgo bąąh yishdééh ńt'ę́ę́' kodéé' front line iikááh. Box ńdii'ąa ńt'ę́ę́' Japanese dabikee' shı́į́ daalzhin. Ła' ńdiinil. Hashtł'ish bąąh yishdééh ńt'ę́ę́' George hodoo'niidgo kéhę́ę́ t'óó nahjı̨' ahéłtł'íídgo Japanese bikee' yę́ę́ biihí'eez. Áko be'eldǫǫh éí t'áá nidaojaah nihidi'nóo. Ákóó níyá. Marine atah yisháął. Ákǫ́ǫ́ yisháął ńt'ę́ę́' be'eldǫǫh shidadiijil. Four Marine daats'í. Be'eldǫǫh yę́ę́ shílák'ee hadayiisxan. "I want to see George. I'm from HNS Company," dishnóo kót'áo. Ńt'ę́ę́ kodi ła' shinéł'į. "Yeah, George is over here." Áko shéédoochid.

[The marines] treated me all right. A lot of teasing. Ayóo nihídaneedłį. T'ááyó Indianígíí war dayiichxįįh danízin daats'í nisin łeh áko. T'áá íyisíí ałk'ináájiijahgo éí t'ááyó, they know what to do danízin łeh nahalin. Ákót'áo jó shik'i nahayáhígíí t'áá bínáshniih nahalin. Doo hózhǫ́ baa áháyą̨a da. T'áá íyisíí kǫ́ǫ́ da'dildon ndi. Áko ndi safego náshdááhgo t'ááyó shiya nahalyiz łeh. Áko díídi náás deiikai dóó ńléídi doo chxohoo'įįgóó nááda'diłdongo. Fox hole íílyaa. Kojí éí t'ááyó tsé. Hodiłch'il. Ááji Bilagáana ła' nii'nil. Ááji éí army ła' eekai lá ńléíjį'. That night t'ah ńt'ę́ę́' hááhgóshį́į́ da'diłdon. Áko Bilagáana kojí foxhole ádayiilaa yę́ę t'óóyó t'ą́ą́' dahideeskai lá. Nihí t'éí t'áá ńléídi. T'ah ńt'ę́ę́' hááhgóshį́į́ da'dildon t'ááyó nihik'ijį'. Áko shį́į́ bisóódi da áádóó goat dóó chicken da, they let it loose. Áko ńléídi t'áá hodilkǫ́ǫ́h. Ńléídi éí holiłch'il. Áádę́ę́' shį́į́ ch'éédaalzho'go da'diłdon. Ńt'ę́ę́' kojoo naashghal. Ła' áshiłni, "Ashkii, hey, t'áádoo t'óówáhádzoo yadindoní," shiłnóó. "Nił da'didoołdǫǫł." Áádóó ch'ah be'eldooh biihítsih. Dah diitą́h díí át'áo. Ńt'ę́ę́' hááhgóshį́į́ kodéé' nihik'ih yadayiiyį́. Be'eldǫǫh. Áádóó t'óó tsé'yaa shiitéézhgo foxholegóyaa shiiljool. T'ah ńt'ę́ę́' foxhole yii' sik'az nahalǫo shik'ih yayiiyį́ nahalin. Hajoobá'igo índa nahidésh'náá'. Ch'ał kónildííl léí' hak'i dah sidá. Kodóó ti'joo'nį́įhgo. Ałdó' shį́į́ noochééłgo. Ch'ał át'į́į́ lá. Atah shį́į́ nanichéo. Ákwe'é ałdó' ákódzaa. T'áá áádóó ch'ééh ádeiit'ǫo. T'ah ńt'ę́ę́' Dan next day daats'í shaa niyá radio yésdá ńt'ę́ę́'. Shí éí kwe'é foxholegi. T'ááyó yaa adeez'áo shaa níyá. "You and me are going to the spot where the Japanese are," nii lá. Then I looked at Captain, nihicommander. Radio station ááji yínahááStą́ ła'. Ń léídę́ę́' ayóo shídaneedłį daazłį́į́ Bilagáana, especially Colonel. Éí t'áá áádę́ę́' nihił oo'oołgo ayóo shídaneedłį. Geronimo shiłnii łeh. Captain McCaine ałdó'. Éí ání nóo. "Dooda sha'shin," dishní. "Dooda. Díí t'áá áníídlahgo éí Japanese nahoniidlin bidishní. Áádę́ę́' ałdó' t'áá ałch'ihdę́ę́' nihienemy hólǫo dooleeł," bidishní. "T'óó Bilagáana ła' biłgo éí t'áá," áko bidishní. Hodíína' ńt'ę́ę́' Bilagáana ła' nihaa ní'áázh. Ła' shaa ní'áázh. "Let's go, Chief." Éí dah diikai. Kojí dził si'ą́. T'óó dah daask'id. Ła' foxholegóyaa naazdáá léí' ałdó'. Áko díídi ła' be'eldǫǫh neetin. Éí alą́ą́jį' yigáálgo. Ła'ígíí éí radio yoołjiłgo. Nihilą́ą́jį' yilwoł. Ńt'ę́ę́' naaltsoos áyiilaa lá. T'áá ákwe'é locationgi Japanese da'diłdonígi. Ła' bich'i' áshlaa. Áko t'áá íídą́ą́' da'deesdǫǫh Navajo bizaadígíí éí daashíínílmą'ii. Áko ádíshní: "Tł'ohchin bikáá' wóldonígíí." That's all I said. That means "I'm retiring now." Or you could say: "Ak'ah bikáá' wóldonígíí."

Áko Iwo Jimadi dahalne'go Navajo. Nléídi náániijéé'. T'óó áádęę' łeezh dóó łid. Three days later daats'i áádi niikaii. Be'eldǫǫh yęę naaztį, Japanese dó'. Ániid ndaakai ńt'ęę' léí' naazhjéé'. Haashįį shiilaa. T'ááyó shitah hodiiłnáá'. Nésh'ǫ. They look like Navajos. Japanese t'óó ahayói. I was wearing my uniform. Ashkii shaa níyá. "Thank you." Shináznii'. T'óówáhádzoo chah shii' deeyá. Shinák'eeshto' náálį. Éí ákódaat'éi nihizaad bee nidasiiltseed. Áádóó éí ákódzaa. T'ááyó ak'ehdadeedłǫo náás deekai. Ńt'ęę' bikooh. Valley. A lot of bushes and trees. The whole company, we were advancing on the hill. The Major stopped. Ńt'ęę' ánii lá, "Geronimo, grab some hand grenades. Let's go down there. I think there's some snipers down there." Áádóó éí bił dah dii'áázh. Hand grenade naaki ńdiinil. T'óówáhádzii ádaníłdáás. Ákǫǫ niit'áázh. Hodiłch'il. Tsé da daní'á. T'ááyó neesélíí'. Shiláájį' yigááł. T'ah ńt'ęę' tsé nahalin. Ch'ilígíí t'ááyó łahgo át'é nahalin. Hand grenade yęę ła' héé'á dóó t'áá baahat'aadí biyi' ch'ídahwiis'á nahalin. Ákóne' ahíiłxan. Booh! yiists'ą́ą́'. Japanese bizaadjí, "Come out with your hands up," díiniid.

Saadíí shįį t'áá íyisíí diyingo nihaa dahaasyá ńt'ęę'. Diyingo. Éí biniinaa nihizaadígíí ts'ídá doo bich'į' át'éhi da, the person very sickgo da. Ts'ídá yéo nizhónígo bich'į' yáti'go you can feel it. Náádidoodáálgo át'é. Medicine man niidłǫo át'é. Jó t'áá íyisíí bee hinii'ná. Bee yéélti' dóó nihitsodizin. Ákohgo nááná haashįįt'áo diné doo bił hózhǫǫo da ndi bich'ahoshiikéégo yíiníídziihgo háádishįį nidiiltéélgo át'é. Saad t'áálá'í ndi doo chxohoo'įįgóó bidziil. Kót'áo éí shił hóóne' shizhé'é shik'ih nahałao. Nihizaadígíí dínsingo át'é shí. Nááná niha'áłchíní shí sha'áłchíní t'áá ałk'idą́ą́' Bilagáana tahdi t'éí naakai. T'áá bił hashne' ndi t'áá bił haada ádaat'é nahalin. Ako ndi Bilagáana k'ehji t'éí aghá. Baa náshdááhgo díí doo ájíł'įį da dishní łeh. T'ah ńt'ęę' áłts'ísí yéédą́ą́' "Grandpa, tell us about the war, what you did," nóo. Doo bee nísht'įi da. Áádóó ólta'di shįį yaa nááhálne' ałdó'. Íídą́ą́' nihił dahodíílnih shidoo'niid. Áłchíní ádaałts'íísíí. T'ááyó nanitł'ah áłchíní yázhí bich'į' yájíłti'go. Doo hózhǫ́ íínisin da ndi. When I was discharged, Ts'ídá t'áá ká baa hóólne' shidoo'niid. "Don't talk about what you did in the war, what you used," shidoo'niid. "We might use it again," shidoo'niid íídą́ą́'. Éí biniinaa t'áá áníiltso ákónihidoo'niid. Biniinaa doo bééhozin da. Éí biniinaa áłchíní bił hashne'go hahoolzhiizh. Today díí t'áá át'é ńdee'nih Bilagáana doo bił béédahózin da yęę ndi. Binahjį' Navajos béého'dólzin dóó t'ááyó dah naajaahgo bee hii'na' nahalin ałdó'.

Shizhé'é hataałii nilįi ńt'ęę'. Áko ndi doo hazhó'ó yish'įį da. Áko ndi shizhé'é shik'i nahasáh. K'adę́ę́ ákǫ́ǫ́ dah diishááhgo. Áádóó nánísdzáo. Tsodizin shábíighah dahodííníílzingo. Áádóó tł'éé'go dó' nááná. Éí shį́į́ Anaa'jí. Áájí tsohadizinígíí nááná. Éí shį́į́ t'áá ałtso biyi'jį' ná'ookąąh át'é. Dahodiyinígíí t'áá át'é: Four Sacred Mountains áádóó Nítch'i Diyinii, shą́ą́' nítch'i łigai daaníí łeh ha'a'aahdę́ę́. Nítch'i Dootł'izh. Nítch'i Łitso. Áádóó náánáá Nítch'i Dilxiłii, náhookǫsdéé'go. Díí kéyah bee dahodiyinígíí t'áá át'é. Dził naaznilíí. Nááná tó. Tó éí nááná tó niteel, t'áá át'é há náokąąh. Ákót'áo tsohodizin. Ákót'áo áádi atah naashá.

■ ■ ■

My clans are Bitterwater People clan. You are probably my daughter. I am born for Folded Arms People clan, and Many Goats People clan are my paternal grandparents. Black Streak Wood People clan are my maternal grandfathers. It is said that my father met another woman when I was still a baby. I was raised by my mother, so I was alone with my sister, also my younger sister. This is how I was raised at Monument Valley. All I know is herding sheep, and sometime I work on my home. Back then, all we had was our home, and there was no water. Back then, from a long distance, we used to haul water with a donkey. That's all we used to bring water. That's what we used, too, to haul wood. That's how I was raised. We grew up in Navajo tradition. [My mother] used to wake us up early in the morning with white cornmeal; she used to get us up before sunrise. I used to hate it a lot. "Here," she used to say, giving us the white cornmeal. That was probably for safety and to do things well again. Prayers were even done for sheep and plants. Back then, there was a lot of vegetation. It used to rain all the time. Even that was medicine. There was no doctor. That's how I was raised at Monument Valley. And then when we went for walks, she used to tell us more things like, "That plant is good for this. And there's one called *jilt'oi* which has water on it," she used to say. There was nothing from the store. We only had cornmeal flour, also milk and meat. She used to prepare it in different ways. That's all we had. She would go to the store by herself, and sometimes we went with her. The closest one was *Ooljee' To,* about twenty-five miles away. It took her one day to get there. Now it's near. Sometimes she would walk there. Only one day.

She used to tell about the Anglos. One day she said, "There was an Anglo visiting homes. They say he collects children," she used to say. "They take children away from their parents, take them to a boarding school." I became terrified of it. So the reason I'm afraid of the white man is that she told us about Hwéeldi, Fort Sumner. My great-great-grandma and my great-grandma were going to Hwéeldi when she [great-great-grandma] died, they say. When that happened to them, they used to just leave them anywhere. They were going to do that to my great-great-grandma, but my great-grandma made a fuss about it. Four years. Many of them were sold, they said. "Navajos," she said. They were leaving with the Anglos. "And the Mexicans gathered the young, beautiful girls," she said. "There are probably relatives of ours there, even in Mexico." She used to tell about it. That's why I was very terrified of the Anglos. My grandmother and the rest returned from there. "She was one of them who used to get very angry," she said. "They used to really throw her around," she said. So when they returned, she used to get nightmares. She used to scream, "They're coming on horseback again! I can hear them!" She used to tell these stories, and for that reason we used to be very frightened. Then one day we brought in the sheep, and there were mules tied up, about four of them. And there was a wagon, an old army wagon. And then he was standing outside. I thought, "What is going on?" Then my mother met me outside. She said, "The man sitting over there is who I'm with now." And I went inside with her. And then I just went back out. I just continued herding sheep around there. My stepfather, he's from Kayenta area somewhere. That's where his relatives reside.

So when I was about ten years old at Kayenta, it used to rain a lot back then. I was herding over there. It was very hot. The sheep were returning. I was to put them back in the corral. There was a rock protruding from afar. The water had filled. When I crawled back out of the water, there was blood. I barely made it back. I was dragging my leg when my mom came out smelling like food. Some men were working for her. One of them came and picked me up to go to Kayenta. I returned to consciousness there. I spent about three months there. Some of the kids who were patients [in the hospital] had gotten well but were also attending school. Some were very small. Then I was told to go to school too. I was carrying my leg around. The kids didn't like me. "Here comes Leg Man again," they used to taunt me, kicking me, as our beds were being made for us in the evenings. They used to kick me. That's how I was raised. I spent about three months there. Then I was told to go to school at Tuba City. And I learned very little, things like "no," "yes," "ABC," and naming dogs. I became quite good. And it was very strict. The dorm assistants were Gary Jones and a woman.

I was enrolled in the boys' dorm. And then I was told not to speak Navajo, only English. And it was very difficult for me. But I've been trying my best. I made a friend. When we ate at the kitchen, I put cookies in my pocket. I used to give them to him. We walked around there. I tried my best to learn. I know what you mean in Navajo, but in English I didn't know. It was about two months that way, and then they promoted me to second grade. And then from there it got easier. And then the boys were very mischievous. I used to carry things secretively because they used to say, "I'm going to hit you in the face." They were eventually expelled. First year they were playing football and boxing. And then I joined boxing. Next year I returned. I was in boxing. No more bullies after that. That's what I did for four years.

When I went home, the recruiters came. "How old is he?" they asked. My mother said, "He recently turned eighteen." Then they said, "There's a war. They are fighting with the Japanese. So we need boys to go there," they told my mother. My mother tried her hardest. "No. He's the only one who herds sheep. He's the only one I depend on," she said. "He was at the hospital and then he went to school; he came back okay." That's how the Anglo recruiters came. Then I went ahead and left for Provo, Utah, to school, where they said there was a trade school for carpenters and welders and mechanics. I spent about five months there. Then I received a letter. Report to Flagstaff, it said. Then I got on the bus. And then we went to Phoenix for exams. So I passed it. Then to San Diego. We were learning things at the boot camp, even climbing ropes. A few were difficult. Then that was completed. Then we were transported to Camp Pendleton. Then we learned wrestling again, and guns. And a little bit of Japanese language, like, "Come out with your hands up," "Lay down your arms." I spent about two months there.

We got on the ship again at night. We landed in Hawaii. We left again. They told us we were at Saipan. We were told there were Japanese there again. I was in the Second Wave. Then suddenly there were gunshots. They were shooting with machine guns. I just listened. Planes appeared above us far away. Some Anglos were killed. Suicide. We were told to report those. Time passed until evening came. Then the one they called Road Man called for the "Second Wave." It was dreadfully windy. The ocean waves kept rising like this [gestures upward]. Water fell on us. It was my pack. When I threw it, I noticed it was heavy. I was dragging the gas mask when I crawled away from it. When I rose,

Navajo Code Talker Day, August 14, 2009, Window Rock, Arizona.
Left to right: Samuel Tsosie, Sr., Samuel Holiday, Alfred Peaches, Teddy Draper, Sr.

the water was knocking me over. The canteen was around my neck. One of the beach patrolmen cut it off for me. So some of them had crawled back to rejoin. We reunited. Some of the guns were missing. I was bruised from here. The next day we packed, even the guns. I went down there with him. Some were already dead lying around. Some went off to the clinic. We just patrolled around.

It was jungle-like, and the Japanese had already made holes. I went down there. The sound came nearby again. I didn't really know what happened from there. I was kind of dizzy. But I wasn't telling anyone about myself. I hid it. From there the Red Cross were just transporting them back. I just endured it. The shooting lasted about two days. It was far away. Then I was being taken to the Japanese airport. Something was still very wrong with me. We helped shoot there. I'm not sure how many we killed there. Then we, H&S [Headquarters and Service] Company, were told to go back. I was among them. I returned with them. Something was wrong with me. I was dizzy. The dirt and sand seemed black and it was very hot. The air seemed sticky. When we returned, a Japanese prisoner was standing with about two or three MPs. We stopped near them. Then one of our company was washing in the shell hole where there was water. He was washing in there. I was hesitant. I thought it would be okay. I washed quickly. I went like this [gestures upward] when suddenly he was putting a Band-Aid on me. They don't tell this correctly. Remember the movie they call *Windtalkers?* Some were telling me, the book they wrote is not correct. And then that's what he said to me. "I'm a marine," I said. "Get out of here, Jap!" "Don't give them a chance. Japanese are really tricky," they had told us. Although I was still nude, I ran to the Japanese. The Anglos used to really tease us and we used to tease them. So they were looking at me. "Hey, hey, that's our man," they said to me. I said, "I'm a marine. Then they let me go." That's where they changed it in the *Windtalkers* movie.

I also found a slingshot. I'm not sure how many days passed, maybe about eight days. Then we moved to another spot. It was a place where the Japanese lived. Their homes were demolished. They had exploded bombs there. There were scared chickens. So we were stuck there. The other company was trying to catch the chickens. I remembered the slingshot I found. So after we killed the chickens, another regiment moved in. And I knew another Navajo among them. There were two of them. I haven't seen them for a long time after all this happened. Even though it looks like just grass, underneath it is mud. I started toward them and I stepped in the mud. When they moved over there, we moved from here again. They were shooting over there. "I want to see George," I thought. Then as I was cleaning my muddy military boots, the front line was just right here. I picked up a box, and the Japanese's boots were black. I got a couple of them. I was cleaning the mud off of them when they called George. I just threw my boots aside and I put on the Japanese boots. So they were telling us to keep our guns. I went over there. I was walking among the marines. As I was walking over there, guns were pointed at me by about four marines. They knocked the gun out of my hand. "I want to see George. I'm from H&S Company," I said. One of them looked at me. "Yeah, George is over here." Then they let me go.

[The marines] treated me all right. A lot of teasing. They were very interested in us. I used to wonder if they thought that Indians were good at fighting in a war. When the fighting began, it seemed as though they thought, they know what to do. The ceremony I had is what I remembered at those times. All this fighting didn't really affect you. Even though the shootings are happening right here. But when I returned safely, I started to get jumpy. We made a foxhole. Over there was a bit rocky. It was jungle-like. That night there was shooting. And the shooting progressed toward us. Then they let the pigs and goats and chickens loose. Over there was flat. That side was brush. They were sliding out from there, shooting. I was looking this way. One said to me, "Boy, hey, don't be standing out so much. They might shoot you." Then I pointed my gun into my hat. I raised it like this. Then they poured it on us. Rifles. We lay downward in the foxhole. Then it felt like they poured something cold on me. I finally moved again. There was a huge frog sitting on me. Here, he was suffering too. It was probably escaping too. It was probably running scared, too. That's what happened there also.

Then Dan was watching the radio and the next day he visited me. I was in the foxhole. He came when it was sunset. "You and me are going to the spot where the Japanese are," he said. Then I looked up at the captain, our commander. They were monitoring the radio station. They had become interested in me long before, especially the colonel. Ever since we were coming by boat they began teasing me. He used to call me Geronimo. Captain McCaine also. "I don't think so," I said, "No. Both of us will look like Japanese. We will create more enemies. It'll be okay if I go with another Anglo," I said. Shortly after that a couple of Anglos came. They came to me and said, "Let's go, Chief." And we left. There was a mountain on this side. There were hills. Some were sitting in foxholes. One of them had a gun. He was in front. The other one was packing the radios. He walked in front of us. Then there was a message, right there where the Japanese were shooting. I sent one to them. And they had already shot a fire. The Navajo language wasn't working out right. So I said "onion—on top of it—shooting." That's all I said. That means, "I'm retiring now." Or you could say "oil—on top of it—shooting."

The Navajos were sending messages at Iwo Jima. We arrived over there again. There was dirt and smoke from there. Three days later we arrived there. The guns were laying everywhere, Japanese too. They were so young. It did something to me. It affected me. As I looked at them, they look like Navajos. There were many Japanese. I was wearing my uniform. The guy came over to me. "Thank you." He put his arm around me. I really got emotional. My tears were running. "We used our language to kill them," I said. That's what happened. So we advanced and marched on. Then there was a valley. A lot of bushes and trees. The whole company, we were advancing on the hill. The major stopped. Then he said, "Geronimo, grab some hand grenades. Let's go down there. I think there's some snipers down there." Then I took off with him. I grabbed two hand grenades. They were very heavy. We went there. Very thick brush. Rocks were jutting out. I suspected something. He was in front of me. Then it looked like a rock. The plants looked different. I took out a hand grenade, and it was obvious that there was a trail through the brush. I threw it in there. *Booh!* It exploded. I said in Japanese, "Come out with your hands up!"

■ ■ ■

My father was a medicine man, and I didn't see him much. But he conducted a ceremony on me when I was ready to leave. Then when I returned. We prayed. Then at night again. That was probably the Enemy Way [ceremony]. Prayers for that one again. Within that offerings are made. Sacred things, all of them: Four Sacred Mountains and Sacred Air Being, the one they call White Wind from the east. Blue Wind. Yellow Wind. And then the Glittering Wind, from the north. Everything that is keeps this land holy. Mountains. And water. Water to ocean, an offering is made to everything. That's how the prayers go. That's how I was among them there.

Our language was given to us as a sacred language. It was holy. That's why our language can withstand anything, even when a person is very sick. You can feel it when you really talk to the sick person. It feels like he or she will become well from it. We are in fact medicine men. We thrive on it. We use it to speak and pray with. As another example, when someone is very upset and we continue to yell at him or her, we will greatly negatively affect that person. Even one word is powerful. This is what I was told when my father used to perform ceremonies on me. I keep our language sacred. And our children, my children, have been among the Anglos for a long time. Even though I talk to them, they still don't understand, it seems. They speak mostly English. When I visit them, I say, "These are things you don't do." When [my granddaughter] was small, she said to me, "Grandpa, tell us about the war." I didn't bother. And then she talked about it at school. That is when they asked me to talk about it. The students were very small. It can be difficult when speaking to small children. I really didn't want to. When I was discharged, I was told never to talk about it. "Don't talk about what you did in the war, what you used," I was told. "We might use it again," is what I was told then. That's why all of us were told that. That's why it was confusing. That's when I started telling children. Today we are known all over, even the Anglos who were never aware of us. From that we have educated many about the Navajo people and now it seems that we are highly admired as well.

George James, Sr.

April 23, 2010, Tsaile, Arizona

I MET GEORGE JAMES, SR. when he came to Arizona State University to give a talk in the fall of 2009. His son George James, Jr. drove him from Tsaile, Arizona, where he lives. I made an appointment with Mr. James to come to his home in November. George, Jr. said his father didn't live far from the road and he drew me a map. On the appointed day, we were coming from Farmington and planned to drive over the mountain to Tsaile. One of the roadside vendors at the junction advised us that snow might have fallen and it would be dangerous to drive through Buffalo Pass. It would have been a shortcut from Shiprock, but indeed dark clouds covered the mountain. We took the longer route past Mexican Water and Rock Point instead. As we drove parallel to the community of Lukachukai, white and gray clouds created a halo on the red rocks. Snow had fallen on the highest points. Winter arrived bringing *Niłch'its'ósí*, November, the time of the Slim Wind, when the wind becomes colder. I grew up at the base of the *Ch'ooshgai*, Chuska Mountains, southeast of Tsaile, and knew what it was like to drive on the roads wet with rain or snow. One must be prepared with a shovel and other items. Once stuck, it could take hours to get out. The rental car was from the city and no match for the drenched roads, even though it was an all-wheel-drive SUV. The steady rain made the dirt road to Mr. James' house treacherous. The vehicle was too light and it slid all over the road. One wrong move and we could have slipped off the embankment and without cellular service we would be stranded. The sun was less than an hour from dropping into darkness. It was best not to take risks with the road, so I managed to turn the vehicle around only yards away from Mr. James's house and try for another time.

Our next meeting was set for April 2010. I thought the snow would be gone by then, but it had been an unusually wet winter. We arrived in Tsaile only to find the roads once again muddy. With some quick changes we met Mr. James, Sr. and his son at Diné College. Mr. James remembered my father as "a tall, slim fellow" at Fort Wingate when they were students. Although he didn't speak of it, Mr. James had been in Japan when the atomic bomb was dropped. I decided to respect his privacy and did not ask him to elaborate.

As an elder statesman, Mr. James expressed insightful ideas about the direction of Navajo education and the issues of administering a community college grounded in Navajo philosophy. While he did not elaborate, I had the sense that he had much to express on these topics, as well as the direction of the religious and spiritual life of The People on the reservation.

The lack of employment on the rez led many like Mr. James to seek employment far away from the homeland. In his younger years, Mr. James worked in Kansas for Beech Aircraft. When the company's contract expired and the work dried up, he returned home and found employment with the Bureau of Indian Affairs (BIA). He became active in community service as a Board of Regents member for Diné College, the first tribally controlled community college in the United States, and was elected by his community to serve for twelve years as a Council Delegate to the Navajo Nation. A plaque hangs on the wall of the college with his name on it.

■ ■ ■

I am *Tóhtsohnii,* Big Water clan and I am born for the *Ma'ii deeshgiizhnii,* Coyote Pass People clan. My maternal grandfather clan is *Tó'áhaní,* Near the Water People clan and my paternal grandfather clan is the *Tóhdich'iinii,* Bitter Water clan.

My name is George James, Sr. I have lived here in Tsaile [most] of my life. I was seventeen years old when I went into the military, but before that I went down to Morenci, Arizona. During that time they discovered a copper mine, so they were hauling people from here to Morenci. I was seventeen and I took a chance. I took a physical and they hired me. I only worked July and August. Then I went back to school at Fort Wingate. That's where I went to school with your dad, Benson Tohe. I went back my sophomore year. I only stayed in school for about a month and then they drafted me. So I went into the service. You get up at 5:30 in the morning to drill. I was just a young fellow then. The first day I

didn't know how to swim. I thought I did. But I went across the swimming pool and coming back halfway, I went down.

I believe I went in November 23. I got out in July 1946. I spent about ten months training and then they shipped us out to Camp Matthews rifle range. They take you out there for a week and show you how to use an M1 and hit those targets. On qualifying day I hit 298. My instructor was really glad. He said if you hit three hundred tomorrow, you will beat all of these guys. The next day at six hundred yards I missed the whole target. So I got out of the rifle range and then they took us out to the sea. You get on a LST, little bitty boat. A lot of guys got sick. I never felt it. All these things you got to do before they ship you over. They ship us out to Hilo, Hawaii. We spent a little over ten months there. Then they told us that we were going to Iwo Jima. Mount Suribachi, they said, is where we are going. I was in communication and I carried the radio and my gun and my sleeping bag and my clothes. It's pretty heavy. I was in the eighth wave when we hit Iwo. I was on the beach and there was a machine gun sitting way down there, and it was spraying all those guys. The water was up to here when we got off the boat. They had barbed wire over here and you had to go through all of that stuff. I was lucky that I got through there. They told us what to do. I was with the radio. We spent, I don't remember, forty-five days or something like that on Iwo. They sent me out with another fellow.

There was a big guy who got wounded out there. They told us to bring him back. He was almost on the front line. So we went out there to get this guy. He weighed about two hundred pounds. I only weighed about a hundred and sixty-five pounds. This guy was trying to get into a little foxhole. He was unconscious and he didn't know what he was doing. Just when we got there, this guy who was helping me went combat fatigue on me. *Hááhgóóshį́į́ ditsxiz díí át' áó.* [Shakes his hand] *Ch'į́įndii! Hánáásgóó yíínsdziih.* He was shaking like this. Damn it! I started cussing him. I said, "What the hell is the matter here? Let's get this guy out of here, *bidishnóo,*" I was saying to him. Every time the mortar hit, *hááhgóshį́į́ ditsxiz.* He was shaking. *Áko éí t' áádoo ndi baahweeshn' da.* I didn't report it. Should've reported him. *Áko daat'éhíí baa dahane'léí.* Apparently one is supposed to report such things. We took that guy and rolled him over and got him on a stretcher and took him out. He was gone; he was unconscious. *Kwe'é binii'dahalzhin.* His face was a black hole. Part of his face was all gone. And we took him back to the headquarters. And they took him from there. They had a big Red Cross ship sitting out there and you could see it at night, you know. It had lights on it. It's got a big cross on it.

One time, most of the platoon in F Company got wounded or got killed. They wanted to get someone as a temporary communication man. A friend of mine, I don't remember these guys' names now, but he said, "Why don't you go with me?" He said, "Just cover me—I'm going to run way over here under the brush." The mortars started coming and the trucks started going zigzag. I don't know if they got hit. We spent the night there. I didn't see anything, so we went back to the camp. There's a ridge there, and a string, *kónízahdi nít'i',* it was stretched this far. So much distance apart. So I don't know how that guy got over somehow. *Ńt'ę́ę́ kónizahdę́ę́ nihich'į́ nii'na'lá.* Apparently he crawled up to us from a distance. The next morning, blood on the rocks. There were a lot of guys, young guys, that I guess they went to sleep in the foxhole and got their throats cut.

We stayed there for about four or five days on Iwo. Then they took us back to Honolulu. We spent another ten months training. And they took us out on a big ship again. We stayed out on the ocean for forty-five days. We didn't see anything; looking north, south, east, west it was just ocean, forty-five days. So finally they told us we were going to hit Sasebo, Japan. The very next day was V-J day; the Japanese unconditionally surrendered. We were lucky. Just before we got on the ship there at the camp, I was laying there. *Tł'óó'óósétį́í ńt'ę́ę' ha'át'íishį́į́ áshiłnii lá.* I was laying outside when something said to me, "You can't do it. You're not going to make it this time. You're not going to come back." Some spirit told me. I remember that.

George James, Sr.

The next day everybody went crazy. They were drinking and hitting a drum. A lot of them got thrown in jail. My captain was there. His name, I don't remember. He was sort of a missionary type. He came up to me the next morning and asked, "Did you get thrown in jail?" I said, "No, I didn't go any place." I was pretty lucky. But he died. Those are some of the experiences that I went through. I had a rough time. A lot of the time you had to sleep on the ground, any place you camp. You carry your own clothes. You carry your own dishes. You wash your own dishes. You wash your own clothes. You carry a little bitty tent and pitch a tent and go to sleep there. But you don't realize it though, what we went through. What we learned at Camp Pendleton there, we got words for boats, guns, enemy, and all that. I forgot it there.

They gave that flag to Colonel Johnson there in the morning to take up to Iwo on Mount Suribachi. He didn't accept that flag. There was Ira Hayes and there was a corpsman. He was a navy guy, real good corpsman. He treated a lot of guys that got wounded. I remember that. I think that there were five of them. These guys came up and got the flag and they started going up. I just radioed that these guys are going to put the flag up there on Mount Suribachi. They were almost up there and my assistant commander Major Pierce said, "Let's go." So I took the telephone and a spool. They put the flag on this hideous stick. They had decorated it. I just missed raising the flag into history by about two or three minutes. I met Ira Hayes twice. I think he was in F Company. After we secured Iwo, I met him in Hilo. He said he was going back to the states. I never followed up on him. Did you know he had a big parade in New York? But he told me that he was going to go back to Washington. He went back to Washington and within two or three weeks I saw him again. They told him, you don't need to come back. He said no, he's coming back. So he came back and he said that one of the movie stars tried to kiss him out there. He was a heavyset guy. He was a BAR man. It's a machine gun. I don't know how much they weighed. He's lucky he got out of there too.

I got out of the service and I fooled around for about two or three years. Then I finally went back to school and got my high school [diploma]. I went back to Wingate for one year and then they sent me to Chilocco, Oklahoma [Indian School]. In 1952 is when I got out. I was discharged in '46. I didn't do anything. I didn't know what I was doing, see. I didn't look at the future and what I was going to do, how I was going to make a career out of what. Here I was just playing around, a young man. So I went on the GI [Bill] and finished there. After I got out of high school in Chilocco, there were all kinds of jobs. Then I came back and I started working. I got married. I had nine kids. My wife is gone now. My youngest boy, he was an electrician. He got killed in a car accident. Then my youngest girl, the youngest of the whole family, died about five years ago. I got one that works at Shiprock.

I had different types of jobs. I went to Wichita. I worked for Beech Aircraft, commercial aircraft. I was making pretty good money. Every three months I got an extra check. You know the aircraft, they work under contracts. So if you don't have any contract with the government, there is no work. So that's what happened to Beechcraft. They laid me off. Then I went to work for Boeing in Wichita. I didn't like that. Then Beechcraft wrote back to me and said, "Come back over here and work for us." I didn't go back there, so I just went home.

The government hired me to work at the BIA. Then I started substitute teaching. They sent me to Flagstaff on a scholarship. Then one summer I didn't cut the mustard, but I should have stayed there. I didn't finish. Oh, I worked for the state of Arizona for ten years in Chinle. I was an employment interviewer. People would come to me for work and I would place them. I had a pretty decent job.

These young kids that are going to school now have more opportunity to learn than when I went to school. I think a lot of these kids are a lot brighter than when I went to school, because of the technology they have now. Their mom and dad are more educated. You don't have a good chance to get a good job unless you got a college degree. I admire these kids. They have all the opportunities. Now the tribe, I don't like the way they are running these educational programs, like the college here. I hired I don't know how many presidents when I was on the board here. Something goes wrong and then we get rid of them. It's always from the council or the [president]. That's not too good. I would like to develop something here. When we donated 1,200 acres of land here, they said they would put in housing, a high school, elementary, and many other things. But they are not doing that. So we sent it to Washington two or three times. This could be a pretty place for a bigger college where kids could go to school with better buildings and recreational activities. It's all right; it's going slowly. I think the trouble is that they change the president all the time. Right now everything is focused on the Navajo way of life. That's all they're doing now. They're teaching Navajo basket weaving and mostly about Navajo things. That is what's happening now. It takes a lot of time. I kind of disagree with it a little bit.

I think it's good to educate the kids about where they come from using the language and what their clans are. The medicine man is a part of the tradition. Right now The People have separated themselves from Navajo [spiritual] beliefs. There are all kinds of churches having services and even peyote ceremonies. I don't belong with that peyote. I got nothing against that. The different denomination of churches, you got them here and you can't do anything about them.

I told my son to write the history of this whole thing. He gave me part of it. I was Councilman[1] for twelve years from here. You can see my plaque there. I had some pretty good responsibilities. These guys want me to go back into politics again, but I'm staying home and watching my sheep and my cattle and horses. I got a little farm.

---

[1] Elected representative and also called Council Delegate to the Navajo Nation.

Jack Jones

July 11, 2009, San Juan Pueblo, New Mexico

WE ARRIVED AT JACK JONES'S HOME IN SAN JUAN PUEBLO, New Mexico, on a warm summer afternoon. His daughter gave us directions, which seemed complicated at first, but the turns by sight markers and speed bumps directed us to his home. We found Mr. Jones sitting under the large umbrella tree in his front yard waiting for us. He wore a crisp striped shirt and a single-strand white shell and turquoise necklace. He had married a woman from this pueblo and, according to Navajo tradition, moved into his wife's community. Navajo women warn that "no good" would come to the wife if she moves into her mother-in-law's home. Mr. Jones was a widower and his two daughters took care of him. After Mr. Jones's storytelling, they invited us into their home for lunch for one of the most tasty meals the Pueblo women are known for—chili stew, oven baked Pueblo bread, salads, and other dishes that rival the best cooks. It was the first home-cooked meal we had had since we began the project. We were grateful to have been treated to Pueblo hospitality, to feed those who come to your home.

■ ■ ■

It is said that it will be known what one's clan is when one comes across a Navajo. I am *Tahneszahnii Dine'é,* Tangle People clan, and born for the *Tábąąhá,* Water's Edge People clan. My maternal grandfather clan is the *Tódich'ii'nii,* Bitter Water People clan, and my paternal grandfather clan is the *Deeshchii'nii,* Start of the Red Streak People clan. My dad's name was Albert Jones and my mother's name was John Red's Sister. My late grandmother was *Tó'aheedlíinii,* the Water Flows Together People clan. A woman who was Bitter Water was called *Asdzą́ą́ dee'dį́į́',* Woman Four Horns, because she had a lot of those rams that had four horns, it is said. She was the mother of my grandfather. I am from

73

these people. We are originally from the people from Monument Valley. We separated from them and moved to the Montezuma Creek area.

My mom said I was born during the month of May, 1919. I was about seven years old I think, maybe two years behind my age when I went to Shiprock [New Mexico], to the boarding school there. We were asked not to speak our language no matter if we were advanced in our English language. So that left it very hard. We had to sneak around to talk to someone, a friend, or whoever we were with. We had to wander way away from the school. We'd get over there and we'd talk Navajo and as soon as we got back to the school campus, we were not allowed to speak Navajo. If they were heard, some of the boys would tell the officer that we were speaking Navajo. They would get their names written down and we were punished for Saturday and Sunday. We would be in line all day. So that went on over time. I don't know how I picked up a few English words, but anyway we continued to learn our English words by having the teacher say, "Say this word," and "Give me a pencil." After a time, well, you begin to pick up a few more English words and we got along all right. During the summer we went home. They didn't have a school bus like today. In those days they had a big old three-quarter truck that had those boards around the sides like that, and we would be all packed inside to take us home. Everything was very difficult, like the road. It was rough; no road grader went through there.

They took me to Phoenix, Arizona, to go to boarding school. I was there '35 through '37. And during Christmas, at the end of '36, there were some people that were Indians from South Dakota that worked there at the school. They were doing construction work and when they got done they said, "We are going to travel to Washington." One of the men was from Washington state. The other two were from South Dakota and they were brothers. We said we were going to take a trip, so we caught a freight train and we went to Buckeye, Phoenix, Yuma, Redding, Barstow, and to Sacramento. I remember I was fifteen years old at that time. They had their bedroll and everything like that in the days of tough times that year. So after going to Sacramento my friend said, "All right, this morning you are going to go to that house and from there you check those houses and get some food." Well, I thought to myself, I never begged for food in my life. So I went and knocked at the door. A woman came to the door and asked me what I want and I said, "I would like to work. I'm very hungry. I would like to work if I can earn my breakfast or some food." She said, "Wait." She brought a big sack package of, I don't know, all the food that was in it. I left and went on. I hid that bag. I went to another house and repeated what I had to say to the first woman. Again she said, "I have some meat here. We didn't eat those yesterday and I'll gladly give you some." She made a big package. I said, "I'm traveling for days to go to Oregon and up that way to get to the state of Washington." So she said "I'll give you a big package so you can eat from time to time as you go." Those two bags I took back to my friends and said, "This is what I got," and we had a good meal for breakfast that morning. They said, "You have done all right." They were happy about me bringing food. We never got beyond Klamath Falls. We were in the timber area, and we cut those trees that are dead. We chopped the limbs and we were there for some time.

I went to school at the Indian School and graduated from there. After that, I learned to be a house painter. I got into it after going to school. That was '37 or '38. And from there I worked different places out that way. I thought to myself, the war was already on so, I'm going to go to San Francisco. I took that chance and I worked at a shipyard. What I did over there is I learned how to shrink metal. They called it flanger. I saw service personnel: marines, army, navy, merchant marines, seabees and all that. I thought to myself, you know, they might ask me to get in the service or arrest me for not being in the service. So I volunteered.

They sent me to San Diego from there. Samuel Tso, Thomas Claw, he's the one that died just recently, and I came in together, and I was with a whole bunch of Anglos and Blacks that were getting into the marines. One officer there asked me, "What kind of Indian are you?" I said I was a Navajo. He asked, "Do you speak the language?" "Oh yes, I speak the language," I said. He said, "You know there is a platoon of Navajos over here and they are studying to be taken in to be Code Talkers." Then he asked, "Do you want to join them?" He took me over there and I was accepted.

Many of the Navajos did not make the grade to be a Code Talker, so they sent them off to either rifle platoon or somewhere else. One morning, they said, "Tomorrow get all of your stuff to go to the ship over there." So we got in the ship and off we went. We didn't know where we were going and we sailed for days. All you see is maybe islands way off in the distance, nothing but water. We went to New Caledonia. That island belongs to the French, I think. And there were different kinds of Asian people there. Our group stayed many

weeks. Then they said, "Get in the ship again." So we sailed for Australia. We got to Brisbane, Australia. How many days or how much time we spent over there, I don't know, but we met up with a group that fought on Guadalcanal. That was the First Marine Division that fought on Guadalcanal at that time, the nearest island to Australia. They made all those air raids against the Australia. And sooner or later, they were to move the ground troops to hit Australia but they never did. So the U.S. Marine First Division was assigned to fight on Guadalcanal. So they took it. No more Japanese raiding the Australians. There were six divisions of marines and these Navajo Code Talkers were assigned to different divisions.

I was with the First Marine Division, First Signal Battalion. That's a communication setup. From there we moved and got in the ship again. In Brisbane, we met up with some of the boys. They went out into that city and they roamed around maybe for the night and came back in the morning. Some of those boys came back and said, "Yeah, you know those black Seabees out there are telling girls that they are American Indian." From there we moved on to Cape Gloucester, New Britain, and another city up north occupied by the Japanese. We saw some of those Japanese prisons over here. They have them all fenced in with no way to get out. Another Navajo—his name is Edward McCabe—and I went all over different places. And we saw some of those natives out there chasing great big long lizards. They ran up those big palm trees. They put rope around their feet and tied them like you do a horse. They got up to where that lizard is and they chase it and that lizard has to fall all the way to the bottom. They catch the lizard and, I think, eat those lizards. We were told not to be visiting those natives because you might contract some of those jungle diseases or whatever they may have. We did see them in the distance. Some of the women, they don't wear top clothing. All they have is skin. They expose everything and some of them carry babies and nurse them.

So finally we moved to another island to exercise what we trained for. We went to another island called Russell Island and we sent messages. We did this so that we could renew our code language. At the same time we learned that the army and the navy were operating over there. They had Morse code, so every day they changed to a different code, and we found out that the Japanese have code breakers. They said we better not use that Morse code. So they quit that and from that time they used Navajo code. They found out that the Japanese were recording those code languages and they couldn't break it. The Japanese that studied language, they asked them, "What kind of a language is that you hear sending messages?" They said, "It sounds like a Chinese dialect." They said the Japanese took those recordings and sent them to Japan.

They took a lot of American soldiers somewhere to the northern part of Japan, somewhere and had them in a concentration [camp] there. So they took those recordings to see if anyone would recognize the language over there in that prison. They found that two Navajos were there. One's name was Kayone. I don't remember what his first name is, and then there was another one. After the war these two prisoners that heard the recording of the Code Talkers in the prison camp testified to the Code Talkers that they were under torture. One of them said they put baling wire around his head and they twisted it like that. They wanted him to reveal what the message said. He told them, "I can't. I know what the words are, but what is the meaning of it? How can I tell you?" That was the testimony that they gave to the Code Talkers. They couldn't reveal the secret. Even if I were to give a code today from what we learned during the war, if I gave a message to a fluent speaking Navajo, you wouldn't understand. The order in our outfit, I don't know about other outfits, was if you see a Code Talker captured by the enemy, shoot the Code Talker. That was the order.

I was in the service from March 1943 and I came back in March 1945. After being wounded, I was hospitalized at Hunters Point in San Francisco Navy Hospital. [This is my] Purple Heart. But it was not recorded that I was wounded. I had a hard time trying to get compensation from the government. I finally had to get a lawyer from Albuquerque to work on it for me and he finally did.

A few of the Navajos were taken as Japanese because they thought maybe they picked up a marine's clothes and put them on. They had to run them up to an officer to be recognized as a Code Talker. You go to that prison camp at Cape Gloucester and you see them and some of them look like Navajos. From Russell Island, they said, "Get your stuff because we are going to invade another island; we don't know which island." I was on a troop ship. The first group that came off the ship got on that amphibious tractor that floats on water and can maneuver on land. The first wave went onto the beach and then the second wave and then the third wave; I was in there. From the ship, we got into the amphibious tractor to the beach. When you get down to the beach, at the edge of the water, you look down and you see bodies floating all over. They still had their packs, some of them upside down. Some of them upward like that. And then, on the beach, you see some of them moving around; they were wounded. Some are just dead. So Ben Manuelito and me—I don't know if he is still alive—we were in that First Signal Battalion together. So we both got over there. There was kind of this rock ledge. A group of us got to the beach and sat there. The officers said, "Let's go."

We took off from that beach and we were instructed, "When you get past those palm trees, shoot up there at the palm tree because some of those palm trees have snipers. They tie themselves up there and you have a chance to kill one or two up there." So we went on and got to about three hundred yards from the beach, from the water's edge. And out in the distance there is a high hill. You know those rocks they call coral? You can get your hatchet and chop on it and it breaks easy and you can make a hole in that rock. They have all of the hill, which is big. They had their machine gun nests, some for cross range and some for long distance range. They had their setup and they threw bombs. And we were pretty well singled out, I would say. They bombed constantly. We couldn't move out of there. We dug a foxhole and I went down about that deep and I stood in there, me and my partner. We hid out and we saw *Boom! Boom!* all over. It was kind of dark. We heard a bunch of noise. And here, it was a suicide attack. It was a bunch of Japanese coming and they are running with a gun and some of the boys were awakened from their sleep, and we shot. You could see them fall all that first morning. Later that day, I would say maybe 8:30 or somewhere in that time, I stood up and I was facing that direction and I heard a bomb. All I heard was just a blast. How far it was, I don't know. All I know is just *Boom!*

The blast was so tremendous it gave me a concussion. The blast hit me and knocked me back. Maybe they found me lying there in the hole to see if I was dead or if I was breathing.

They got me on a boat and they gathered those wounded marines and they took them back to the aircraft carrier. I might have spent one or two days without my mind. I was lying on a cot and I looked up and there was canvas spread out. I looked this way and rolled over and looked that way. I thought to myself, "Where am I?" Immediately, I guess my subconscious made me jump. They said I was running and staggering around and hollering. I don't know what I said. These navy corpsmen brought me back. They said, "Go back and take it easy; lay down." So I did that. It was not until the afternoon that I fully gained my normal consciousness. The next morning the doctor made his rounds with those navy corpsmen. The doctor told me, "You are in no condition to go back to active duty, so we're going to send you back to the United States." I don't know how I felt about that announcement. We got back to the Golden Gate Bridge on March 11, 1945. They transferred me to Oceanside Naval Hospital. I spent five and a half months in the hospital for recovery.

During those years, I went out with my friends, the boys, you know. We would go from Oceanside to Los Angeles or San Diego. I went with the fellows that drank and I used to take a little. After a time, they gave me furlough to go home. I got back to Gallup and from there to Montezuma Creek. I went before my mom, and she was happy to see me. After a time she said, "Son, you look awful thin, what seems to be the reason?" "Well, I don't know," I said. I thought I was physically built like I should be. "But you're awful thin," she said, "No doubt that you have been drinking." "Yeah, I drink a little," I said. She said, "Son, I want to tell you that you don't know what you are getting into when you drink that liquor. You get too much of it, maybe you get hurt. Maybe somebody kill you or you might be made disabled for life because of damage to your health or you could get hurt somehow. You will be that way for life." So I thought about it and told her, "Thank you for the advice." So I went back to the hospital in Oceanside, California. I found my friends there and we go out and go to different bars and I thought about my mom. My mom says, "Don't drink." I'm going to keep her word from now on. It was kind of a promise to my mom that I won't drink anymore. That was way back in '45. I never drank from then up until this time. I did smoke at one time. I was working up there in Raton, New Mexico. We were working on painting a post office up there and I got so sick with a cough. I felt real bad, but I worked all day for several days. I got all right and then I thought that I don't want to smoke no more. From there on I never smoked. It's been maybe forty-five years. So I have been in good health from then on.

■ ■ ■

At age ninety-one, Mr. Jones is fighting another battle to save his homeland. He is putting forth a legal petition to get land restored to the *Kaayellii Diné*[1] people who lived in the Montezuma Creek area before Utah became a state in 1896. The petition is a long and complex land issue that involves the Treaty of Guadalupe Hidalgo, the U.S., the Navajo Nation, and the *Kaayellii* people. According to the agreements that were made between Mexico and the U.S., one article in the Guadalupe Hidalgo treaty states that the Native inhabitants in the Montezuma Creek area were not to be driven out. Later when the Bureau of Land Management (BLM) came into the picture, the people were ordered to leave their homes and farmlands in an area rich in coal and gas reserves. Mr. Jones says that, since the people around the Colorado River did not go on the Long Walk to Fort Sumner, the treaty of 1868 that the Navajo leaders signed, does not apply to the *Kaayellii* people. This forced removal took place during the era when many Indigenous American peoples were relocated to places far away from their original homeland, often to inhospitable places that did not support human habitation. Mr. Jones says that the treaty of 1868 and the treaty of Guadalupe Hidalgo are the basis for the petition on behalf of the *Kaayellii Diné,* who are an independent group.

As we sat under the shade of a large tree in his front yard, he showed me legal documents and letters on the land claim. At his advanced age, he was still fighting the good fight for his country and homeland. This time, the fight involved courts, treaties, and the language of the law. I was deeply moved by his commitment to try to reclaim the lands and resources for his community. Mr. Jones was fighting in the same spirit he took with him when he was willing to sacrifice his life in the battles he fought and when he used the Navajo language as a weapon to help save America and its allies. Ironically, the country he put his life on the line for was the country that was now denying his land claims. Nevertheless, there was no bitterness, no regrets, but a warrior still fighting with

---

[1] Name of the people who live in the Montezuma Creek, Utah, area.

a passion for his people and country. Here was a man who truly deserved to be called a warrior, though I think he would prefer not to call attention to himself and do his work in humility.

■ ■ ■

There was such a land loss. We lived out beyond the Colorado River. *Ńléí Dził Bízhi' Áden Hoolyé.* The place is called The Mountain with No Name. *Áádóó yówohjį'* from there on the western part there is a place called *Dził Binii' Łigai,* Mountain with White Face. Over there is another place called Green River, Utah. *Áádóó kót'áo Dził Naajiin hoolyé. Táchééh naaznil. Dibé da dabighan. Diné kéédahat'įi ńt'ę́ę́'.* And then Black Streak Mountain it is called. There are sweat lodges. Sheep corrals. Navajos used to live there. They drove us back from there. So these are some of the issues that I refer to of our living areas during the years before and after coming back [from Fort Sumner].

From Montezuma Creek to Bluff, Utah, that highway is built with Navajo money. The Navajo money that comes out of that oil field is at 37.5 percent. 62.5 percent may be somewhere in Washington. I don't know. But we want that 62.5 percent for my people over there. The Spaniards had ownership of part of the eastern part of New Mexico and what are now the states of Colorado, Utah, Nevada, California, Arizona, and New Mexico. The Spaniards claimed that when they first came during that war and after that war, they made peace. And after they made a treaty, they agreed that they are not going to go to war. So in other words, the United States and the Mexico group ratified that agreement. All that fuss about land grant and all these Pueblos are living on land grant. Up north the whole state, even the state of Utah, is under land grant including Nevada, California, and Arizona. This Treaty of 1848 that Mexico and the American government agreed on it. It's a ratified treaty, so that's what this is. This is another letter to be taken to my people. When we get the agreement we'll send it to Native American Rights Fund in Boulder, Colorado. And there is another group in Alaska and Washington, D.C. This one is House Memorial 91 and it's been approved here. The lawyer made the document here to be recognized for my people. There are nine offices to be notified on this. The governors of Utah, New Mexico, the Navajo Nation, and then there are six other agencies or offices that have to be notified to bring the Navajo people, the *Kaayellii* people, from Utah together to discuss the issue about lost land and oil resources that we want to get back.

My grandpa settled there. He was ninety-two years old and must have been born in 1823. Okay, then you count back this way and Utah became a state in 1892. My mom said my grandpa died about three years before I was born. The year my grandpa was seventy-two years old is when Utah became a state. According to the Guadalupe Hidalgo Treaty, in a book I have, Article 11 states that the Natives that are inhabitants of the area will not be driven from their inhabited area. So that's the way it states. The BLM said, "Get out. Take your horses; take your cattle; take your sheep. Move!" There was a Navajo interpreter that was with them to give them all the instructions of what the concern was about, so they moved them out. So we have that complaint against the Navajo Agency for being a representative that gave the instructions to get out. The whole setup is under [the violation of] Human Rights, that's what this is. I just humble myself before my people. So we took it to Salt Lake City. We had a lawyer there. He was an Anglo, and he represented us and we won the case. So we moved back up that way, not too far though. After that, about a year and a half or more, they re-appealed this case again at Salt Lake City. We believe that it was over in no time and the government, I think, shelled out some and gave it to the lawyer and the lawyer accepted it. What do you call it, a bribe? So that's what happened, I think. So we lost the case and from that time, there has been no re-appeal of that land concern up to now.

But what I'm doing is, I've been in the service and I said that I fought for my country. I fought for my every right of my people and we lost that land. I said there was oil and gas found. Plenty of it more and more in the ground and the government says, "You have service rights but the depth of the earth is mine." So I told my people, "Look what we should have done or what you people should have done is that when the driller comes, he taps the earth right here. So, you tell him to put the money down right here. You can go as far as you want and whatever you find down there, but before you bring it up, put some more money down." That should have been done. We didn't know anything about the whole thing, or what they were doing. We didn't know. They took a lot of things away from us and they made roads all over that place. No place for the cattle to nibble on the grass or the sheep. Roads all over in that area. And some people are living there with all those machinery tools. They have an oil pump working and it's an awful stink.

So what I'm doing is somehow to gain something back for my own people, my relatives. That is my aim. I am not a councilman; I don't have any kind of representation. But because I served my country and my people, I want to see if they can get some compensation for my people, so they can be happy. They lived throughout those lands and they were driven back years ago. That's for the *Kaayellii* people from Montezuma Creek.

The duty we performed went beyond the call of duty. Those were the words of the officers while we were in the service. They said if it were not for the Code Talkers, the war would not have been won, because communication is so important to make contact, to move, and to act. If anybody questions the Navajo weapon, I will say:

Ha'át'íísh éí bee nisiníbaa'? Ha'á't'íí éí bee adíłt'ohgo anaa'í nisíníłtseed? Áádóó t'áá át'é baa nitsáhákéézgo honeeznáadi éish ha'á't'íí nilíigo áko nizaad bee yáníłti' ńt'éé'? All in all, wolyéego éí hózhǫ́ náhásdlį́į' wolyé. Nihikéyah bá ádeiit'į́įd. Nihidine'é bá ádeiit'į́įd. Iiná wolyéii bee sézį́įgo kót'áo dahwiilne' ńt'éé'. Bee atí'doolnííł wolyéego éí saad nanil'inii. 'Áá éí saad nanil'inii bee atí'doolnííł éí hózhǫ́ náhásdlį́į' násdlį́į'. Nizéé' dóó kót'áo. Be'eldǫǫh éí dooda. Nizéé'dóó ati'doolnííł biniiyé nizaad diits'a'go bee enemy atélyaa, atídaołaa. T'áá éí bee atélyaa hozhǫ́ náhásdlį́į' wolyéego nihikékah bá ádadohníí ńt'éé' lá. Jó kót'é. You write that down.

What did you use to fight in the war? What did you use to kill the enemy? With all in mind, what did you value as you used your language in the war that was won? All in all, it is called "harmony is restored." We did it for our land. We did it for our people. I stood as life when we used our language. Secrecy of words was a weapon. That same secrecy of words restored the restoration of harmony. For the good of the people, for the security purpose, and for the freedom of America and its allies, that's what it is, Navajo weapon. From your mouth, it is this way. Not with guns. From your mouth, your words were heard to destroy the enemy; you destroyed all. With that, harmony was restored for our land. This is how it is. You write that down.

Tom Jones

July 16, 2010, Hogback, New Mexico

BY VISUAL LANDMARKS, we managed to find Tom Jones's home in Hogback, New Mexico. It was late morning when we set our equipment out in front of his home for the interview session. Mr. Jones is now eighty-four years old and using a cane. His son settled him into the chair. He wore a baseball cap that said "Iwo Jima Survivor." He had served in the Thirty-second Battalion, Division Headquarters from 1943 to 1945. He was only sixteen when he enlisted. His childhood was difficult without his mother, who passed in 1935, and an absent father. To support two sisters and one brother, he worked at a coal mine and attended high school.

After his discharge, he worked briefly as a prison guard for German and Japanese POWs at Alcatraz Island. "They were friendly, all those prisoners. They didn't even act like they were in war or being captured. They were kind, every one of them. They were nice people. I don't know what they did afterwards." After this brief stint, he headed home to find his siblings had grown and had mostly lived alone during his absence. Right then, he decided to take responsibility for raising them rather than finishing high school.

He found work at a mining company in Colorado. He was injured, but returned to work for a coal mining company in the area. Later, he found dangerous work in the uranium mine. One of his sons helps him get around now. "I lost my memory in 2008. I forget things too," he added. Still, he learned the code words and had to be retrained in it when he wasn't in combat. More than three hundred code words had to be committed to memory, a feat that relied on the power of accurate memory, concentration, and being quick, while simultaneously fighting in combat. *"Tsíílgo bee ndashiilnish."* "We had to be quick," he said.

Following in the footsteps of their father and grandfather, Mr. Jones's son was a Vietnam vet, one of his grandsons and two of his great-grandsons are also in the marines. "We are a marine family," he says. "You have to think first for them. I probably forgot a lot of things, but that's how I am—forgetful. That's how my ears are, too. That's why I don't hear very well. I tried reporting it. I returned, disabled." It also left him pondering the cost of human life and if monetary gain can ever replace the toll a war takes.

■ ■ ■

My clan is Táchii'nii. Kinyaa'áánii éí báshíshchíín. Dashinálí shíí éí ha'át'íí sha'shin. I never did get that one. Áshįįhí éí dashicheii. Hashtł'ishnii dóó Hooghan Łání éí shįį t'áá łá'í Kinyaa'áánii. T'áá éí t'éí shił bééhózin.

Ashiiké bił da'íínishta' nt'ę́ę́'. T'óó ahayói: Charley Y. Begay. Cosey Brown, John Chee, Fleming Begaye, Stewart Clah da dayolyé nt'ę́ę́'. Éí ałtso dahdiikai. Nihí under ageígíí.

■ ■ ■

My clan is Red Running Into the Water People clan. I am born for Towering House People clan. My maternal grandfathers are Salt People Clan. I'm not sure what my paternal grandfathers are. I never did get that one. Mud Clan and Many Houses are the same as Towering House. That's all I know.

We went to school at the Shiprock agency high school. I went to school with many of the boys: Charley Y. Begay, Cosey Brown, John Chee, Fleming Begaye, Stewart Clah were their names. They all left. Others of us who were underage [stayed behind].

■ ■ ■

So I decided too, I was just going to join up. There were over sixty of us. We left Gallup for San Diego, for basic training. Another physical examination there. Then there were only fifty-eight of us left. Some went on to something else. Then we went on: start training, physical training. We finished there and graduated. Then they shipped us out to the Camp Elliott for the rifle range. Then we went to Camp Pendleton. From there on we went overseas. I guess it was almost a month, went through all these islands. We were all together, all the Navajos. We spent two weeks there, and then they finally separated us by group.

Áádóó, and then, we departed again for Guam. After we went to Guam, it was too scary. All these rocks. We used to carry a radio all the time. Where the enemies were located, they had to reposition all these areas; send the word back

to our command. That's what we did. These radios, carry them around. You have to really watch what you're doing, where you're going, where you're at. Snipers nest up there in the trees. So you had to look around every move you make. There was all kinds of booby traps. After Guam, we secured that island in so many days. We stayed there for so many months. Then we were ready to go again. While we were at Guam, we did a lot of things, unloaded the ship, things to be used. It was ready to be shipped to Iwo Jima. And then we went back to Hawaii. They loaded us up again and headed for the rough land, bloody one. And then we hit the beach again on February 19. Everything was floating around, bodies, first day we landed. Too scary. You didn't really know where [the Japanese plane] was going to land. The only thing they looked for, the Japanese, is how to get to our radio station. It was the main thing. We really had to watch. The beach was pretty sandy, stinky; you couldn't hardly climb up. You slid back down. It was too cold, windy. You had to use the radio all the time. You stood by it, day and night. That's what we did. It took so many days to secure that island. We used everything that we had. Mortar shells, combat, shooting, all kinds of tunnels. That's what they used against us, whatever they could get. There were all kinds of booby traps. Even the rain, couldn't get out of it. They used really fine wire for booby traps.

After we secured Iwo Jima, everybody stayed there for a few months more. Then we went back to Guam again. And then we were ready to be shipped again to Okinawa. It was the last bunch. Then back to San Diego. Back to Camp Pendleton. That's where we get discharged, December 30, 1945. After we got discharged, we spent two days in San Francisco, then Gallup. Back to Gallup again, then back to Farmington. And back to here.

[After I was discharged] I went to work in Colorado. After that, I fell off the timber when I worked for the timber mill. I worked for iron mining. While I was doing that, I lost my arm. Bothers me. I went around a lot of places then came back to reservation and worked in the uranium mines.

When I was ready to leave for the service in Santa Fe, the day before I was leaving, I got help from a medicine man.

■ ■ ■

Shik'i doo iiłhaazh da. All night long he gave me a ceremony. Éí ákót'áo yee shich'į' haadzíí'. "Díí bee ńdíídááł. Azhą shįį ndahonitł'ah dóó haashįį néélą́ą́' bitahgóó díníyá ndi." "I want you to come back," shiłnóo shik'i doo iiłhaazh da. Áádóó dah diiyá Farmingtongóó. Áádóó áádi ahidahidiikai. Éí ákódzaa. Nináhaakaigo áá ákót'áo shá ánááyiidlaa. Nánísdzáo shił ná'ílwodgo Farmingtondi. Éí bee nánisdzá. T'áá ákót'áo shá ánááyiidlaa. "Tł'óó'déę' t'ááká yah anáodza'. Éí ni'ę́ę́' bii'sínítínígíí bee yah anáodááh," shiłní.

T'áá tł'óó'di t'áá áádi ałch'į' hóshlaa dóó yah anáásdzáh. "Ei éí háádi da ndíínił. T'óó da nániníl'įįh doo," shiłní. "Ńléídę́ę́' łeezh naazhjaa'go áádę́ę́' nadą́'áłgai ak'áán bee hahodiilyaago tádídíín dó'. Ei bikáá' yínáálgo yah anídíídááł." Kót'áo yee shinináánáshnish. Nát'ohígíí yee shinaashnish. "Díí éí bił hada'astsih yę́ę́ háádoolyéél éí doo bee kananináá doo k'ad ná'áshlééh," shiłní. "Ná'áshlaadóó éí bííghahi baa nináánídáá dooleeł. T'áásh Diné honááł ádaat'íinii bináál ájít'įi dooleeł."

"Bee yínáál dooleeł," shidííniid. Éí ákót'áo shik'i doo náá'iiłhaazh da. Éí díishjį́idi bee yishááł. Doo łahgo áshlééh da ałdó'. K'ad éí ałtso aná'iisdee' kót'áo yéédahósin yę́ę́. Éí biniinaa askiiké ła' doo bá ákódaalyaágíí dadahizhdiikai dóó ninájiiskaigo t'óó bik'ee hahizhdínééskai. Doo ákót'áo hwá ada'alyaa da.

If they want to readjust, they have to be done. *K'ad ákót'é. Ła' t'ahdii bik'ee nidajikai. Doo bá ádaalyaa da.*

Jó bee n'doonishgi át'áo. Éí binahjį́'go. T'áá'isíí bee ak'ihodoodooł dóó ak'ihodidoodleeł. Éí t'éí atis áníłtsoo bee nitsídeiikees. Kót'áo ádeiilyaa. Ashiiké t'áá ałtso. K'ad éí ádingi át'é. Ts'idá áájį'go éí hodínóónééł. Łahda íínisin łeh: I wonder how much a person is worth? *Ákót'áo bich'ą́ąh ádeiit'įįdígíí. Kót'áo éí jó haadait'áo nijilnishgo honaanish yá'át'ééhgo ájiił'įįhgo bonus wolyéhígíí t'áá éí t'éí doo bee nitsáháskéézda doo nisin, World War loyalty. How much does a person cost? T'áá łá'í jizinígíí baa nitsáhákees. Kót'áo nidashiilnish. Éí dó' baa nitséskees łeh. Jó insurance shį́į́ dahóló̦o. A hundred thousand áádi neeskid. Bonus wolyéhígíí doo bee nihaa nitsáhákees da. Jó when we went in there, fifty dollar, díí bik'éh áhodííł'áál dóó bik'éh tádidíínaał. Tsé'naa dah diniyáo you can have it, only ten percent. To me, fifty dollar yéę́ ádin, ten percent, háájí? You lose your mind, lost part of your body, does that cost ten dollars? Ákót'áo baa nitséskees.*

Jo nihizaadígíí éí alááhdi yéégo baa nitsáhákees dooleeł. Binahjį' ádeiilyaágíí éí t'áá ájiłtso hoł béédahózin. Government hojoo'báá'ígo recognize ádajiilaa. Diné bizaadígíí yee ádínálniih doo. Yee náás yigáάł doo. Yee át'éé dooleeł. Yinahjį' t'áá ałtso k'é yó'níí dooleeł. That's what I'm thinking. Jó éí nihí nihaadeet'á̦. Nihí nihizaad. Háádę́ę́' shį́į́ nihaa deet'ánígíí éí nihí. Bee yéiilti'ígíí éí nihił da'íló̦o bee yéiilt'i'. Bee da'íldééh dóó iiná bee deélt'ééh. Jó ákót'áo baa nitséskees.

■ ■ ■

He performed a Blessing Way on me. All night long he gave me a ceremony. That's how he explained it to me. "You will return with this. No matter how difficult it will be and what you will encounter. I want you to come back," he said as he sang for me. And then I left for Farmington. That's where we all met. That's what happened. When we returned, he did the same thing for me when I returned to Farmington. That's what I came back with. He did the same thing for me. "Do not come in from outside. Don't enter with those clothes that you are wearing," he said. "You're home. I don't want you to wear it anymore. You did your job. You accomplished what you did, what you learned, your job."

I gathered it all outside and came back in. "Put those somewhere. Maybe you can just look at them time to time," he said. From there, forms of sand were placed with ground white corn and corn pollen. "Enter while placing your feet on top of them." That's how he performed for me again. He helped me by offering tobacco. "This will help you readjust by loosening the prayers before. After I am done helping you, you can do whatever you want again. Don't do what others are doing negatively. Take care of yourself. Do what you want. Do what you learned."

"You will walk this path," he said. That's how he did the Blessing Way for me again. That's what I am living on today. I'm not changing it. Those who knew these ceremonies are gone now. That's why some of our people who go to service and do not have these ceremonies are struggling. They didn't have this kind of ceremony. If they want to readjust, they have to be done. That's how it is now. Some are still suffering. They didn't get it done.

It [the Navajo language] was a tool to do the job. On behalf of it, to win the war. That was priority. That's how we did it. All the boys. I'm not sure about now. It was all about winning. Sometimes I think: I wonder how much a person is worth? What we defended there. Like when you do a very good job, you receive some type of bonus, World War loyalty. How much does a person cost? Consider every single person. That's how we worked. I also think about that. There is probably insurance. It was about a hundred thousand. The concept of bonus was not even considered for us. Let's say, for example, when we went in there, fifty dollars would be what we were promised to get paid to do our job. But when you leave across the ocean, you'll only receive ten percent of that. To me, the fifty dollars disappeared, and where is the ten percent? You lose your mind, lost part of your body, does that cost ten dollars? That's how I think of it.

Our language will be considered most important. Everyone knows why we used it. The government finally recognized it. They will remember themselves with the Navajo language. They will live forth with it. It will sustain them. With it they will address people with it. That's what I'm thinking. Well, it was given to us. It is our language. From where it was created is ours. When we speak with it, it is sacred. It is carried on, and from it life continues. That's how I think about it.

LEFT: *Tom Jones with his wife Alice.*

Joe Kellwood

August 2008, Phoenix, Arizona

JOE KELLWOOD IS A WIDOWER and lives alone in his home near the Phoenix Mountain Preserve. His living room walls are covered with Code Talker memorabilia. Unlike most of the Code Talkers, Mr. Kellwood settled in Phoenix, where he worked for most of his life and raised his family of five children. His wife was a nurse and a Norwegian. He jokes that his children are the "Navewegian tribe." Shortly after they began living together, Joe and Adrena encountered jealousy and racism when their place was set afire. They moved away and bought an acre of land for $35.00 a month. It had no modern conveniences, so Joe had to rely on how he once lived on the rez—hauling water and wood for heat and cooking. His home has all the conveniences now and even gets help from the local VFW (Veterans of Foreign Wars) to repair his home. One of his five children lives next door. After his discharge he took up vocational training in Phoenix to learn the carpentry trade. Like some others of the Code Talkers, both of his parents passed on when he was growing up. His father died of pneumonia when Joe was in the eighth grade. Nevertheless, he and his siblings have longevity. He was eighty-seven years old when he told this story. One of his brothers is one hundred years old and another one nearly ninety. He had some trouble recalling names, but he wanted to tell about his life in the marines. Before boarding the ship that would carry him into battle, he repeated the prayer for protection that his uncle taught him. He sometimes spoke of himself in third person. Mr. Kellwood believes that the younger generation is losing the Navajo language and that it will become part of history, but he wants people to remember that the Code Talkers used The People's language to help America win the war.

■ ■ ■

I am *Naakaii Dine'é,* Mexican clan and born for *Tábąąhá,* Water's Edge People clan. My maternal grandfather clan is the *Tsi'naajinii,* Black Streak Wood People clan and the *Tótsohnii,* Big Water People clan are my paternal grandfather clan.

I saw the movie about Guadalcanal in Gallup, New Mexico. Those people in the movie looked real neat and I wanted to be one, so that's why I enlisted when I was twenty years old, not drafted. I did make it to the outfit that hit Guadalcanal. First Marine Division, that's the one I joined at Camp Elliott. We were not to tell anybody what we were doing. It was all secret, you know. I worked at the Wingate Ordnance Depot when I decided to enlist. I asked the boss that ran the ammunition depot and he said I could do it. I had to go to Albuquerque to enlist. I passed the grade and they told me to come back in two weeks. They said, "Put your things away and then come back." I took my things home and then I told my sister that I was going into the service. I could go to where they can teach me to fight in the war. That made her cry. So after that two weeks, I went back to Albuquerque and I got on the train. We stopped at Gallup and in the evening heard all these guys coming aboard that went to school at Wingate, a vocational high school.

I enlisted in 1942, got through boot camp, and then went to Camp Elliott communication school. And you studied a lot. I tell you that you had to learn all those hard words, long words that you don't know what it means. But at the end, you learned what they mean, you know. The spelling had to be perfect. And your writing has got to be clear. You had to talk loud and clear. It was extra work for me because I only have an eighth grade education. A lot of words are military and I didn't know what they mean. So after graduating from Code Talker school, you went on a ship with all the loaded things: seabag, pack, and a blanket that was wrapped around your pack and the rifle.

I had to say a prayer to get on the ship that my uncle repeated to me when I went to South Pacific. *"Tóhniteel, Shimá, shaa'á halyą́ą́ dooléél."* Mother Water, take care of me. That's your prayer and you put the corn pollen to the ocean, which I just put on chewing gum. I don't throw it, you know. I just spit it to the side when walking onto the boat. That's the way I did mine. And the rest of the time, I ran out of corn pollen but I just pretended I had it. You do the same way when you say a prayer on the Navajoland. That's what I did many times because I was out for a long time. Somewhere we hit a hurricane, and I tell you the hurricane was really bad. You go downhill one time and then you go uphill again. You know, it's like big waves of hills. There are blasts under the ship. A lot of people just walked around carrying a bucket, puking. We went through that hurricane and from there we went across the equator where the navy put on a show for us.

From there we stopped in Australia. I don't remember the name of the place where we stopped. There were a lot of Australian boys, you know, waiting around out there. They wanted you to throw some cheese in the ocean. So they jumped in and they picked it up [laughter]. They always teased. We had to join the First Marine Division. The first group of Code Talkers was there. There was also Dennis Cattle Chaser from Tuba City, Andrew Toledo, and Joe Kellwood from Steamboat. You had to change your money to Aussie money. They got a lot of sheep. We split up in the end. I met up with John Chee from Shiprock, New Mexico. So that's two of us and then I caught up with one of my relatives from Steamboat. His name is Bill Cadman. We got sent back into the Pacific to New Guinea. That's where we were stationed for a while. We learned a lot of maneuvers. When we walked in the river, the Japs couldn't know where you go. One of my brothers was stationed in Italy too, with the air crew. They had B-17 and B-24 bombers that they used over there in that area. I tell you, in the jungle you couldn't see much. A lot of vines and you couldn't see the Japanese. The air corps bombed the area. The rain and wind hit us, and then those trees fell. We lost a couple Code Talkers, from what I understand.

We were at the edge of the river when I lost my shoes for a couple days. I guess they found somebody my size that got killed, so I got shoes, because there was no quartermaster there. When I looked down the river, I found one Japanese who died. He got washed out. Skinny, I guess, from the mountain. The mountain is big and the water comes out from it. So the Japanese were up in the mountains and the troops down below all scattered around the mountain. The air base was there. The Japanese set up a trap. Yeah, they led us, but I was glad we didn't go. Some of those that washed out, like the one I was telling you about, they were all skinny, you know. I guess they didn't have any food up there in that area. We went back to Russell Island. I tell you that it was a stinking jungle. A lot of rotten coconuts and a lot of mud and mice. But we built the camp there. Everywhere we went we used the code. I'm with the Fifth Regiment. We had three battalions and three Code Talkers, one to each battalion. I don't remember but the one, Joe Gatewood. We used to work together at Wingate in our early time. He's a good buddy, a brother. *Ahidiilchį*, we're born for the same clan. So that makes him

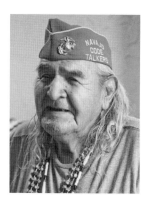

my brother. *Tábąąhí yáshchíín*. He was born for Near the Water. I talked to him a lot, almost two hours to make the report, because they were on the other side of the river. A lot of times they couldn't contact the unit, usually a mountain interfered. You had to call another unit to send a message that way.

After Cape Gloucester, New Britain, in 1944, we hit the hot one, Peleliu Island group. We landed about five hundred miles from it. It is just a small island, but inside the mountain, it was just full of Japanese. I don't remember how many they said was inside the mountain. It was hollow and outside of the mountain it was like a battleship with the cement pocket. I tell you that we lost a lot of marines there. And the water, we didn't have because they say twenty-six Higgins boats got hit with mortar. The water splashed in our Higgins boat in an amphibious tracker and got us all wet. I was lucky to get to the beach a little early. Later on, one of the units with a Code Talker said they lost all their communication [equipment]. Those are some of the things that happened there on September 15.

I guess they started landing troops on the beach at eight in the morning. I was there with the second wave. One was still lying with his feet in the ocean. I dragged that one out of the water. All marines that were there were on their bellies. They told me not to walk around. They can shoot that far from the other side of the airport. The airport was wide open and the three regiments landed in that area. The First Division landed west of us and we were in the middle. The Fifth Regiment and the Seventh Marine were to our right. At night we got shot at by mortars and artillery. Our communication commander's ears started bleeding so we had to leave. One of the three Code Talkers, John Chee, he was going to finish this one and he was heading home. We spent the night there. We lost our communication commander and the Fifth Regiment too. So early in the morning, when it was still dark, we got up. They told us we got to get out of there because soon it would open up and there would be shooting in the area. Anyhow, the Sherman tank was on the beach. The guy was running with the toilet paper to guide where the tank is supposed to go, because there were a lot of mines.

The Japanese broke a lot of codes, you know. They tell me, "Don't say any more than you have to." But we didn't have a problem. They banged a lot of tins and things like that on the radio when they listened. That didn't bother me all that much. I got my message through okay. You know you are dealing with your enemy and you have to do things like that to get that message through.

[I was never wounded except] later in Okinawa, a chunk of metal fell in my foxhole. It was so hot. That's the only close one. And other than that, you heard things bang but you just kept going. You're a marine; you're supposed to be tough [laughs.] We didn't have a bodyguard. The First Marine Division knew that in the surrender in the Philippines some went through a lot of torture, things like: got their fingernails out, took their teeth out, castrated. All those things they went through and they didn't let on. At Bougainville a lot of Code Talkers got their picture taken. The same photographer came to the First Marine division. If the Code Talker got captured, we didn't want to see him tortured, so I didn't get my photo. Otherwise, I would be dead too, because the Japanese would have my photo. The air force requested Navajo Code Talkers to keep the Japanese from knowing when they are coming. But they didn't [allow] that because they can be shot down and be in Japanese hands. So those are the reasons the Code Talker can't be on the air corps bombers, too dangerous. So marines really protected the code. They called me "Chief" and they called me "Geronimo." I got a lot of buddies; we are just like family. The First Marine Division, they're all white, but there are two Indians in there, Joe Kellwood and John Chee.

You have to remember, you don't tell anybody [that you were a Code Talker]. Keep it secret. So I was glad I returned home. My sister was scared because she didn't go to school and she knew the Japanese were coming this way. So I returned home and that was all nice for my two sisters. I was over there three years and one month. I had a one-night prayer when I came back, *Hózhǫ́ojí*, Blessing Way. They

more or less tell you, you're a Navajo and you live in the middle of this mountain, the east, west, south, north. And they gave you that mountain and that's where you belong. I came through well. My mind was made up to be a carpenter that I learned here in Phoenix. I've been driving nails for forty-three years.

Well, the way it goes, I think they're going to just let it [Navajo language] fade away. I know they want to keep it, but kids have to know English to get a good job. If you're going to talk Navajo and can't learn a trade, it's no good. You have to learn the English. I know we're losing our language. It's going to be history. That's it, so that's okay with me. Just let it be history that we did that job. It's good that we did the job and I don't really ask for anything.

John Kinsel

July 6, 2010, Lukachukai, Arizona

JOHN KINSEL LIVES IN ONE OF THE MOST BEAUTIFUL PLACES in Lukachukai, Arizona, at the base of a mountain pass. His home is surrounded by red rocks and red earth. In every direction, the eye meets natural beauty. I met Mr. Kinsel through his son, Ron, whom I knew from high school and college and who has worked actively for the Code Talker Association. Mr. Kinsel was dressed in his Navajo Code Talker uniform. He looked dramatic in his yellow shirt decorated with his medals and red hat. He wore a strand of turquoise and a white bone necklace. My equipment needed an electric outlet source. Mr. Kinsel said there was one behind the cabinet that was full of cookware and food supplies. My collaborator and I tried to move it away from the wall just a few inches but it was like moving a U-Haul truck. Suddenly he stepped in and moved it! Later I saw him easily pick up a heavy wheelbarrow. Mr. Kinsel, in his eighties, still ranches and takes care of his horses. One of the qualities that impressed the military about the Navajo soldiers was their heartiness and strength that came from living without modern conveniences. One had to be a sturdy individual to meet the demands of the Navajo homeland that could be harsh. Mr. Kinsel was still exemplifying those qualities in his advanced elder years. He didn't need a gym to pump iron. There was plenty of work for him on his land that gave him endurance and kept him strong.

The war that he spoke of left an indelible mark on him. A man pledges his life to become a warrior, a soldier in the name of his country and its ideals. While Mr. Kinsel volunteered to leave his homeland to help America, the pledge he made was not necessarily a moral agreement. The bombing of Nagasaki and Hiroshima that wiped out thousands of children and old people still resonates with him. Moreover, he didn't want to bring home the atrocities he had seen and participated in. Mr. Kinsel referred to the stories of the mythic warriors, Monster Slayer and Child Born for Water, who returned home from their battles depressed and spiritually wounded. This story parallels some of Code Talkers and veterans who suffered from PTSD. It is said that the Holy People gave The People a sacred ceremony that would help the veteran recover from the violence and bloodshed of war. Mr. Kinsel had such a ceremony after he returned as a way to restore him to spiritual health.

■ ■ ■

One day I was herding sheep and he said, "How many sheep do you own?" I said, "I don't know." "What do you really want to do in life?" he said. "Well, I want to go to school," I said. "Okay," he said. When I turned six, they put me in Fort Defiance. I went to school there for two years. My tongue wouldn't go the white man way. In 1933 I went to St. Michaels. There were sisters [nuns] over there. Every morning they are always praying. We sing and that's where I start getting the lingo, start getting the English language. I sang in the choir. Then, somehow, I was a good athlete playing football. I was a quarterback. I was only about fourteen or fifteen years old then. Then these guys that we played, this team at Fort Wingate, they called them teddy bears. We beat them. I guess I was a pretty good kicker. I threw short passes like a bullet. There's still a guy over here that still says that he tried to beat me, but he couldn't outrun me. I will tell you his name later. When I graduated from St. Michaels, I went to Fort Wingate. I didn't like the school because it was a government school. Catholic school is different. You learn a lot of respect from those nuns. Then they treat you like your mama does.

But Wingate was different. One day, I packed up my things and I started walking down that way. I went to [Highway] 66. And here comes a bus and it stopped. This bus driver says, "Where you going, Son?" I said I want to go to Santa Fe. He asked, "Do you have three dollars and seventy-five cents?" "Yeah, I got some money." So I paid right there and got to Santa Fe. That's how I ended up at St. Catherine's High School. On December 7, Sunday morning, they bombed Pearl Harbor. It's a good thing I graduated in '42. I knew Bill Toledo who was in eighth grade.

We went to Camp Elliott. Up to this day, I don't know where Camp Elliott was. We trained at San Diego for two months and at Camp Elliott for two months for Code Talker. I got in the Marine Corps by volunteering. They sent us back home and I told my mom and she cried. We used to live over about three miles down that way. That's where I'm from. I have two older sisters and one little brother. Right now, there is only one sister left, but she's a stepmother to me. Her father's Kinsel—that's how I got Kinsel, adopted the name. And then I found out that it's a German name.

I volunteered and didn't know anything about Code Talkers being recruited. All they wanted was some Indians, Navajos. I wanted to be a marine. After we graduated, I got a letter. It said to report to Camp Elliott. The next day there was a whole bus of Navajos, I guess twenty-five platoons. They shipped us over there to Camp Elliott. There were classes. Joe Kellwood, Bill Toledo and all of them from Crownpoint, Shiprock, Tuba City, and all out that way. Some of them were from way out there in Utah and Navajo Mountain. This guy named Samuel Holiday, he's still going and he's an old guy. There is also another one down here in Chinle but he never goes to association meetings. He is practically forgotten by the Code Talkers. His name is Fleming Begaye. He's from over the mountain there. He talks to me every time I see him. He used to work here.

You know what Philip Johnston said in Navajo? "Hello there, *Hastiin* (man)." "When are we going to have a sweathouse?" he said in Navajo. I was used to talking Navajo too much when I was overseas. But it's all right. I keep my language.

There were a lot of words, and I used to do a lot of practice on that. When I graduated, some of my comrades failed. Some of them needed help. Nobody knows unless you're a Code Talker, not even those guys who were on the combat team. What really saved me was that my dear mom knew a lot of things about ceremonies together with the family. My stepfather was educated. My mom knew all the ceremonies. There was a medicine man and she would do things for him. He did it for me, the warrior ceremony. What you call it, *tádídíín,* corn pollen? They used corn pollen. He said, "Now you can go." After I came back, they did the same thing like that. Of course, you have to have an Enemy Way ceremony dance too. That's different. All of the smells and smoke and killing and all that, that's what they shield you from when you come here and have the ceremony again. That's how I came back a human being, not a killer anymore. Some of those people that went to Vietnam never had anything like that, and that's why they went crazy. Some of them are having a hard time. You got to have those things. The only thing that I believe these days is my Catholic religion and my Navajo religion ceremony and that's it, nothing else.

There's an arrowhead I had on my dog tag for protection, a shield. Another thing is that bear dust *yąąh ndi'nigha'go,* when the bear shakes off dust, they use some kind of a seed or something they call *shash bitł'ool* bear string. They put that corn pollen on and they put it on you. That's how it went. I came back. That's when I got back from Iwo Jima.

When we traveled to New Zealand, we did a lot of maneuvering there and we used the code. On our way to Guadalcanal, we had an amphibious landing. We used our language to get back on the ship and continue to Guadalcanal. At Guadalcanal, they were still bombing it and the code had never been used there. It took seven months to secure it. It needed the language to shorten the war. I guess we were important, handy people at that time. It was the first time that they used it too, after that Tarawa. Two brothers named Morgan from Crownpoint went to New Britain. One of those brothers got killed there. We talked to each other. Navajo language was very powerful. Like Hopis and other Plains Indians, they had Code Talkers, but they say they used it in World War I. They wanted to get the praise, but we don't expect praise. I don't want praise. They just told me to do this. It's gone, so I go about my business until after the war. They asked, "Hey man, what did you do over there, what did you say and all of that?" We realized it after the war. It was something we did. But I never realized it when I was in the war. I saw people get killed; I saw bad things. I saw a lot of dead people. John Walker and I were holding people that had no head and their hands and arms were in the water. That was at Guadalcanal.

When we arrived there were some people, I don't know, pygmy people. One came out of the bushes and "Hey," he says. Then there was another guy and he was looking at his feet. He said, "Hey, how did you get one of those coconuts?" So he went up there like a monkey. He threw that coconut down and we opened it. One time, there was a snake that came out of the water. We found some purified water. So we passed the word around to come and get the water. We had knowledge, which Anglos and other people don't know about, because of our ancestors. One time it was really raining and we were getting cold. They tried to build a fire out there. So we went over there and brought the dry weeds and built a fire. Everybody was standing around and General Walker said, "You guys get your own fire!" He got mad at those guys. I always wonder about the talk about bodyguards; I never had no bodyguard.

One time at Guadalcanal, we got together and said, "Why don't we build a sweathouse?" A week later, they called from over there. There was a message for the Navajos, for Arizona and New Mexico. They said, "Come over. We have a sweathouse ready for you." Down towards the ocean there were crocodiles. Those Anglo guys shot a big one. It could swallow you with just one bite. They cooked and ate it. I don't eat snake. But I ate fish. We said to our company why don't we go over to Seabees and ask for some flour for fry bread. In other words, fry bread went to war. Lucky Strike went to war, and beer went to war. Chester's cigarettes went to war. They gave those free to us. When we came back, we didn't have no sugar, no coffee, no cigarettes. The Navajos call the Camel cigarette, *"dibé sání,"* "the old sheep." That means the old camels; it looks like a sheep. Another thing, Lucky Strike—red hot. Remember it used to have a red spot in the middle but now it's white.

The only thing is they shouldn't have dropped the atom bomb. Why Nagasaki? There's no fighting going on over there. There's children and old people. People who had nothing to do with war. Why should we drop it over there? Why should they drop it in Hiroshima? Yeah, sixty-four years ago it happened.

My medals say: Asian Pacific, four stars here, Battle Campaign, Purple Heart, and this one is Expert Rifle. Marksman, that's the third. All of the Navajos were pretty good shooters; a lot of them made Expert. I used to weigh about 120. When you fire, *Boom! Boom! Boom!* you start going back like this unless you're tall or big. Some of those Navajos, you know, they are big fellows and they make Experts and they shoot for those Anglo boys. *Bikéé' naazínígíí.* Ones that stand behind them. One followed them and one ahead of them. They shoot for them. Those guys made Expert. This one right here is the company. The Striking 9, they call it. And this is a Silver Star. I didn't want the Silver Star, but they said you Code Talkers earned it. I also got the Silver medal. My son has it. This is the Code Talker medal. The jewelry here represents Indian or Navajo. This here represents the earth [tan trousers]. This one here represents *bááshzhinii bistłee'* abalone socks, black abalone. I forgot what the shoe was. Anyway that's what it is. The jewelry, of course, is for Code Talker. [Pointing to the Navajo Code Talker Association patch] And then here is the stratosphere. This is the rainbow. This one represents the twin brothers[1]: *Naayéé' Neezghání dóó Tó Bájíshchíní,* Monster Slayer and Born for Water. These are feathers. This is a large feather right here. Anytime you run into an obstacle or wherever you go, it flies over it. This one they went up there with it and came back down. This is what they went for. This is a weapon, a shield. In the sky or sun, they went up there for the weapon to kill the monsters. Of course, the monsters used to be spirit. This one here is the earth. And then, of course, here is the universe. They create these things with the medicine man. Even the Code Talkers talk about it.

Ńléíjí bikáá'. It says over there. *"Discharge" bikáá'.* It says "discharge." The first thing is to get back alive. Then cleanse your life, and then, of course, a job, education, and things like that. But when they classified [the code], the Code Talkers were told not to talk about it and never say anything about being a Code Talker. But to me, the war is over. That's the way it is. I even forgot about all of the things that I did over there after I had my ceremony. When I used to hear something blow, I hit the deck. It was still in me for a while. That's why I had the ceremony. But I never talked about it. I never said I was a Code Talker. I was just glad to go back home to my mom. Then they declassified the code. That's when I went to Window Rock. They were meeting and I joined the association [Navajo Code Talker Association]. Then all the stories started coming out. They never asked us, but now we talk about it. I went to Chinle and talked to this guy. He's a veteran [at the veterans office.] He took the Purple Heart out. He said, "The [U.S.] doesn't give out Purple Heart for nothing. I'll see what I can do," he says. So I'm expecting some money coming, but I only got a hundred and seventy-two dollars. I was laughing about it, not even enough for one loaf of bread.

---

[1] Mr. Kinsel refers to the story of the mythic Hero Twins' journey to the sun.

One thing was that we became citizens and were allowed to vote. And then the only thing that I didn't like about what the Navajos did is they sell the alcohol. It's not the Navajo tribe's fault. It's the council. It says we will drink too, just like everybody else. We will drink too because we went to World War II. Our clan, our people went to war, we should have that privilege, he says. It isn't the Navajos that vote on it, it's the tribal council that votes on it; I always blame them.

■ ■ ■

Jó t'áá aaníí doo ada'ii'níílgóó doo wólta' da. Táá ałsoní tsodadiilzinígíí church ádaatée da nihich'į' ąą'ádaalyaa. Nihá át'ée dooleeł. Bee ániit'ée dooleeł. T'áádóó ńléí ha'at'iíshįį yee áádęę' nihá hooł'a'ígíí t'áá át'é nihich'į' ąą'át'ée dooleeł. Nihizaadígíí t'áá aaníí diyin. Éí t'áá aaníí bee hoch'ąąh iikai. Jó hoch'ąąh tsodadiilzin nahalingo hoch'ąąh iikai. Ákót'áo níláhdęę'anaa'i nilíníí t'áádoo yéé'dinítąą da; ch'ééh áát'įįd.

■ ■ ■

It is true that if we don't vote, it's not counted. Everything, our prayers, churches, are open for us. They will be for us. They will make us what we are. It will provide us more opportunities. Our language is very spiritual. That's what we used to win the war. We prayed for them as we fought for them. That's why the enemy didn't decode; they were unsuccessful.

■ ■ ■

Táá łá'í 'áshlaa. Ts'ída t'áá łá'í. I only made one, just one. "Route." There's a path. What are we going to call it? After that we call it R for rabbit . . . o-u-t-e. You have to imagine little things like a little rabbit den. Sometimes the wind blows or sometimes a little snow comes around and you see rabbit tracks, a bunch of them. Why don't we call it *gah bitiin,* rabbit trail? That's how we made the code out of little things like house, plant, birds, animal, things that we eat, stars, and all the things that we used.

We did something, we guided, and things like that. *My children and grandchildren yéédaalniih dooleeł. Yee náás yikah dooleeł.* My children and grandchildren will remember it. It will keep them going in the future. Even right now we have the privilege of getting scholarships for our kids and grandchildren. They are thinking about building a museum in [Window Rock] to carry our legacy. I sure hope that I get to see that thing in two more years. I'm still in good health.

Keith Little

August 2008, Crystal, New Mexico

the road to Crystal, New Mexico, led past summer wildflowers blooming on either side of the road. A gentle female rain fell early in the day and left the earth soft with colors. The highway wound through the red earth to the small village of Crystal. The chapter house is one of the first buildings you see upon arrival. I grew up in this community and knew that the roads spread in all directions to homes and ranches throughout the base of the Chuska Mountains. Today I especially regretted that my mother had moved away when I was at boarding school. Crystal still held strong memories of growing up in a place where we didn't lock our doors and knew everyone in the community. I stepped inside the chapter house and asked directions to Keith Little's house. I came prepared with a spiral notebook. A woman drew a map for me and we followed it down a sandy road. It's always a good idea to have paper available for someone to draw a quick map because there are no road or street signs in remote areas of the rez. I have a collection of hand-drawn maps to the Code Talkers' homes.

The map didn't turn out to be helpful, so we retraced our path back toward the chapter house. Suddenly a car appeared and it was Mr. Little on his way to the chapter house to vote. I said we'd wait for him there and follow him home on his return. My ulterior motive was to pick wild tea that was ready for harvesting and we were near a field of it. We picked a large bundle to save for the winter and to give away to friends who were not fortunate to have a tea field growing near them.

Mr. Little's home overlooks a valley of red rocks and red earth. His wife's family had picked one of the most beautiful places in which to settle. He invited us into his office that was filled with photographs and Code Talker memorabilia that we found in almost all the Code Talkers' homes we visited. Among my late father's effects, I found a photograph of Mr. Little as a high school student, which I showed him. We spoke of my father, who had passed over ten years ago. They were friends and classmates at the school in Ganado, Arizona, the day Pearl Harbor was attacked. Both enlisted and became Code Talkers. Mr. Little is the current president of the Navajo Code Talkers Association and, though he is into his eighties, he is still a strong presence.

■ ■ ■

I am from the Navajo Reservation. I am identified by clan, and in Navajo I am a *Tódích'íinii* and then *Tłízí łahní éí dah shizhé'í. Áádoo 'indidah Haltsohí Táhbąąhá 'éíya shicheii 'ádaat'é. Kinyaa'aanii 'éí shinalí 'adaat'é.* I am Bitter Water People clan and born for the Many Goats People clan. And then the Meadow People of the Near the Water People clan are my maternal grandfathers. Towering House People are my paternal grandfathers. This is my identification in clanship relations to my fellow Navajos.

I was a Navajo Code Talker with the United States Marine Corps from May 18, 1943, to November 1945. On December 7, 1941, it was a real ordinary Sunday. You might say, a fine day. That morning I remember I had to go to work at five o'clock in the morning down at the school farm. I was going to school at Ganado Mission School, Ganado, Arizona. One of my jobs to pay the cost of education was working on a farm. One of the primary duties was milking the dairy cows in the morning and delivering them to the dining room for the students and also for the patients at the hospital. So by about seven o'clock I was done. And then we usually went to breakfast, and then after breakfast we spent our time getting ready for church.

Now this was a Presbyterian mission school, so they had the real strong disciplinary rule that we don't talk our native language, and that we were there to be converted to Christianity, and to take us away from our cultural religions and our beliefs. So a lot of us were convinced that that was the way to do and forget to be an Indian. This was primarily drilled in to us, and as Christian learning, one of the primary teachings is that you get along with every human being, regardless of what color they are. So that was one of the integral ideas they put into our mind, so we kind of believe in that. We usually had poor food at this mission school because they were always, I guess, conserving, and were always short of good food. Usually we think we got the worst end of the food that they served to the staff and the other people at the mission.

In order to get other food, because we were always hungry, we were always looking for something to eat. So my friends, my buddies, and I usually went hunting on Saturdays and Sundays to get some rabbits and dress them out on trees down at the wash. When we got hungry, we went down there and built a fire, made some good coal, and had some real good rabbit meat. This is what we were doing Sunday afternoon on December 7, 1941. We got our dry sandwiches from the Sunday lunch and we took it down there to have it with the meat that we had cooked down there, and discovered that we didn't have any salt. So one guy named Willie Hiyi ran back to the dormitory to get hold of some salt any way he could, steal it if he had to. So he made a run and came back panting real hard. He didn't have to run that hard, but this time I guess he really ran because he had heard some exciting and terrible news through the radio. He wanted to get back to us quickly to tell us what had happened. He came back and stood in front of us and we looked at him.

He was breathing hard and trying to catch his breath and I said, "What in the world is wrong with you, Willie?"

He said, "Something, something bad happened."

"Okay, what?"

"United States was bombed." And we all looked at him, you know, shocked, astonished at what he said.

So somebody asked him, "Who done it?"

"Japan."

"Well, how did they get to the United States?"

"I don't know," he says, "but they say Japan bombed Pearl Harbor!"

"So where is Pearl Harbor anyway?"

And somebody knew, so he says, "Hawaii."

Then somebody else said, "Hawaii is not the United States."

So we circled around that for a while. Anyway that was the bad news and so instead of eating down there, we grabbed all the food that we had spread out to eat and took it back up to the dormitory. On the way, we took a bite of the sandwich. We had a radio in our living room. The radio was on real loud and there was a broadcast coming in from Washington, D.C. that Pearl Harbor had been bombed. They gave the casualties of the day and President Roosevelt was coming on so

everybody waited around. Our matron was standing there listening with us. Once in a while she would moan and say, "Ohhh," something like that, you know. The President came on and I don't know what he really talked about but the one phrase that I caught clearly that day was ". . . this is the day of infamy." I don't know what all that meant, but whatever it was, it wasn't good. Then he says the Congress—I didn't even know there was a Congress—but he says the Congress may declare war and our house mother moaned "Ohhh" real loud. Instead of listening, she was moaning at almost everything that was said. So when things kind of quieted down, I asked her, "Mrs. Simon, why are you making that noise?" "Ohhh, how awful," she said. "I'm thinking, I'm looking at all of you and some of you may have to fight in the war and it would be terrible if some of you get killed or get wounded, because lots of people will get killed, if this war comes to the United States." I guess she was thinking ahead all that time.

I remember some of the boys that day. There was Willie Hiyi, a Laguna boy, and there was Paul Daniel from Oklahoma. I don't know what tribe he was, but he was a pretty husky boy, and Benson Tohe. He and I chummed around together. He was the one that milked the cows with me that morning and delivered the milk at five o'clock in the morning. And we delivered it in a wagon. You hitched a mule team to a horse; you threw about ten gallons of milk cans in the back of the wagon, and then you ran and you delivered some to the main kitchen for the students and the staff. Then the others they delivered to the hospital. That was our job early in the morning. So he was with me and another guy. I think it may have been a guy named Larry Barney. He was one of my friends. Those were the people that we chummed around with.

So after all that, we got back together. We were so doggone hungry that day. But we had forgotten to eat. After things quieted down, we sat down to eat. We talked and said, "Do you think we will go to war? What outfit are you going to join if you do go into the service?" At that time, we had never heard of United States Marine Corps. It was the army and the navy and the Army Air Corps. Those were the prime armed forces of the United States. We all decided that we were going to join the outfit that was fighting the Japanese. The war was going bad for the Allied Forces, and come July 1942, I noticed that a lot of the boys that I knew, boys that had just maybe turned eighteen, had gone into the Marine Corps. So that's how I got to know something about the United States Marine Corps. So that's what we did. That's how Benson wound up in the Marine Corps too. [Laughter]

I finally became seventeen years old and I got into the Marine Corps the day after my birthday in Gallup. They told me to report to Fort Defiance. There was a bus going down to St. Johns and then were being shipped to Phoenix. Then after they were done with their physical they either went on or they came back home for ten days. But anyway, down there I passed everything and the recruiter asked me if I was going to school. I said, "Yeah, I'm going to school." So he sent me back. He said, "You finish out your school year and come back and report for duty." Instead of going right on, I was sent back to Ganado Mission. That's how I got into the Marine Corps on May 1943 when I was seventeen years old. It took a long time to get there from being fifteen on December 7.

So I went through boot camp and then I ended up in Camp Pendleton in July or August. Well, towards the end of our boot camp training the D.I. [drill instructor] called everybody into formation and, normally, when he calls us into formation, we have to have a clean rifle because he's going to inspect. There was a procedure and a way to give it to him. You didn't just give it to him. When he stood in front of you, you shoved the rifle at him and he would catch it and he would inspect it. Then, when he threw it back at you, you had to catch it. That's what he did. And I shoved the rifle at him. He just looked up and down, from one end to the other and gave it back to me instead of shoving it. Then he said, "Chief Little, are you an American Indian?" I said, "Yes sir." And then he said, "Are you by any chance a Navajo?" I said, "Yes, sir." And then he said, "I understand the Marine Corps needs Navajos real badly because they make good scouts. That's all." That was an astonishing, baffling question to ask. What in the world is that anyway, a scout? Because you only have scouts at the school where I was attending, not in the Marine Corps. Then my platoon mates really got a kick out of that.

When the D.I. dismissed us, they started picking on me, saying, "Chief, you got promoted. The D.I. called you 'chief' and then he gives you a job that you're going to be a scout." They said, "I feel sorry for you, when you join an outfit they're going to shove you across enemy lines, and you're going to have to scout it out," which I guess meant reconnaissance work. "And when you're doing it, you're going to get your butt shot off and get killed or something, you know." So that was another baffling thing that I came across. What in the world did I do that for? I didn't want to get killed. When we graduated from boot camp, I was told by my D.I., "Wait there and somebody will come pick you up." There were about four or five Navajos with their seabags waiting there. One of them I knew. We had been together at Tuba City going to school. We both asked, "What are you doing here?" at the same time. That's how I got into the communication school up in Camp Pendleton.

At the barracks that we went to, nobody knew what was going on. Didn't even know where the company was or where the men were. They came marching back about five o'clock, and to my astonishment, they were all Navajos. I asked, "What are you guys doing?" "Well, you'll find out. You'll be sorry." [Laughter] They didn't tell you anything, and then the next day we waited. They told us to wait in the building. "There will be other Navajos coming in from boot camp, and when we get enough, we'll start a new class." What that was, we didn't know. Finally, about a week or so later, we got about sixteen to twenty Navajos, usually about twenty per class. We asked these other Navajos, "What are you guys doing?" They went off in the morning, marched to another building, and that's where they spent all day. They came back at noontime, but they went right back or they went out on the field. "You'll find out," was always the answer.

About a week and a half later, we finally got into class. We were working with the Navajo language. There was a list of English words in one column. The code word was in the middle column. What it really meant in the Navajo code was in the third column. I found out that you had to memorize all of it. You had to familiarize yourself with that English vocabulary. By the way, it was the battlefield language. For every word in the middle there is a Navajo coded name to this vocabulary word like bivouac. For the word bivouac, the name was *ił názt'í,* branch shelter. It can be built anytime out of tree branches like piñon and juniper. There were other words, like grenades were potatoes, and the letter T was *tązhii,* turkey, and then the letter A had several codes. One of them was *wóláchíí',* ant. Then there was the anti-tank gun and that one was *wóláchíí' yihxéés,* ant itch. Every word had to be memorized. There were names for countries like Japan, Italy, Germany, Russia, units of the military, like division, regiment, battalion, companies, platoon, and on down to squad. The squad was your *yo',* bead. Those were the words that we had to memorize. They really drilled you. You had to know how to spell each one, so that you could write a message when you were talking on the radio. If you were talking into the mic, you were encoding the English vocabulary into Navajo code. The receiver down there, he was decoding it into Navajo code. When he heard *"ił názt'í,* branch shelter" this guy here, wrote down "bivouac." Or he said "grenade" over there. He'd say, *"nímasii"* and then over there he wrote "grenade." The tools that were used in a war—a lot of them did not have Navajo words, so they were given names. Those that could not be translated or if you translated it, it would take a long phrase. So they made it one word. That's the way it was and you have to be really precise. They tested to see if you could make it in so many words a minute. You couldn't miss some spelling or the required time to write a message. The time on the radio has to be short and precise. So that's the way it was. I passed my examination, and finally got into the Fourth Marine Division.

I went overseas in January 1944. My first stop was Pearl Harbor. It was famous for the day it was bombed, but there was no sign of the harbor ever being bombed. There were ships of all kinds. Then we went on to Roi-Namur and Marshall Islands. It was my first battle on February 2nd and 3rd. I was a radioman for the battalion commander. Wherever the battalion commander went, I went with him. We spent about four or five days on that island and left and came back to Maui in Hawaii. And then in June we ended up in Saipan in the Mariana Islands. That took about two weeks to clean up. And then a week or two later we went to Tinian adjacent to Saipan, and we spent about a week there. Then we got aboard ship and come on back to Hawaii again. In the meantime we had heard that the B29 had built up bases in the Marianas like Saipan, Tinian, and Guam. They say big planes flew from the Mariana Islands all the way to Japan and back. I don't know how long it took. It must have taken more than ten hours to fly. At that time planes didn't fly six hundred miles an hour. We heard about Iwo Jima and how it was being bombed and raided, and the airplanes that bombed it. Then the navy comes in and shells it. Thoughts come into your mind. Maybe that's our next target and, sure enough, we ended up at Iwo Jima in February 1945.

According to the reports, they were going to take seven days to get it all cleaned up. At the end of seven days, we were only about two or three hundred yards or less than half a mile from the shore where we landed. The resistance was so fierce and the garrison forces—the defending enemies— were living in caves and tunnels. Every time we made a move, they took a shot at us. They didn't live on the land, and I can say that I have never seen a Japanese in combat there, but I have seen those that were captured. Very few that were captured came out. They were all well camouflaged, and we read about it, as it was one of the fiercest battles that the Marine Corps had ever encountered. Somewhere along the line, some communication officer made a remark that if it wasn't for the Navajo Code Talkers, the Marine Corps wouldn't have ever taken Iwo Jima. To me, that was a lot of exaggeration because the Marine Corps would have taken Iwo Jima, but it might have taken them longer, but it would have been done. But anyway those are my own thoughts undercutting the Marine Corps and giving credit to the Navajo Code Talkers, which is good because the code that we used had worked beyond expectation. Its use had primarily become a prevailing language of battlefield communication. In comparison to the conventional codes at that time, the Navajo code completely outdid the conventional code in accuracy, in speed, and in saving countless American lives.

On Iwo Jima, I was also radioman for the battalion commander who went to the front. Somehow or another, I always ended up with him. A lot of times we made a trip across no man's land. One of the primary places that I went was the rock quarry right on the north side of where we landed. They had us pinned down for almost a week before it was shattered. Then another place that we went was a place called "Meat grinder." I think that's number 382-something. Those are the places that are so thoroughly camouflaged that you don't even know that it was there until you walk into it or walk on it or you see a hole where you're walking. That is an air vent for the tunnel down below. You don't even know whether the enemy was behind you or around you or somewhere. It was somewhere around there that we mixed up with them. Maybe they were sleeping in the tunnel and we stepped right up on top. That was Iwo Jima. It was only seven hundred miles from Tokyo.

So after about a month, thirty-some-odd days, I remember we boarded ship on March 26. We were back aboard the troop ship that brought us back to Maui several days later. You have these memories all the time. You have memories of losing your friends; you have memories of trying to rescue your wounded friend. You don't forget these things. You live with it. We finally came back to Maui in April of 1945 and they give us about two weeks' rest. In the meantime, a lot of replacements had come in and after two weeks, we started training again: walking all the time, simulating battles in town or up the mountains. Then we went out in the ship and we practiced landing. And by August, we were ready to go again. This time we knew where we were going. We're going to land somewhere in Japan, the land of the people we were fighting. When we made a promise, when the war started, to fight the Japanese, we didn't even know what kind of soldiers they were. We knew nothing about them, but I have a lot of respect for Japanese soldiers. They were well trained and they fought to the death. They left their wounded, and we rescued a lot of wounded Japanese. These are the memories I have of Iwo Jima. Like I said, we were walking over them while they were down in the tunnels. Somebody had to watch your back all the time because somebody's going to come up and take a shot at you. This is the way Iwo Jima was.

We were all ready to go again. One day we had a tent town. At the end of it was the communication tent that was guarded and manned twenty-four hours a day. We took our turns over there watching the communication. You know, you listened for news that came in, communication that came in. Once in a while, I took my turn on that communication chat. One day early in the morning, about three or four o'clock in the morning, somebody was running up and down the street yelling, "We're going home! We're going home! The war is over! Yeah, yeah, you guys, the war is over!" We were really sound asleep. Here this guy was interfering with our sleep, so somebody piped up and says, "Hey, you son of a bitch, get off our street, we're sleeping good!" "No," he says, "No, no, come on down to the communication tent. You listen in on the broadcast." And we reluctantly got up and put our pants on. Some guys just went in their shorts, barefooted, and listened. There was a broadcast coming in that Japan was offering unconditional surrender and wanted the United States to negotiate terms. Of course, instead of being half asleep, we all jumped up and down and yelled. Somebody said, "Let's go open the beer garden."

So that was my memorable day of the end of the war and that turned out to be Navajo Code Talkers Day. Today, we observe it as Navajo Code Talkers Day. Instead of training intensely, everything slowed up. I guess all the ships that were available for troop movement were in the Far East, loaded with cargo or were on the open ocean. We all knew we were going home and we all wanted to know, "When do we board ship for the United States?" It took me almost through the month of February to get on a ship and come on back. Finally, I got out of the Marine Corps at Camp Pendleton. When we arrived in San Diego in the States, the people that were there as we came off the ship were ladies who were giving out ice cream. Some guys went and touched the land and blessed themselves with our land, so I did the same thing. I went to Camp Pendleton to be discharged. I waited and waited until I think it was November 28, after Thanksgiving Day, in November 1945 when I got out. Before I left the Corps I was told, "Don't ever tell anybody what you have done." So as it was in the communication school when we first entered, this was a military secret that you don't tell anybody. They told us not to air what we had done. We went home and had no celebration of any kind.

When we got home, of course, the family is glad to see you. They don't meet you at the train station. They don't even know you're coming home. So you had to go to the trading post and leave your stuff there and walk home or somebody that knows you gives you a horseback ride home. My sisters were glad to see me, so we had a lot of mutton feast for several days and they never said anything about a blessing or anything like that. So it stayed that way. Then I went back to school and graduated high school and went to work. Went to school again and my kids grew up. They knew nothing about me just like you. They didn't know what I did until twenty, twenty-four, maybe twenty-five years after World War II, when the code was declassified and revealed. And we still didn't know what to do with it. My kids don't even know that I was a Code Talker; my own kids the ones that are born for me. I don't believe my ex-wife knew I was a Code Talker when she died. The secret part of it is we didn't even know that the code was devised by a group of men who were recruited on the

Navajo reservation back in early 1942. Thirty of them were selected out of a volunteer list the Marine Corps had recruited on the reservation. Of the over six hundred men, only thirty were selected and the other guys were waiting to be called into the Marine Corps. In the summer of 1942 there was a flock of Navajos going into the Marine Corps. I noticed that a lot of them probably just went through boot camp and went overseas. The original twenty-nine that were selected went to training somewhere in San Diego. They developed the code and vocabularies. They had to go to the South Pacific to get the bugs out. So in a way, they had to overcome a lot of skepticism. Nobody knows anything about the Navajo marines that devised the code so craftily that it was never deciphered by the Japanese. So in essence we, the qualified Code Talkers, had the code in our mind and the whole secret code was engrained in our physical body. And if we were captured we would have suffered. What do you call that, treacherous? Because of our knowledge, they can't kill us, but they would have, they would have tortured us.

I don't know nothing about bodyguards. The thing is, the Marine Corps also secretly had somebody watching the Navajo Code Talkers wherever they go, whatever they do. If a Navajo Code Talker was captured by the enemy, the Marine Corps would do everything they could to rescue the man. But if they couldn't, they had to shoot him to protect the code. We couldn't carry any notes. Everything was memorized, so in essence we were walking human beings with all the codes of the battlefield. All the previous codes had been broken and deciphered. This is the only one that is not broken, so with that, we probably saved thousands of lives, whereas the atomic bomb killed millions of human beings. So, this is my story.

I think the Navajo language is a highly secret, spiritual language that was given to us by the divine people and it is very important. The Navajo people have contributed beyond expectation with their sons who became Code Talkers who completely confused the Japanese. They were so patriotic. They obeyed orders. Most of them never received recognition of any kind. Some of them are glory hounds, most of them are not. I think they have done something very great as a contribution to our democratic country, to our cause of freedom. And the younger generation should carry the ball from here and pass it on to the next generation, protect the land like we did, like the people of World War II, and Korea, and Vietnam, and the other people.

■ ■ ■

T'áá Diné k'ehjí shı̨́ı̨́ éí hait'áo baa hojilnih. Jó nihik'eh hodidleeh n̲t'ę́ę́' lá. Doo nihił bééhózin da éídí. T'ah n̲t'ę́ę́' ałk'ijiijéé' hodoo'niid t'áádoo hót'é ílíní. Áko éíyá t'óó kéyah bich'ą́ą́h ndadiikah jó hótáo tsízdíkos. Hastóí ádajiníi n̲t'ę́ę́' íídą́ą́' 1941 yeedą́ą́' yówohdę́ę́' t'áá ákódajiní bits'á dahojích'įįdii łeh dajiníi łeh. Doo shą' léí' nihik'eh dazhdidleeh lá. Yówohjı̨́' anídahodíníílkał. Jo kót'áo tsíhodeeskéézígíí át'é.

■ ■ ■

I'm not sure how one tells about it in Navajo. Well, we were ready to lose the war apparently. We were not aware of it. All of a sudden the war started. One thinks, let's defend our land. Back in 1941, elders said, they are usually evil. Let us not have them win over us. Let's chase them back. This is the thinking.

■ ■ ■

It's an automatic choice to defend your land, your people, your loved ones, your home.

■ ■ ■

Kót'áogo éíyá tsízdíkos. Diné kodi hak'éí hólǫ́ǫ, homá holǫ́ǫ, hazhé'é, háí shı̨́ı̨́, hak'éí nilínígíí bee, éí éíyá bee ázhdoonííł, Diné bíká azhdoolwoł, hadine'é bíká azhdoolwoł, hakéyah bíká azhdoolwoł, bich'ą́ą́h tázhdidoogaał. Jó kót'é. Áko díídí Diné bizaad chooz'įįdígi hane' saad doo béédi'dootı̨́ı̨́łígíí, saad nanil'inígíí, kót'áo hadít'éégo ályaa. Diné t'áá bí ádaat'í. Doo háí da át'ji da. Azhą́ Bilagáana bídahólnííh ndi Diné éí bich'į' dajííł'aad. Ádaołééh, dazhdííniid. Naaltsoos biyaa ndajiz'á. Díí bik'ehgo ha'nǫǫ. Áko éí ákódayiilaa. T'áá kǫ́ǫ́ t'áá nihí háíshı̨́ı̨́ nihikéyah bikáá'góó hólǫ́nígíí—nanise' ádaat'éii dóó dibé béégashii łı̨́ı̨́' da ádaat'é áádóó táyi' da nda'aldeeh ha'iíshı̨́ı̨́ táyi' naaghá shı̨́ı̨́ niłch'ih yee nagháhígíí. Éí ts'ídá t'áá át'é chodaoz'įįd ádaolyéhígíí. Dóó nááná t'áá nihí niidlínígíí nihitsodizin ádaat'éhígíí dadííníílzingo bee yéiilti'ígíí ádóóne'é niidlínígíí. Áádóó inda nanise' t'óó ahayóí chodaoz'įįd ádaolyéhígíí. Kót'áo éí nihikéyah bikáá' hólǫ́nígíí éí biniinaa Diné bizaad, Diné bitsodizin, Diné binahat'a' ts'ídá iyisíí ílı̨́i sha'shin daniidzin. Hozhó'ó baa nitsídzíkeesgo ákót'é. Doo háí da yéé'idlééh da. Éí biniinaa éí díí Diné bizaad yee nidaashnishígíí tsiláołtsooí wolyéhígíí éí ts'ídá aláah áníłtsogo daats'í keyah yich'ą́ą́h naaskai bizaad yee. Éí biniinaa Diné bizaadígíí t'áá iyisíí ílı̨́. Áko nihizaad nihił yá'át'ééhgo nihił nizhónígo bee yeiilt'i'go shı̨́ı̨́ niha'áłchíní yéédahósin dooleeł. Háálá na'nitin t'óó ahayóí biyi'. Yits'ą́ą́dóó yee nitsídookosígíí éí hoghandi bee ałch'į' yéiilti'. Ako ákót'áogo shį́į́ ha'át'íí shį́į́ ábidii'ní Bilagáana k'ehjí "legacy" bidii'ní. The legacy of the Navajo Code Talkers. Jó díídi doo ndi nihaa ákohwiinidzingóó łá'í ndi diné doo nihaa ákodanízin da. Nanil'inígíí át'é ałdó'. Secrecy. Doo nihí ádii'níigóó saad nihíyííkeedígíí éí ádaanǫǫ éí bik'ehgo ádeiidzaa tsiláo wolyéhígíí. The armed forces of the United States. Nihinant'a'í Wááshindoondi hólǫ́ ha'níí łeh éí shį́į́ bik'ehgo ádahóót'į́įd ts'ídá ałtso choidoo'į́į́łígíí bee łá ni'iileehgo indá kwe'é chǫǫ'į́. Éí biniinaa haashį́į́ t'áo óólyé ts'ídá niná'níyázhíjį' daats'í wolyé. Diné bizaad ts'ída bik'ehgo áhodooníílgo baa nitsáhákees, ts'ídá ílį́igo, ts'ídá diyingo shį́į́ baa nitsáhákees áko. Kot'áó éí nihizaad hólǫo át'é. Bee k'é ahidii'ní. Éí bee da'ahííníítǫ'. Éí bik'ehgo nihinahat'a' dahólǫ́ ałdó'. Nihitsodizin dahólǫ́. Yá'át'ééhgo baa nitsííkees. T'áá éí t'éí bee neiidá. Tsiláo danilígíí óhoo'aah biyi' nináánát'i' ka'd. T'áá aaníí lá hwiinidzingo. Éí biniinaa shį́į́ éí Diné kót'áo ndaalnishígíí Diné bizaad yee ndaashnishígíí ts'ídá alááh áníłtsogo baa nitsáhákeesgo át'é. Kot'ée lá.

Shimá t'áágééd shiyaa hoo'a' shizhé'é dó'. Áko na'nitin wolyéhígíí, óhoo'aah wolyéhígíí, ts'ídá t'áá haaníłtsóhígo shį́į́ shaa náádiilyá. Áko t'óó íísísts'ą́ą' dóó t'óó t'áá háí shį́į́ t'áá ákondiyę́ę́ ndashizhnitinígíí bik'ehgo shinahat'a' hazlį́į'. Shicheii dajíłį dóó shida' da dajílį́. Shimá yázhí da dajílį́. Shimá sání da. Éí bits'ą́ą́dóó nitsáhákees nilį́nígíí, kót'éego éíyá nitsodizin hólǫo dooleeł ákót'éhíí nanináa dooleeł tádídíín nidi'nilgo dashijinǫo. Áko éí doo hąh bíhoo'aahígíí át'ée lá ałdó'. Homá hálǫo shį́į́ éíyá yee hwił halnih. Hazhé'é da hólǫo. Hacheii dó' ts'ídá t'áá íyisíí hwaa ákonízingo shį́į́ ałdó' ákódoonííł. Hamá sání da. Éí t'óó t'áá bita'góó na'adá nahalingo shiyaa hoo'a' azhą́ shik'éí t'óó ahayói ndi. Hooghan wolyéhígíí ts'ídá alááh áníłtsogo íłįigi át'é. Biyi'dóó óhoo'aah t'óó ahayói.

■ ■ ■

This is how one starts thinking. When one has relatives here, when one has a mother, a father, anyone, family—for them, one will help his/her people, one will help the land and protect it. This is how it is. So the use of the Navajo language, the one that was never decoded, the secret language, was created to help. The Navajo people did it themselves, no one else. Although the Anglos were in charge, the Navajos were the ones who were asked to do it. "Do it," they said. They documented it on paper, according to this, they said. That's how they did it. Those that are here around us on our land—plants, sheep, cows, horses, water animals, mammals. All of their names were used—even us, our prayers

that we hold sacred, our clans. And the names of many vegetations were used. That's why things we have on our land, Navajo language, Navajo prayer, Navajo planning, we value. That's how it is when you really think about it. No one is copying it. That's why these veterans who used the Navajo language used the language to the utmost capability in defending our land. That's why it is very valuable. So if we like our language and consider it beautiful and use it to speak to one another, our children will know it, because there are lots of teachings in it. They will think to use it at home.

The word we use in English, "legacy," the legacy of the Navajo Code Talkers is known for it. It is about secrecy. Secrecy. It wasn't our idea; we were told to use it, we servicemen, and that's what we did, the armed forces of the United States. They always say we have a President in Washington, D.C.; he's probably the one who ordered all of this to happen. He approved everything they used, every single thing to the smallest size depended on the Navajo language; it was considered very valuable, very sacred. This is how our language exists. We address our relatives with it. That's what holds us together. That's what we use to plan with also. We have prayer. We cherish it. That's what we live on. For servicemen now, it has teachings. We consider it very real. That's why we think highly of those who used the language this way. This is how it is.

I was raised without my mother, my father also. So, I was sort of stripped of teachings and learning. So I gained knowledge by listening to whoever wanted to teach me. I had maternal grandfathers and uncles, aunts, and a maternal grandmother. From them came knowledge. "This is how you will have prayer, this is how you will be. Use corn pollen," they said to me. So those are things that you do not learn quickly. If you have a mother, she will probably teach you those things, likewise if you have a father. If you have a grandfather who really cares for you, it probably happens that way, even if you have your grandmother. Although I have many relatives, it seems like I was raised just wandering around. I learned that home is the most important thing. Many teachings come from it. *Eelkid.* It ended.

Alfred Peaches

August 6, 2008, Winslow, Arizona

JIMMY BEGAY OF SAWMILL was not home for our appointment, so I called Mr. Alfred Peaches who lives in Winslow, Arizona. It was a last-minute call, but he agreed to an interview. Mr. Peaches lives north of Winslow, the reservation border town. His wife, Jeanette, opened the door with a smile. "Hello," she said. Like those of many of the Code Talkers, the living room was decorated with military memorabilia and family photos. Mr. Peaches is hard of hearing, his wife informed me. Like many of the Code Talkers, he is in his eighties. He is soft spoken and I didn't want to tire him out asking him too many questions. Mr. Peaches spoke of the battles he had been in, though he had trouble recalling names.

His childhood is not usual for his generation and for many of the Code Talkers. He was still a boy when his father died, leaving his mother to raise him and his siblings. He believes in education and though he was late in enrolling in school, he strongly believes that the younger generation needs an education. He attended Sherman Institute in Riverside, California, after he was discharged, and that is where he met his wife. A large black and white photo of over one hundred students at Sherman Institute hangs on his living room wall. He points to himself standing in the back row. "I was twenty-three at the time," he said. I asked him if he knew my grandmother, who was one of the first Navajo teachers who taught at that school. He thinks he remembers her. Among the many other family photos is one of his son who currently serves in the air force. He tells me that he was never wounded and received a Presidential Unit Citation, the highest medal for his service. He received the rank of corporal after nearly eight years of service. And like many of the Code Talkers, no family members met him at the train or bus station because they didn't know he had been discharged.

■ ■ ■

I am *Tódích'ii'nii*, Bitter Water People clan and born for the *Kinlichii'nii*, The Red House People clan. My maternal grandfather clan is the *Tábááhá*, Water's Edge People clan and my paternal grandfather clan is the *Lók'aa' Dine'é*, Reed People clan.

I was born in Shonto, Arizona, where my mother was raised. My father was from the Kayenta area. My mother and father got married, and I was the first one born to the family. We had to move to Kayenta where my father's ranch was. From the beginning, I supported my parents from about five years old. I took care of the sheep, horses, and cattle some time. When I could, I rode horseback when I was about six years old.

They didn't put me in school until I was thirteen years old. My father and my mother wanted me to be a rancher or a medicine man. One of my younger brothers was already in sixth grade. They finally put me in school with my brother. I am not sure but I remember 1938 to '39, '40, '41 being at the boarding school. I didn't know anything about what was going on in the war. All we heard was there was a war. I didn't know anything about it then until probably I was seventeen. When I was drafted I only finished fifth grade education and I was seventeen and a half.

I enlisted in November 1943. I was called to Phoenix for a physical examination. Then I went home for a week and then I was ready within a week. After that, we had to go through a prayer and Navajo Way [ceremony]. A prayer was made for me. After that I had to get on the train and got off in San Diego. It was December. I was sent to Camp Pendleton, California, for eight weeks' training on communication that included Code Talker training and radio operation. While I was at the examination in Phoenix, I asked to join the navy. But they told me you have to go to Marine Corps. I didn't know much about it. We had to learn everything about radio operation signals before we graduated. They told us that you are here to be a Code Talker and that's all.

Then they shipped me to Guadalcanal. At Guadalcanal we had to go through training again. For three months, we started moving towards some other island that was unknown. I don't know where we sailed. Then we ended up in the invasion of Okinawa right after Iwo Jima. For three months, from April 1 to June 20, we secured the island. From there we went to Saipan. On August 12 Japan was bombed and surrendered. I thought about peace [after the war] was

done. I thought our country's been saved for the people of the USA. So, I was very grateful. Then they sent me back to the U.S.

[Thirteen Code Talkers] got killed in action. One of them got killed by their own men. It was a navy man. I don't know if it was a mistake that he shot the Code Talker because he thought he was Japanese. Some of them got captured too. About two or three got captured. The order was say nothing. We didn't report anything even if they threatened to kill you. So that's how it was. The code was top secret.

I was treated pretty good. Only a few of these guys were kind of funny, you know. They don't like Indians much, I found. There were a few guys who are like that. [The code] saved a lot of people, even on the frontline. The war could have taken longer. But we saved thousands and thousands of people, even our enemies. I'm just proud that I served my country. I served to save my people and country. Now everything is okay.

After the war, I went back to school and finished ninth grade. When [the Korean War] broke out then I had to re-enlist. I was in the reserves. So I re-enlisted and left my education again. I served for five years, one year in South Korea, and two years stateside. Finally my health got me out of service because they found out that I had tuberculosis in my lung. So that's the reason the Marine Corps discharged me.

I was in the hospital for about three years recovering from sickness. Then I worked in the Albuquerque area. And then I came back to reservation to work. Of course, I had a family to support and I had to be closer. So I got a job in Fort Defiance. After eleven years, when I was in the hospital, that's where I finished high school. So I worked for eleven years for the tribal water department. Then

Alfred Peaches with his wife Jeanette.

I decided to go back to school again. I went back to Chinle to the community college where my AA [associate degree] education was completed. From there I went to school here and there. I went to this school, Pawnee College, and went to Phoenix College to learn engineering drafting. Then I came back to the Navajo Nation and worked for a while. I worked for minerals department in Window Rock. Because my school record was good, the University of Louisville gave me a scholarship. So I attended for one semester. One of my oldest kids was graduating from high school and was going to college too. My wife wanted to work instead of going to school, so I came back over here. From there, I went to school in a different area at the University of New Mexico in Roswell [he may have meant Eastern New Mexico University]. I worked at the same time. I became a geologist, finally.

■ ■ ■

Díí da'ahijoogá'ígíí áádóó nihidiné'é ashiiké dóó asdzání, háishį́į́ ndaazbaa', bikéyah yich'ą́ą́h ndaazbaa'. Nihikéyah bich'ą́ą́' nidasiibaa'. Áko t'áá íyisíí baa ahééh hasin shį́į́. Ákót'éego bee łá'í jíłįigo bee łá'í ádlįinii bee atah jizǫo. Doo baa áhwiilyą́ą́góó éí háádida yiilchxoohgo éí t'áá nihik'ijį' nándlį nahalin. Kót'áo baa nitséskees shí.

■ ■ ■

This war and the men and women who fought in the war defended their land. We defended our land. So it is profoundly appreciated. There needs to be unity; one has to believe in unity. If we don't take care of it, we will destroy it and that destruction will return to us in the future. This is how I think about it.

Albert Smith

August 4, 2008, Gallup, New Mexico

ALBERT SMITH SAID HE DIDN'T LIKE TO EAT ALONE, so I invited him to join us for breakfast. It would give us a chance to get acquainted before the interview. We arrived at his house to find him appearing elegant in his Navajo Code Talker yellow shirt and brown shell necklace from one of his trips to Hawaii. Married for fifty-four years to Ellen Louise from Laguna Pueblo, Mr. Smith was now a widower. She had passed not long ago. I joked that that made him an eligible bachelor. He said he was still in a year-long mourning cycle according to traditional belief. They had raised a daughter and ten foster children and have two great-great granddaughters. Some of his great-grandchildren live in Alaska and work for the salmon fishing industry. After breakfast, we drove to Coal Avenue in downtown Gallup to view the Navajo Code Talker mural. Mr. Smith is the one standing in front of the deer. Then we walked to Veterans' Park, which is dedicated to all the local veterans, and to those who fell in the U.S. battles since World War II.

Active in the Navajo Code Talker Association, Mr. Smith has served as president. An articulate and venerable man of eighty-four years, he is in demand as a speaker and has traveled all over the country and internationally. He worked for twenty years in adult education in Crownpoint, New Mexico, where he retired as director. Mr. Smith's wisdom and humility about his service as a Code Talker, like the other Code Talkers, are what impressed me during this oral history project. He spoke profoundly about taking care of the earth. "Give the mountain a drink of water when it's thirsty," he said. Mr. Smith and his older brother George enlisted with the intent of serving together, but their plans were cut short when a military ruling prohibited brothers from serving together. Nevertheless, Albert and George became Code Talkers, but served in different companies.

After we packed our equipment and were readying to leave, Mr. Smith gave me a blessing. It was a special moment that reminded me that this oral history project needed care, nurturing, and guidance. I was being entrusted with Mr. Smith's stories and with the other Code Talkers' stories, public and private, so that they would continue for all.

■ ■ ■

My name is Albert Smith. I'm Salt People clan and born for *Tsi'naajinii,* Black Streak Wood People clan. I am adopted by friends from Zuni and Acoma Pueblos, and I have in-laws from Laguna Pueblo. I have relatives from the northern Pueblos too. I'm a Navajo Code Talker.

I did not know that I was going to be a Code Talker. Military instructors were giving military introduction to seventeen-year-olds at the school. One of my brothers was involved in it. So every now and then, I would listen in to their topic. They also went through some military training. At the end of the year, they were to be inducted into whatever [branch of] service they chose. My brother and I were talking about it and we said, "Let us go in together. Let's get permission from our father," because our mother had passed away when we were little boys. We took a walk on the weekend back home from Wingate to here [Gallup]. We found him at home and told him that we were thinking about going into the service together. But I didn't tell him how old I was or our plan to enter together. He said it was okay because we had two older brothers that were in the service and they were in the Philippines at that time. We walked back to school. My brother put my name down even though I was just in the eighth grade.

So we took the bus from Wingate to Albuquerque and the train from Albuquerque to Santa Fe. We were there for two days. They gave us an exam on the knowledge of our English language. Both of us passed. The second day we were questioned as to which branch of service we wanted to be in. We heard about the marines, so that was our first choice. Some went into the air corps, the army, and the coast guard. The majority of us went into the marines and were sworn in together. Some were told when to report at certain places and some were ready to be sent out. They took the platoon numbers for the Navajos for the marines. We were separated there. Ten of us stayed behind. We were told that we would be called later on after we finished school. There was a second all-Navajo platoon. They continued on to San Diego.

We went back to school and reported in June. We were treated like everybody else, no exceptions. After two months we finished, and then we were told we were going to a code school. When our turn came, they had not sent out that first group, the first twenty-nine. They were still finishing up at Camp Pendleton, so we had to wait a month. While we're waiting at the base in San Diego, they were having a battle with the Japanese on one of the Solomon Islands. It just so happened that there were five navy men on one ship, and they were all brothers, the Sullivan brothers. They were on a battleship and were hit quite heavily. The officer asked them to abandon the ship, and it so happened there was one down at the bottom in the engine room. The other four were way on top. They were ready to jump overboard when they looked around and saw the young brother was missing. Without thinking, they all took off to bring up their brother. And in the process, when they were going down, that part of the ship got hit. They all perished aboard ship. The next day we got word. My brother and I couldn't serve together any more. I guess Washington got the message. No more family members serving together in one unit. So we were separated there when I got to Camp Pendleton. I went into the artillery unit. Part of the first twenty-nine went to the First and Second Divisions. Then, when the next group finished their Code Talker training, they went into the Third Division. Some of them waited for the Fourth Division, and that's when I finished, in December. We were assigned to the Fourth Marine Division and all the Fourth Division was formed on the east coast. They were all men from the eastern states, and when they completed their unit, they moved to California. That's when we were assigned to them.

We shipped out in January '44. While we were in school, we were memorizing the code. The code was a secret because they couldn't stop the Japanese, because they went to American schools, and they knew all the military activities. The Morse code was also taught them. That's why we were called upon and at that time we were the largest tribe. Phillip Johnston had been in the first World War. He knew about the Navajo language because he was raised on the reservation. That's how our language was selected. When the first group made the code, they used everything on the reservation: plant names, minerals, parts of the body, and bird names. Many had been to a two-year college. Many of the first group had that background and were beyond the draft age. They knew of Navajo traditions.

They took all those minerals, plant names, animal names, and parts of the body, so they could easily be translated from Navajo to English. Instead of having just twenty-six-letter alphabets, they had us memorize sixty-six-letter alphabets, because many of the letters we had to change. Like if there's two "e's", we couldn't say "e" twice and use the same name. So, for the first time you might say "elk," the second time you might say "ear," or "eyes."

I remember quite a number. When it came to the military words, they took the planes, the airplanes, and associated them with birds. Like the fighter planes were hummingbirds, and an eagle, a larger bird, were transport planes. And an owl, which sits there and observes—observation plane. And a bomber is a hawk. Then they took the name of the navy ships, and associated them with names of fishes. The only trouble they had was with a submarine so, the only thing they came up with was *béésh łóó'*, iron fish. That's how they did it.

The Navajo language is special because it's a language that was used in time of emergency, because there was no way of stopping the Japanese from continuing their conquest. With the exception of the Hawaiian Islands, they had gone all the way to Australia, and they were even making landings in Alaska. Did you know they never went forward after we started using the code? They were bombing Australia and some of those islands. They were in engagements with the First and Second Divisions. That's as far as they went.

Most of the time, I didn't carry a radio. We were around but not in specific places. The officers knew the Code Talkers, but they never said Code Talker; they would say Arizona, New Mexico, and Talker. That's when we answered the radio. We didn't have a special number. They asked for New Mexico and Arizona. Those were the first two. One of them would be called the Code Talker. That means for us to receive or to send. In a write-up, the officer would write the message and point out what area the help was needed: they need a movement back, a stretcher, medical assistance, that type of information. If there's heavy bombing, if there's support needed from the navy gun power, evacuation of wounded men, we were there. If there was no Navajo word, then you had to spell those out using the Navajo code alphabet.

At the division level, we used heavy radios, those mobile units. Otherwise, at the lower levels, at the division level, sometimes they used Jeep radios. At the company battalion, we used something like walkie-talkies, small radios, about that size, and another one in three pieces, and the generator. There were three divisions working together. And sometimes, it was just too much coming in. There were a lot of kamikazes coming in from Japan, so we were in contact with the ship and the air communication.

To be a warrior means you have to face the enemy; you survive the conflict; and you are the survivor of a battle and engagement with the enemy. Warrior society really came from the Plains Indian. The Plains Indians were the ones that started gourd dancing, and that's why the song is the same way. If you listen to the songs when the drum starts, that's a call for battle. So they come. In those days, they came on horses. So their horses are trotting. The rhythm of the music is the same. They're coming together and that's how it starts off. Then the rhythm changes, and that's when they start hollering. They start yelling and the music also changes. That's when they're charging, and that goes on for some time. Then when they finish, that's victory. It's because of the horses. And then they might go away again. Then it starts again. Bring them back, and there's another scrimmage. That's where they got it. But as for ours, I don't think I've ever heard about us as a tribe having that except the *anaa'ji*, Enemy Way ceremony. You would be able to do that, with your fellow man, when your buddy's wounded, you have to jump and do it, regardless of whether you might be hit or something. But you go and still assist wherever the need is even though the enemy might be coming, yet you still have to tend to the need because you're not by yourself.

Ádóó ńléí ts'ídí bits'á ńjídááhdi 'éí t'áá hwii' hólǫ́ogo bee ńzhdiidzáhą́ą́, bee jiínánę́ę́ 'éídi. Doo hoyi'góógo 'áko 'éí t'áá sáhí joolwoł dooleeł. Ła'ígíí nahgóó 'áhoot'éhígíí doo baa ntsíjíkees da dooleeł. Áłtsé 'éí doo hush baa nitsíjíkees da ákódaat'éhígíí. T'óó níwohda hadziil áyiił'įįh. You become more alert to emergencies. When you become a warrior, you're more stable, more alert. You put your whole energy into whatever you're doing. *Doo shiidą́ą́da baa nitsíjíkeesda. Áádi warrior jiłįįgo 'éíya instant. Dóó doo hush nináhiznilyéés da.* And then when you finally leave, when it's still within you, what you came into being with, what you lived on, you carry all that. If it's not within you, then you can go on by yourself. You would not think about what was around you. At first, you really don't know about those things. It makes you even stronger whatever your emergency is. You become more alert to emergencies. When you have become a warrior, you're more stable, more alert. You put your whole energy into whatever you're doing. You don't think about it. When you become

a warrior, it's instant. No matter how difficult the emergency is, we jump right in. Suddenly some of those things become automatic. When you're over here, you think twice before you do it. Before you become a warrior, you hesitate.

Áko 'éí biniinaa, because of that a lot of our older people don't want to mix in the younger ones; they don't want the children involved in the war dance. The way they put it: *"T'ah dit'ódí.* They're still soft." Their physical, their mental, everything is still soft, and hasn't been distorted. *Áko 'éí biniinaa yaa daasti'.* That's why they're cautious of it. They want to keep those separate yet.

I think what the Code Talkers did is bring out, not only as Navajos but all the natives, what we are and who we are. We are examples of Mother Earth. We use all that we have. We use the plants, the animals, the minerals, and parts of our body. That is the legacy that us Indians are all a part of. We understand nature. We can't get away from that. And we survive no matter what torments we go through; we respond. And that's why we were stable—to be able to face the enemy, without flinching, without withdrawing. And I think that's what we are, a tree. See, when we have Blessing Way, we use that. We put our family pictures in there. We put our jewelry in there. We put our money in there for the Blessing Way, so that we can unite and work in solid togetherness. If one of them gets into some difficulty, if somewhere turmoil is brewing, we bring him back. If he's lost, we use that to bring him home because his mind is put in there—his mind, his whole feeling. And what I usually say is, you know, Mother Earth turns this way, right? We turn this way to welcome her each day. That's a Blessing Way.

Navajos are far advanced because they use the stars. The Navajo medicine men use the stars. And they can tell what plants to use because of the animals. And they said that many of the plants that the medicine men use were taught to them by the deer. They said a deer never used to be sick but now you find them sick.

You know, our elders used to tell us to talk to the early people [sacred spirits]. They're up at four o'clock in the morning. They said if you really want to know them, to speak to you through the mind, you can talk to them at that hour. They're the ones that made our churches, the four sacred mountains. The north is where our protectors are because they can see things at night. They even tell us that they are protectors of things on Mother Earth; they help them; they complete them. And all of us that live on Mother Earth, and all those that are in the sea, and all those that are roaming above us, that's their responsibility.

I am a traditionalist. My father was and most of my family members were traditionalists. My guidance was always from people above, people who had gone on ahead of me to assist me. A lot of people didn't understand that. They ask me at the communication center if I could deliver information, written work, maps and all, to another unit about three or four miles away. They didn't want it to go over the air because the enemy could copy it. They wanted it hand-delivered. When I asked him [a Code Talker] if he could go with me to deliver that, he said, "I'm afraid to go at night." So I had to deliver it myself, and I followed my traditional way. I asked all those people who had gone on before me and my spiritual Father to guide me, because I didn't know the road; it was at night. So I'd ask them to help me, to guide me. Yes, they would come along and I'd go fast. I walked over, found my unit but that was on the other side. The bodyguard didn't come around until *Windtalkers* was filmed. It came out of Hollywood. It never existed. If it was a secret, then I never heard about it. And if there was a bodyguard, I don't know how he would keep track of me.

If I was an outgoing individual, it might have been difficult to re-adjust to coming home. I had a ceremony going into the military. When I got discharged, me and another guy traveled back together here to Gallup, then to Hogan Station east of here. Then I walked home. Nobody was expecting me, you know. I went back to school. I hitchhiked to Wingate and told them I was out of the service and I wanted to go back to school. They called Window Rock and asked what to do. I was a military man, and they asked me if I wanted to take my G.I. Bill. I said, "No, not now, I'll use it later on." So they scratched their heads. They said, "Give him an exam," and I took a two-day exam. They gave me a credit for two years of military service, promoted me from freshman and sophomore grades, and took me into the second year of my junior high school year. I was in the eighth grade when I joined the marines.

I had to take class every other day. Then based on that second semester they called me to Window Rock, gave me a physical exam, and said I was losing too much weight and I wouldn't last very long. So they took me to a sanatorium in Tucson, San Xavier. So three of us went down there from Fort Defiance. I spent a summer there and I came back the second semester of my senior year. I finished my senior year at Fort Wingate. I waited a couple of years before using my G.I. Bill. I wanted to work, but another stumbling block. I was competing against people who were already employed in various fields.

■ ■ ■

Before he ended our conversation, Mr. Smith wanted to tell one last story that he said he hadn't told. We ignored the phone rings and the clock.

■ ■ ■

When I was about between a year and a year-and-a-half, I got hit. Everything went blank. I guess I couldn't talk, couldn't hear. I couldn't move, and my sister, she was a little older than I was, close to eight years old when that happened. She took care of me from there on. No doctor, just the medicine man. The first year, I guess I was just out completely. And then all of a sudden, I'd hear things, and I would see things, just like I was taking a picture, only special ones. I was in a coma for a year. And then things were starting to come out, like special events.

I was going into or being taken into a winter dance to be initiated. And then the light went out again. And the next time I saw a fire.

My sister and I were on the mountainside, way up on top, and I saw a car going across a little opening. Then she said, "There goes our mother." I couldn't speak. My sister said, "She's being taken to a hospital." And that was it. The next picture that came out was a big fire and my sister said, "There's a fire. They're burning an old hogan down. They also killed their best horse." She used to have a special horse that she always rode. "They killed that one yesterday," she said. And then it went out again.

The next one, I was just a little ways from the railroad track because I could hear the train going by. There used to be a station across the highway at Wingate. There was campfire and people sitting in a wagon. They were sitting out by the wagon talking. My sister told me, "We're moving. We're going to our father's relatives," she said. Then she said, "Our mother passed away. Remember the fire that you saw?" I guess she died. "They burned the hogan with her best horse. Now our father's taking us to our relatives over here. Bread Springs." Then it went out again.

The next thing was, I was here in Bread Springs, oh, about five or six miles from the present chapter community. They were boiling water, some in tubs of hot water, soaking their clothing, wash day. Every now and then things would come and later on get blacked out. And all that time, it was just the Indian medicine that we were using to address me. I had a little brother that passed away a long time ago. Each of us was two years apart, and he was just a baby when that happened. We were throwing rocks, and I guess I was too eager to get my share and I got involved too much. That's how I got hurt.

The second time I got that close was when I was at Rehoboth. After the long heavy winter, that's the only winter that I ever saw the snow that deep. There were no arroyos. The fields were just blank all the way across. At the end of the summer, I came down with pneumonia and they took me into the isolation ward. Good thing all I could see was a flowerbed outside my window. I could see outside and I could see the birds. Sometimes I guess they'd be singing for me. Yeah, that's my second time that I ever got that close.

Well, I encourage all members of our country to learn all they can about Mother Earth so they can protect her; they can help her whenever she needs assistance. Mother Earth needs some water, so look upon Mother Earth as the mother. And there's always a mother and father in the rain. When they had sheep, horses, goats, cattle, our elders used to take some of Mother Earth's rain water to a small holding place so the mother rain, father rain would visit the children. Think of Mother Earth as a living being. Regardless of what tradition, type of religion, we all have spiritual people to help us, to strengthen our thoughts, to strengthen our bodies, to strengthen what we live with, what we live by, to be knowledgeable, to obtain all that our spiritual life has provided for us.

George Smith

April 23, 2010, Church Rock, New Mexico

GEORGE SMITH, EIGHTY-EIGHT YEARS OLD, was one of the oldest Code Talkers who spoke with me. He looked fragile and had an infectious smile. His granddaughter, Amber, had driven him to our meeting and brought his collection of medals earned for his military service. He enlisted when he was around sixteen years old. Like many of his peers, he joined the marines when he was enrolled at Fort Wingate government boarding school. At that time he did not speak English and had advanced up to the fifth grade when he joined. The English language was difficult for him, but he said he didn't try that hard to learn it. While in school, he worked simultaneously for the railroad. Though he did not graduate from high school, he learned a trade and said he was treated like an upper division student. He and his younger brother, Albert Smith, decided to join together but were separated due to the military ruling that prohibited brothers from serving in the same unit. Nevertheless, both became Code Talkers. After his return to the States, he continued to do dangerous work in explosives. He spoke mostly in the Navajo language with some English and code switching. Code switching occurs when a native speaker mixes English words in with the native language.

■ ■ ■

George Smith éí yinishyé. Áshįįhí 'éí nishłį. Ts'inaajinii 'éí báshíshchíín.

I was still in school when I enlisted from Fort Wingate. Áadi da'ííníílta'go, Shash Bitóójí. Shinaanish éíyá railroad atah bá nishishnish. Áadi raidlroaddi łą 'í siláo danilínigíí join ádeele'ígíí t'óó bił ahił ndahwiilne' t'óó kót'é danihiłnóo. 'Áadoo ndi draft ádanihi'dilyaa da. Dóó school outgo Na'nízhóózhįį'. Áádóó inda San Diegogóó. 'Áádi training.

Ha'íí béédahoniilzin yéé chidí da 'adaal'inígíígóó bínanhíkíkid áádi ts'idá 'áá niheekaigo. Áádóó Code Talker t'áá 'al'qq 'át'áo nihił dahoolne'. T'áá 'al'qq dadeekaigo, ła' be' eldǫǫh naatinjį́ łá' éí hane' ál'į́į́jí 'ata' hane' da. Shitsilí t'áá bił, Albert Smith. Áádóó łahjį́ dahshdiiyá. Shí 'éí be'eldǫǫh nitsaáji 'áájí atah dah diiyá. T'áá díkwíígóó shį́į́ t'áá 'al'qq bił deéníikááh. Shí 'éí chidí 'ánál'į́į́ dóó 'ata' hane'jí 'áájí. Chidí da niiltłi'go 'ánásh'ǫ́ǫ́. Áko ndi Code Talker éí 'iyisíí. T'ááyó honiitł'ahgo t'áá 'éí bił ałhąąh be' eldǫǫh nitsaágíí. Áájí 'atah tá díiyá.

Éí t'áá 'ałtso ndajijaahgo. Nihaa hees'nil. Kodóó da call ájiił'į́įhgo 'áádę́ę́' da call áhooł'įįh. I go talk to them t'áá Dinéjí hane'ígíí. T'ááyó shá nantł'ah nahalin shí. Chidí niiltłi'go yichoohgo da 'áájį́. Doo 'áhoot'éégóó 'éí da'dildonjí t'éí tá'díldééhjí 'atah tádíiyá. Díį́'niilt'é shį́į́. T'áá honíyóí t'áá nił bééhózingi' át'é saadígíí shi'di'níiłeh ń't'ę́ę́'. Ła' éí yá t'áá 'iyisíí da'iíłta'ígíí da shá nantł'ah daani t'áá bí. "Saadígíí shił nantł'ah," daani." Haashį́į́ t'áó 'ákódaani Bilagáanaají yát'i'gíí.

Nánísdzáágo t'óó naanish yíkeed dóó 'áájí dah diiyá. Demolition t'áá yó deechii' nahaloo bina'anish yę́ę́, t'áá át'é. Éí 'áájí yik'ideeskai. 'Ákó shí 'éí 'ei be'edildon ha'níníí 'éí baa naasháant'éé'. Níléígóó deediłdon jó t'ááyó dááchxǫ' nahalinígíí. Éí 'áádi nináhágeehgo. Éí éíyá bił hahasgéésgo nahjí neheshníił. Łahjí bee'eldǫǫh powderígíí 'éí t'óó deediłid dóó łahgóó ńdeełbéézh áádóó haashį́į́ t'áó ninádayiijááh chonéédoot'įįł ha'níígo. Hastiin naat'áanii nilínígíí armyjí; shí éí marines. Ńt'ę́ę́' saad hazlį́į́', shí doo bee nísht'į́įda ndi. "Łahjí náádíídáał díí łahjí nináándléé dooleeł kojí t'ááyó kót'é," shidíiniid. "Łą'qq," jó ni army nílį, shí marines nishłį́, shígo 'áájí haashį́į́t'áó 'ánílééh níláah," bidíiniid. "Shí k'ad nílóó t'óó dah ńdiishdááh," bidishní. Éí t'éí 'áádóó t'óó dah ńdiisdzáh. Éí railroadjí bá nishishnish t'óó níghán[į]'.

Díí 'éí yá t'áá 'ąą nihaa dayiisznil. Dóó díí ła' t'áá 'áád[ę́ę́' nináhaakaigo 'índa nihich'į' ádayiilaa. Jó díí níléídi tádadiikaigo 'áádi nihaa dayiin[į́į́ł ńt'[ę́ę́'], be'eld[ǫǫh naajaahjí 'ááji. Díídíí éí t'óó 'atahígíí 'át'é, Code Talker daniidl[į́į́ dóó Second Marine Division. Díí 'éí bee bééhózin biniiyé, honaanishígíí ájiilaą. Ákót'áó 'atah tádííyá. Doo t'áá shí t'éíyá da. Diné bił tádíshkááh áko ndi doo t'áá ła' da. Ahíłká anéíjahgo. Éí áko t'ee ńt'[ę́ę́'].

■ ■ ■

My name is George Smith. I am Salt People clan. I am born for Black Streak People clan.

I was still in school when I enlisted from Fort Wingate. We were going to school there at Wingate. My work involved working for the railroad. There we were talking with lots of other servicemen. They were telling us what it was like. We didn't get drafted. When school was out, we went to Gallup and then to San Diego for training.

As soon as we arrived there, we were asked about our skills, like repairing cars. And then they told us about the various things about Code Talkers. We were to separate, some to rifle training, some to sending codes, some to interpreting. I was with my younger brother, Albert Smith. He left a different way. I joined the heavy artillery group. There were different types of groups. I joined the mechanic repair and coding groups. When a vehicle stalled, I fixed it. But being a Code Talker was the main thing, for emergencies and such. And for heavy artillery, it was the same amount of work. These things are what I did.

Everyone had to carry those [radios]. They were given to us. When you call from here or when they call you from there. I go talk to them in Navajo. It was kind of hard for me. When a vehicle stalled, when I wasn't needed, I was in combat. There were about four of us. I was told, you look reliable, you look like you know the codes. Those who were educated said it was difficult for them. "The words are difficult for me," they said. I'm not sure why they said that, since they spoke English.

When I returned, I just asked for work and went that way. Demolition that is a bit rusted was my work, all of it. They don't do that anymore. I worked on the explosives. They explode them there, the ones that are defective. Where I

George Smith shows his medals.

worked is where they hauled them. I unscrewed them and placed them aside. On the other side, they burned the gun powder and some were re-boiled then declared reusable. The boss was in the army; I was in the marines. There was a disagreement, although I did not bother him. He told me to begin another work duty because he complained about something. "Okay, since you're in the army, and I'm in the marines, why don't you do it," I said. "I'm going to leave now," I told him. And then I left. I worked for the railroad for a short time.

These [medals] they gave to us over there. And some of these they sent to us when we came back. These they gave to us while we were there working with artillery and such. This is for just being in it, being a Code Talker and in the Second Marine Division. This is for recognition, for the work you accomplished. That's how I participated. It wasn't only me. I was with some Navajos, but we were not all together at once. We helped each other. That's how it was.

Samuel Jesse Smith

April 22, 2010, Lupton, Arizona

WE GAVE OURSELVES EXTRA TIME to find the elusive Samuel Jesse Smith. Finding him was a challenge from the start. On our third attempt, we managed to track him down near Lupton, Arizona. It was by hit and miss that we arrived at the gate that had no number. The gate looked like it was locked, but having grown up on the rez, I knew one had to be creative and have patience when looking for an individual. Sure enough, the padlock only looked like it was locked. The gate swung open and I drove in feeling like I had passed the last of a series of tests to find Mr. Smith. Mr. Smith has nine children and was living with one of his daughters now. His granddaughter was home and doing her homework. He told us that his first wife passed away five years ago and, sadly, his second wife passed only a few weeks before. He joked that his daughter looked to him for advice "now that both of the bosses are gone." Like many Native people of his generation, he attended a government boarding school. He received his high school diploma from the Albuquerque Indian School. Much of his career was in law enforcement as a chief ranger and as a BIA special officer. He also worked as an auto mechanic and in administration.

A few years ago, Mr. Smith, his son Michael, and several of the Code Talkers traveled to Iwo Jima. They stood once again on the black beaches of Iwo Jima under Mount Suribachi and had their photos taken. This time they weren't carrying radios and guns and protecting themselves from Japanese artillery fire. Transformed from a war-ravaged island to a place that was "nice and smooth like an apple" is the image that Mr. Smith recalled. It must have been startling, perhaps shocking, to see it changed and how peaceful it looked after carrying violent memories of it for more than sixty years. Mr. Smith spoke briefly of the costs of war and the battles that took thousands of lives. In the end, the memories of war, even when motivated by vengeance for events like the attack on Pearl Harbor, is much to bear for anyone. Mr. Smith said what he wanted to say and that ended our visit.

Mr. Smith is *Naaneesht'ézhi táchii'nii*, the Charcoal Streaked Division of the Red Running Into the Water People clan and born for the *Tódích'iinii*, Bitter Water People clan.

■ ■ ■

My name is Samuel J. Smith. I am over ninety years old. I'm a lifetime member of the Navajo Code Talkers. I'm beginning to dislike long trips and long flights and long stretches between plane stops. I don't do that much any more, but I'm going to New York. Not long ago, I went back to Japan with one of my daughters.

I would like to share my story with some of the relatives of the marines that I served with. I don't have a picture of my group. They told us they were going to give us a test for promotion. I did my best, and I must have scored high, because they put me with the general of the Marine Force Division. I happened to be picked to be with the general, the flagship. Twenty-two or twenty-three Navajos were chosen from Navajo communication. They were the ones that were scattered among the division to be scouts and to do the communication for the First Marine Division. That's how I got to be with the First Marine Division. I thought I had it made to be with the general, but no way, that's the worst place to be. That's where the message starts. Anything going on with troops on the battle, anything going around, anything that needs to be corrected, the general gives the word. There was a big tent put up by the general and that's where we gathered to practice communication with Navajo language. [But] over here they told us, "You talk Navajo, you'll get punished." I got punished a lot of times for talking Navajo. So that's the way it was. It was not hard to learn the code. I was familiar with things in Navajo growing up that way, which was better than the white way. Growing up, that's all you talk is the Navajo language, until school prevented us from talking Navajo.

I grew up in Cornfield, Arizona. That's where I was born. That's where I was herding sheep. I didn't have an English name until I went to school and they asked me, "What do you want?" I said, "I want to go to school." That's when I got my name. I grew up talking Navajo and listening to [stories about] the tribal wars. In those days, a long time ago, all you hear about is war: war with the

Mexicans and war with the other tribes that came through Navajo [land]. I don't know what they were looking for. They were looking for some place to hide, a place to live, a nice place to plant, and all that. We had other ideas when they came to take our things, our horses, our cows, our sheep. That's what we thought and we fought them.

My brothers were all older and they went to work off the reservation. I wanted to work. Finally, I got a chance to do the same. So I hauled wood. All my uncles and brothers worked on the railroad. My uncle built a hogan. When it was complete, I told my mother that I had been drafted.

I was sixteen. My driver's license and my discharge paper are a year older and I don't mind. I don't care. I told the recruiter that I had made a mistake in my birth year. He said, "Oh, you did? Then why don't you change it?" So he gave me the papers and I changed it. Washington wanted to get rid of all the Indians, and I was one of those gotten rid of. Ha. So that's how I joined the marines. They thought I was seventeen. I went. I didn't care. The Japanese were just kids. They were kids, just a few older-looking Japanese that were of some kind of rank. I didn't really know that, but I figured that's the way they worked it.

The most memorable thing is that I'm a scout. That's what I was. Actually I never knew that I was a Code Talker. I was practicing that language. When I was in the war, I notice what we needed to send messages in the Navajo language to fool the Japanese. I wanted to get even with the Japanese. The USS *Arizona,* (I'm from Arizona) was sunk in Pearl Harbor and USS *Oklahoma* was sunk too. They are still down there somewhere. So I made up my mind, I'm going to get even with the Japanese. I didn't know how I was going to, but this is how I did it.

Grazing pony near Lupton, Arizona.

I was on Roi-Namur on the first Marshall Island; the second island was Saipan and then Tinian, those three. After we rested a bit, we went and hit Iwo Jima. How small it was, five miles long and three miles wide. The big shots said we're going to take that in one week. One week went into thirty-two days. That's how long we were there. We were almost taken on that island.

I didn't like [going back to Iwo Jima]. I didn't like eating with the Japanese general. He's sitting over there eating and we were sitting over here eating on this side. I didn't like that at all. And then the island was nice and smooth like an apple. No more cliffs, no more foxholes. My son went on a walk to where they raised the flag. I told him that this is not the way it was. He felt real bad about it. That's when he joined me to tell my stories. That's how war is. War is a dirty thing. They say marines killed kids on some island. I forget where it was, Saipan, I think. I had to. We had to. Anything goes. Let 'em have it. They interviewed the captured Japanese on Saipan. They nod their heads on the good ones, and the no-good ones, you take them away and you shoot them. Shoot them in the back, that's how they did it. They were young. We had to get even. I was getting even all that time. Now I don't feel that way. I don't feel that I am glad [for what] I did, but I do tell people that if I had to do it again, I won't do it again. That's how bad it was.

I hear singing at Enemy Way ceremonies. Young boys, young men, they sing: "*Binaa' adałts' ósí bitaaníyá,* I went among the Slant-Eyed people." That is some of the songs that they have. I know they didn't like it. They saw the movie about Pearl Harbor and what happened Sunday morning when the United States was praying and the Japanese flew over and killed them and [the ships] sunk. It's all bad. We lost a lot of our good relatives and good men. I lost an uncle who was there with the Japanese. They told me that he used to tie the Japanese up on some island. He tied up the Japanese and threw them down the cliff. Then he passed away himself. We never used to talk about war for over twenty-two years. Now that's all.

Bill Toledo

August 3, 2008, Laguna, New Mexico

BILL TOLEDO KINDLY OFFERED TO MEET US at the Conoco gas station to bring us to his home in Laguna, New Mexico. We followed him along a complex set of dirt roads to his mobile home that sits on the side of a hill near Arrowhead Hill. Inside his home were memorabilia of the Code Talkers and photos of his children and grandchildren. One photo showed his Laguna wife smiling and dressed in the traditional Navajo clothing style. She stood next to Bill who looked equally happy. She was a nurse and had made a list of things they were going to do when she retired. Sadly, they never got to do any of them because she passed on shortly after she retired, leaving Bill a widower. Bill is eighty-four years old and lives in his wife's community. Like the Navajos, the Laguna people believe in the strength of a matrilineal society. A baby swing stood near the memorabilia of his numerous awards and recognitions. He said it's for his grandchild's visits. One of the photos shows him and his bodyguard embracing at a Code Talker reunion. Of the Code Talkers I interviewed, Mr. Toledo was the only one who said he met and reunited with his bodyguard.

Bill's parents died when he was a child and he was raised by his grandmother, who taught him Navajo traditional ways and how to live without modern conveniences. He chopped wood for his grandmother to use for cooking and heating. A recruiter came to his school one day and that's when he decided to join the military. Bill spoke of the warrior's role—to help family, to have compassion for community, and people. Before landing at the battle sites, he prayed with corn pollen that "turned hard like a rock." His prayers were for a good landing at the battle sites in Bougainville, Guam, and Iwo Jima.

After spending a few hours in Mr. Toledo's company, I came to feel like he was a favorite uncle who takes time to visit and tell stories. I am a quarter Laguna Pueblo myself, my mother's father having come from one of the villages. Bill lives alone with his dog that greeted us, but he says his children and grandchildren visit him often. When we left I felt saddened to leave him, as if I were deserting him. The railroad tracks follow an east and west direction below his home. The sacred mountain of the south, *Tsoodził,* Mount Taylor, sits north of his home on Arrowhead Hill. It is appropriate that he would live on this hill, because the arrowhead symbolizes protection and was used in warfare.

■ ■ ■

I am *Ta'neeszahnii,* Tangle clan born for the *Hashtł'ishnii,* Mud People clan. My maternal grandparent clan is the *Naakaii Dine'é,* the Mexican clan and my paternal grandfather clan is the *Kinyaa'áanii,* the Towering House People clan.

In Pearl Harbor, the Japanese broke the Armed Forces code. So the Marine Corps was looking for another code that was more secure. There was a man named Phillip Johnston who was an Anglo and the son of a Presbyterian missionary. He had learned to speak Navajo when he was on the reservation at Leupp, Arizona, when he was four years old. He contacted the commander of the communication outfit at Camp Elliott who was Colonel Jones. He told him that he can understand and speak Navajo, and he thought Navajo language could make a good code, if it was made in a certain way that nobody could break. Colonel Jones told him, "Why don't you come back in about two days and we'll bring in a commanding general here and you can demonstrate your idea for him."

So in two days he came back and brought a few Navajos to help him develop his idea for General Vogel. The general told Phillip Johnston to practice his idea for about an hour. So after an hour, one Navajo went into another room with an officer. The general wrote a message in English and then the Navajo with him, using the code, sent the message to the other Navajo in the other room with the officer. The first message came. So he wrote a longer message, and then he wrote it in English and the Navajo sent it over the phone to the other Navajo. The message came out the same. So the third message, he made it a little longer. Then the Navajo sent that message over the phone again to the second Navajo, and then wrote another one this time, a longer combat message. And then he sent it again and it came out the same. And then the general said that Mr. Johnston's idea caught on.

So that's how they got started. The next thing was to get permission from the Commandant Hokum who had his office in Washington. They were allowed

to recruit two hundred Navajos for this program. The general asked some other officers about using two hundred Navajos, but then after thinking about it, thought two hundred recruits will be too many. If the program didn't come out right, he said we might lose some money over it. He suggested recruiting thirty Navajos for this program. So that was agreed on. The next thing was getting permission from the Navajo tribe. So they sent a recruiter over to Window Rock and told the chairman at that time what they were doing, that they wanted to recruit Navajos into the Marine Corps.

They approved it, and the next thing was to go out and recruit thirty Navajos. So they sent recruiters out there to all five agencies: Tuba City, Chinle, Fort Defiance, Shiprock, Crownpoint. Then only twenty-nine showed up at the Marine Corps base in San Diego. They didn't know what happened to the thirtieth man. Today, they haven't found out yet what happened to him. This group went through boot camp and graduated in July 1942. On August 7, 1942, the First Marine Division landed on an island called Guadalcanal located by New Guinea. There's an island group they call British Solomon Islands and on that island group is Guadalcanal, which is located on the southeast side of the tip of the island group.

They said that there was a tiny little island where three marine divisions were going to land on this island. Two marine divisions would land first. The Third Marine Division would be the floating reserve out there and the air corps would bomb it. [The Japanese] had an airfield out there, and that's what we're after. The Japanese also had this volcano, Mount Suribachi. On top of Suribachi, they had anti-aircraft guns. They could shoot an airplane down with them. They had their bombers and their fighter planes on the airfield too. They intercepted these bombers when they were coming from Saipan and Guam to bomb Japan. So, that's why they want to take that island. The First Division and the air corps were bombing it for thirty days and the navy was shelling them for that length of time too. They told us that we were going to take the island in about a week. So, on February 19 the Fourth and Fifth landed and then they start advancing.

Mount Suribachi is about 550 feet high, has black sand, and a cone in the back. As the marines were advancing inland, the Japanese came out of the caves. They found out that they had inter-connected tunnels underneath the island. There was shelling and bombing in the air. There were over 20,000 Japanese, and I guess they had been digging under there for a long time. And that was one of their primary defenses. They came out into the open now, out of the caves, at Mount Suribachi and started shelling the marines that were coming. The casualty [rate] was over 33 percent with 6,000 marines lost. That division that landed there helped the two divisions about three or four days later. We took the middle part of Iwo Jima; the Fifth on the left side, and Fourth on the right side. Instead of taking it in one week, it took us thirty-six days before we finally secured it. During that time we lost our President Roosevelt. We lost a lot of men, and that's where John Kinsel [Navajo Code Talker] got hurt. Towards the end, I guess they planned to dynamite this cave. John was in there when they blew that up, so John got hurt. It was towards the end, so we never used the code again after that. We moved back to Guam and we started training again.

Then, one day, they called all the Third Battalion to a meeting. They told us that some of us are going back to the States, the ones that have 140 points or two or three combat landings. So, they start naming off the list and got down to the "T's" and called my name. I took off to the tent area, got my seabag out, and started packing. Even though I had a week to go yet, I was ready. While we were training, they told us that all six marine divisions are going to land on Japan. I guess towards the end of August they had made a bomb over at Los Alamos, an atomic bomb. They shipped it over there and had two of them. Then they took us down to Guam harbor and we boarded ship and headed for Pearl Harbor. We headed for Honolulu and went downtown. After that we got back on the ship and then we set sail for San Francisco. This was in May '45. About halfway to the States, the planes were ready to bomb Japan. They used firebombs. And they [Japanese] gave up on August 14. And that's how they quit. I was in San Diego when this happened. All the traffic in town stopped. All the people got out and hugged each other and were hollering and honking their horn. I guess that happened all over the world, all over the country. And on that date, August 14, President Reagan gave us National Code Talker Day.

When I was discharged, the colonel said, "When you go home, you must keep your mouth shut about what you did with the code in the war." He said, "Even your relatives or people that you know, anybody, don't talk about it." I went home and the folks at home, you know, they never asked me any questions. They just knew that I served my country. They didn't ask me where I went, you know. They knew that I've been in the war and all that, and I guess they don't want to bring it up. Now they know.

The things we did, using our language in the war saved our country, our people, the American people, and all our allies in the World War II. Don't forget the Navajo language. There's a lot that are not talking Navajo anymore like they used to a while back, you know. We would want them to carry it on. Maybe someday we might lose it. Yeah, that's why I always mention that in my presentation to the Navajo kids to keep it going. It's a beautiful language. I think the main thing [is to teach about] our clans and all that. There's a lot of people that I've met all over the country in my talks. It was such a wonderful code that we used, such a unique code that included the snake and the goats and the ship and the donkeys [laughter]. One time I was making a presentation in Dallas and there were these black students, about five hundred of them in this auditorium. And I was mentioning how the code was made. I was coming down from the "A's" and when I got down to "J," I said, "We say *"jaa'nééz"* [donkey]. They all laughed. I guess it sounds kind of funny to them.

One day one of the Code Talkers' wives brought some papers. It was the "Marine Hymn" in English and Navajo. He said, "You guys really learn this. When you go on parade you must sing this song." Whenever I go to presentations people always ask me to sing the "Marine Hymn" so I sing it. Then they always say that was the icing on the cake, you know [laughter].

> From the Halls of Montezuma,
> To the shores of Tripoli;
> We fight our country's battles
> In the air, on land, and sea;
> First to fight for right and freedom
> And to keep our honor clean;
> We are proud to claim the title
> Of United States Marine.

Samuel Tso

July 7, 2009, Lukachukai, Arizona

IT WAS EARLY JULY, and the summer heat bore down as I drove up to Samuel Tso's home. I found him in his orchard. His family had been reluctant to do an interview when I first spoke to him at the Code Talkers' monthly meeting. Early one afternoon, I dropped by his home to introduce myself and to chat with him in hopes that he would change his mind. He was putting up fence posts to keep the animals away from the fruit tree he planted. Even though he is in his eighties, he was digging a hole with a posthole digger! It was work for a younger man, but Mr. Tso was not letting that deter him. Hard work like this is what gave the Code Talkers their stamina and resilience to survive a war and live into their elder years. I shared with him a bag of oranges and grapefruit from my backyard.

We spoke easily of things and I explained my project, that my father had also been a Code Talker, in hopes that he would open up. After more small talk, Mr. Tso started talking about being on active duty, but mostly about his life after he was discharged. He spoke of a young fellow marine who asked him many questions about his life on the rez and always seemed to be nearby. After awhile he began to take a liking for him. Then suddenly during an attack, the young man was hit. Mr. Tso scrambled to help him, but it was too late. As he held him, he came to the realization that this man may have been his bodyguard, though it was never revealed to him until years later. He also spoke of having a vision of a young woman. Soon after, he received a mysterious mailing containing a cedar bead necklace that he wore as protection. He took these signs to mean he would return home safely. He suffered from PTSD and part of his therapy was to return to Iwo Jima, where he found it transformed from a war-ravaged battleground into an orderly and calm island.

Mr. Tso turned out to be a most interesting storyteller. One story led into another. It was as if he was growing a tree of stories, each branch connected to another until the tree bloomed with stories. I could have sat under his tree all day listening to him. I intended to stay only a short while, but it had been almost two hours. By then, Mr. Tso's reluctance turned into permission for me to return. "I'll do it," he said. I returned a few days later and he continued his storytelling under the cottonwood tree.

As I left Mr. Tso to tend to his orchard, I was struck by his resiliency and his self-determination to earn a college degree, given all the odds against him. He was from the generation of *Diné* that expected to work hard to accomplish goals. Part of his motivation for enlisting was to help his family, who was barely eking out a living. Sadly and ironically, when he returned home to the land of his birth that he protected and fought for, it was taken and he had received no word of his parents' and sister's deaths. His final wish was to return to the place that he cherished, his birthplace under the tree. Ever the warrior, the soldier of his destiny, he took advantage of the G.I. Bill, earned a college degree from Utah State University, and returned to his Lukachukai community as an educator before he retired. He was *Zuni Táchii'nii,* Zuni Red Running into Water People clan and born for *Naakaii Dine'é,* Mexican People clan.

■ ■ ■

Why they sent us back all the way to Hawaii is beyond me. They could have sent us either to Guam or some of those islands that had been reclaimed to recuperate there. We were brought back to Hawaii. We were there to retrain for I don't know what. Anyway, we were being made ready to invade mainland Japan. By that time, President Roosevelt died and President Truman took over. As we're getting ready to invade mainland Japan, President Truman asked his chief of staff, "How many American soldiers will die if we invade mainland Japan?" His chief of staff estimated about a million of us would be killed. So on that basis, we found out, he decided to drop those two atomic bombs over there. The first one was on August 6, I believe. They dropped that bomb on Hiroshima with approximately 360,000 population in that city. The second one was on August 9. They took off from somewhere in Tinian or Saipan. Just before they reached the target area, the weather really changed the clouds. They couldn't see the target. They veered off and dropped that atomic bomb on Nagasaki. Nagasaki, I believe, only had 60,000 people. The weather saved all that population, instead it went to Nagasaki.

I've forgotten how many days later we were on our way to mainland Japan to invade it. We were on the ocean on a ship, going to Japan. Japan quit. So all we had to do was to go there and serve as occupation duty. Instead of going direct to Nagasaki, we went to a place called Sasebo, Japan. It's a little town. And then we settled there in the old building on top; that's where we're stationed. At that place, I was assigned to an officer called Major Woods; he was in charge. He had a jeep all his own with drivers, radio in the jeep, and I was assigned to that radio. Whatever came up, I was supposed to transmit messages through that. So we traveled all over that area. We went to Nagasaki, where they're bringing in Japanese prisoners of war. They hauled them in; they stripped all their clothing and de-fumigated them, the hair and the body. And I found out that a lot of Japanese had lice [in] their hair, their clothes. They took all their stuff away, gave them new clothes, and then got them ready to ship them home. They took their swords and rifles and all that stuff away from them.

One day we were going back to Nagasaki and we stopped at the town of Sasebo. And I noticed there's a Japanese woman who walked into the store with a string tied around her head. I never saw those before and some of the marines there said, "What's with those ladies with the string tied around their head?" And they said, "They have a headache." It just so happened I had aspirin in my pocket, so I got it out and thought I'll give them some aspirin. One of the ladies came in. I followed her into the store and the guy that's the proprietor was dispensing things. She came and talked to that guy. All of a sudden, the guy turned around and went over to a water trough, like a fish bowl, a square one. And I noticed there's a lot of water snakes in there. He just reached down in there, pulled one out, took the head off, turned it upside down, and all the blood drained out into the glass, about that much. And he gave it to the lady and the lady took it and drank it. Oh, I almost went through the ceiling!

And that's one shocking thing that I learned there. The only thing that I cannot forgive myself for is this. We visited a Japanese home. I didn't know you have to take your shoes off to walk in and here I walked in there with muddy shoes. Somehow, somewhere, I need to apologize to the people that I didn't know their culture at the time. I mentioned this to Kenji Kawano[1]. If he

---

[1] Portrait photographer of the Navajo Code Talkers and the Navajo people

ever goes back over there, tell your people that I'm very sorry for that. I didn't know their culture. And what shocked me most was that men and woman use the same restroom, the shower or the hot bath. They go in naked, all mixed. They don't think nothing of it. But me, boy, I couldn't believe it. That's quite shocking to me.

We mostly visited Nagasaki, where they dropped the atomic bomb. We went over there and took a look. Almost all the buildings were flattened out, except some with the foundation, and the rest of it seemed like it was all black. And there was sort of a mountain. There was one running down this way and all the trees burned, nothing left. As I walked close to it, they told us not to walk to the center of it. You can walk around on the edges there. I noticed on the beach the sand was sort of crusty like glass. And I looked at it and I thought to myself, "Oh, that bomb must be really hot to melt all the crystal on the sand." We stayed around that area until sometime in February. While waiting there, the marines told each other they were wondering if they would have survived invading mainland Japan. And that brought a curiosity, what about the civilians? "They say, hey Chief, even those little kids are trained to shoot you." Even young children, they're trained to fight back. As we went through one town, that whole town was completely burnt and I asked, "What happened here? Did they drop a bomb here?" He said, "No, they dropped incendiary bombs." When it hits the ground, it bursts into flames. Then they said these Japanese buildings are made of real thin plywood. They just burn like matchboxes. It burns up in no time. I asked, "Where would the people go?" They just left. He said, "Some of them burned to death right there." Oh my goodness! I keep thinking, how can a war be so cruel and here we Native Americans, we were given a name, "savages." Savages? Anybody, any animal, they protect their own area. They're going to fight and we Native Americans did the same thing. We tried anyway, and they used to say, "Bunch of dumb Indians there. We whip your butt that's why that belongs to us now." So I said we were so far behind in developing any technologies we didn't know about it. At that time, people came over and took our land away from us and we tried to fight back. All we did was just use bean shooters and yet they have rifles and some of them even had Gatling guns. It's just like taking candy away from little children. All those things went through my mind there.

I kept thinking, "I wonder what's happening back home." Back home I had brothers and sisters. I had a father and a mother. We were so poor that our father had to keep on working from dawn to dusk to at least put some food on the table. Sometimes, we used to go to bed without food, and I kept wondering how they're doing. But at least during that war, jobs were plentiful for common laborers. People left the reservation and went to work. They earned enough money and came back and then went out again. That's what they were doing. That bothered me all the time. I just wondered how my mother was doing. I tell you, my mother didn't have shoes at all. My father couldn't afford to buy shoes for us, so we grew up barefooted. My sister, the oldest one, she always complained, complained, complained, and was always getting after us. "Do some work! If you don't do any work, you won't eat!" Somewhere along the line, she discovered that I was growing up, beginning to notice girls, and she got after me about that. And she told me, she said, "You leave them alone. When you start having children, how are you going to feed them? We are having a real rough time as it is." And boy! That really sunk into my mind. How am I going to feed them? So from then on, I left them alone and I don't even take a second look anymore, because I don't have any job, no money. That really bothered me.

I said I got to be home and get a job and contribute some to the family. But I never got any letter from home, none at all until something like 1998 from the Veterans Office in Chinle. They called me and said, "Would you come to the office?" I said, "What for?" "We have to give you something." So I went over there, and then I found out there was a letter that they kept there all those years that should have come to me. But it was still there. And then I found out it was my mother. She found somebody to write for her to me, asking for help, that they really needed help with money. But by that time, I had already signed a paper that part of my military pay will go to her, whatever is left it comes to me. That was in, I believe it was in 1998, that's when I found it and I read it. That was something way over fifty years ago. Why they never sent it earlier is beyond me, and right now I just don't know what to think about it. I could have been helping my mother, but it never came around.

We stayed on occupation duty until sometime in February 1946. Some young marines that were there were being discharged, sending them home, and they kept me over there. One was a marine who was a general's son in the army. He was in the marines with us at Iwo Jima. Right after Iwo Jima, they sent him home. I guess you have to be somebody to do that. Me, they kept me over there and I kept wondering, "How come I don't get discharged? The war is over." And then one of the marines said, "Hey Chief, you don't have a family, that's why." Those guys being sent home, they already had families. I didn't have any, so they kept me there all that time. Until sometime in February 1946, they sent me home.

When we went across, the first time the ship went forward, to the right, forward, to the left, forward all the way across the ocean. But this time, coming back, we just went straight and I asked, "What was that for?" They said that is to evade a Japanese submarine. If they release a torpedo, they will miss at least fifty yards. That was the reason why we went across so slow. Some time in February, we got back to San Diego, the same place where we left the United States. We stayed until the sun came up in the morning. Finally, we got off the ship, and they loaded us in the convoy truck and we got off just outside of San Diego. All the trucks stopped and they told us they are going to feed us ice cream. So we got out. We went over to get ice cream. While we're eating ice cream, all of a sudden the marines and the civilians got into a fight. I said, "My buddy is getting into a fight," so I decided to go over there, and the guy said, "Hey Chief, this is not your fight. This is between us palefaces." So I asked, "What gives?" These guys working here, they're supposed to be doing a defense job. They're packing ammunition to go across and here they went on strike and don't want to produce any more ammunition. Ammunition depends on us here.

Oh yeah, I remember now. We were trained to ride surfboards from the submarine or ship to the beach—surfboards! We go and surf to the beach, come back, surf again. On our final training, I found out they put boxes on the surfboard and we take that to the beach. I guess I didn't really think far ahead. I said, "What's that empty box for?" "Hey Chief, that's supposed to be ammunition. You're taking ammunition over to the beach. If the marines get pinned down on the beach, they need ammunition. That's what you're taking over there, see." We had to go through all that training there. I never really figured out a lot of things until afterwards. So I said, "When I joined the service, I didn't know whether I was coming or going. I didn't have any idea at all, but I learned though." When we got back to San Diego, people got into a fight and they told me it's not my fight, so I stayed out of it.

We went to Camp Pendleton. At Camp Pendleton we stayed a whole month before they started discharging us. On March 29, 1946, I finally got my discharge papers. I just took off with my seabag to Oceanside, California. I went to the bus depot and, man! marines, sailors, and army personnel are just standing in line over at the bus depot, train depot. It's all full! Why they discharged us, all of us, at the same time, is beyond me. They could have staggered it so that we wouldn't have to stand in line overnight. The road that I know I came in on goes to Los Angeles. From Los Angeles, you go to Flagstaff, Winslow, and Gallup. That's the only way I know, so I bought a ticket to Los Angeles. Same thing—soldiers, marines, and all others are standing in line there; some are even about a mile long. Every now and then you move your seabag about, I would say fifty yards, and you wait again. I had to wait the whole night in line there. The next day just before noon, all of a sudden a group of Navajo people came around. And they stopped by me and said, "Are you going home?" and I said, "Yes." "Why don't you take your seabag and take our place way up there?" So I grabbed my seabag and I went over there and took their place. They said they're out and going to stay for a while. They had relatives there at Los Angeles.

So I went ahead of the line and got on the bus about noontime. Took off, went as far as Winslow, Arizona. And they took all of us out of the bus at Winslow. "Unless you're going south," they said, "this bus is going south. There is another bus behind us. You can wait for that and catch it to Gallup." So I got off and I decided not to wait for the next bus. I just took my seabag out to the highway and hitchhiked from there. Before long, someone stopped for me. I got in and we took off. I found out the guy was from New York City, but he wanted to stop at the Painted Desert and see some of those petrified woods there. I said, "Okay, we'll get to Gallup in time." So we went and looked around the Petrified Forest. He decided to have something to eat. We sat down to eat and to my surprise I found out he ordered two bottles of beer and the proprietor said, "I am not serving that Indian any liquor." And the guy was so surprised, he said, "What? A returning hero and you can't even sell him a beer!" "I'm sorry, that's the law." So they started arguing right there. I thought they were going to get into a fight or something. So I said, "Oh, never mind. Let's eat something and go on." Finally, the proprietor gave in and said, "Okay, you be responsible for him" [Laughs]. And we said, "Nothing will happen. We'll just eat and drink and go on." And sure enough, we ate and had a beer with it and we went on; nothing happened. I guess that's what you call being prejudiced or something. Finally, we got to Gallup and we said goodbye. I should have asked him for his address and I could have been in contact with him all the time.

From Gallup back home it's about, I would say, over a hundred miles. And I didn't have any vehicle. My parents were so poor they couldn't come meet me, so I stayed in Gallup that night. The next day, in the morning about ten o'clock, the mail truck from Chinle Catholic Church comes in, picks up the mail and takes it back to Chinle. So I was waiting for that. It finally came; I put my stuff in, and I rode the truck in the back. We went to Chinle, and from Chinle I hitchhiked again.

There was a guy by the name of Naat'áanii Jumbo. He had an old Model T Ford. I found him sitting in the shade. I went over to greet him and I asked him, "I'd like to catch a ride with you back to Many Farms." He said, "Okay, as soon as the lady fixes the tire." He's just sitting in the shade and the lady's repairing the tire. So they finally fixed it, and we took off to Many Farms. Many Farms is a summer home. I stopped there and they went on. And then I found out that no one was there. All were at the winter home, way over by Black Mesa. So all I did was I just took my seabag, walked about a hundred yards, and then I set the seabag among the tall—they call it seaweeds—the tall ones about that high. I hid it there. When you're sitting down, you can't see anything from a little distance. At the Catholic church [possibly St. Anthony's] there's a stack of rocks about that high and on the south side, there's a rock. Underneath it, they usually hide a mirror. When the sun goes down in the afternoon, you can flash that mirror back and forth to my home. That's what it's there for. Then I went on foot until I reach that stack of rocks. And then I found the mirror, and I started flashing and kept flashing until I saw a horse coming across the valley towards me. They saw my flash, so I put it back underneath the rock and I walk a little ways. And he met me there and that was my brother.

We rode on home, just waiting to see my mother, my father, my brothers and sisters. Right away I noticed that my mother wasn't there. My father wasn't there. My other sisters weren't there. The only one I noticed was my oldest sister. She was there, and I asked, "Where's Mom and Dad?" As soon as I said that, she burst into crying. And I just wondered what happened. She finally told me that my father passed away, my mother died too, and my sister died too.

Oh! I just couldn't believe it. Here I went to war for them. And that place where I went back to a little ways from there, that's where I was born. There was a tree there. Right underneath it, that's where I was born. And that tree was no longer there. And I notice there's a family right there. And I asked, "What are they doing there?" And my sister said, "They moved there." "You mean to tell me without even letting me know? They moved on there?" She said, "Yes." Oh! That was something that I could not face. All I did was I stayed that night. Sometime before dawn I got up and I just walked out of there.

Either a mile or a couple miles down the trail, my brother came on a horse and he asked me, "Where are you going?" I said, "I don't know, I'm just going. There's nothing there left for me. Everybody took over and without my knowledge and all that. I'm just leaving here." And then he said, "Are you going to catch the bus?" I said, "Yes." So he got off his horse and gave me the reins. He said, "You ride this to Chinle. When you get there, leave the saddle, the bridle, and everything at the church, and just release the horse. The horse will turn back over there." Because they feed the horse very good, that's why they always come back. So I did that. As soon as I got there, I know the truck was getting warmed up. So I left the saddle and all that stuff there and put the names on it, and turned the horse loose. I could see the horse just start walking down the road toward home.

Before I got on the truck, I noticed there were some Navajos wanting to go into Gallup with that truck. I knew one distant family and I asked, "Is one of my sisters still living over at Fort Defiance?" They said, "No. During the war, they moved out of there and moved to somewhere toward Kingman." And then finally, I got on the truck, went into Gallup. I got off and I went to the train station and asked about my sister. That Fred Harvey used to run a string of hotels and restaurants. And then they told me that she used to work at the Fred Harvey Café. So I asked and then I found out, they moved out of Kingman and moved to San Francisco, and she has a family over there now. And then I found out my sister didn't know that her father and mother died and her sister. So I decided to go there first. I'll let her know and then I'll see what I find out about any kind of job.

So I went over there and at least I knew how to ask for directions and all that stuff. Then I found out her husband works at the National Biscuit Company. I went over there to the National Biscuit Company and they gave me all the

information where he lives. I got that and looked for it and sure enough it was on Olvera Street, in an apartment. That's where I found them and then, she had three children by that time. That's where I found them and I told her about it. What really bugged me was that her husband became an alcoholic, and then to myself I said, "That's not good." So I stayed around with that mustering pay I kept until it ran out. So right there, at National Biscuit Company, there was an opening. I asked for that job and they gave it to me, and I start working there at nighttime. I worked from eight o'clock in the evening to eight o'clock in the morning. I was going out the door while their workers were coming in.

From then on, I couldn't find a job at all. Every time I asked for a job, they said, "Why don't you come back a week later or something?" It became a routine, "Come back later, come back later." I found out that that means you won't get hired. Oh, that was really frustrating, "Come back later." So the only thing I could do was to go back to the railroad and ask for a job there. They hire people for railroad jobs, just plain common labor. So I start working for the railroad again. And I found out, working on the railroad, it only lasts about a couple of months, then they lay you off again. Whatever you save, you wait and look for another job. Ah shucks, I don't know how many miles I walked during the day. It was really frustrating. No job. I had to cut on whatever I consumed. When I went into the service, coffee was a nickel. Hamburger was twenty-five cents. With thirty cents you can have a hamburger and coffee. It will sustain you at least a half a day. But this time, the prices of that were going up, up, and up.

Working on the railroad, I found out that you constantly ask for transfers. If your job stops there, you can ask for transfer for somewhere, any place in the

United States there is an opening. So I transferred from Richmond, California. That's where I worked for the railroad, and I asked for a transfer down to Fresno, California. I worked there and then they laid me off again. And I asked, "Is there any other job there?" They said, "There are some Mexicans quitting work. You can take their place in an ice plant." Where they have the icehouse is where they freeze water. They freeze [the blocks] and then they stack them inside the building and that's where I started working. And after we filled up the ice plant with ice, during the spring, the trains started coming in. They called it "meat wagon." They had all those beef, mutton, pork. It was all lined up in there and then you had to put ice over at the end with the fan blowing in with cold air. They hauled them between big cities and that's where I started working again. It didn't last very long; I got laid off then.

And then I found out it's not good for family life. So the only thing to do was to maybe go on back to school. Even then, I was still single, and then I heard about this Haskell Institute in Lawrence, Kansas. Since I had a little money, I called over there and then they said, "We will send you the application." So I got the application, filled it out, and sent it in, and I got accepted over there. I said, "How do I get there?" and he said, "The usual thing." "What's the usual thing?" "Buy your own ticket and go over there [laughs]." So I bought my own bus ticket and went over there to Lawrence, Kansas. I got off at the bus depot in Lawrence, Kansas, and I asked, "How far is Haskell Institute?" "There is a bus that goes back and forth there. Just get on that and where it turns around, you get off there and that's where the Indian school is." So I put my suitcase in and when we stopped and turned around, I got off there, looking for Indian people.

There was a young lady; I remember her name was Beverly Morrison. She was blond. I thought she was a teacher there, and there was another one. She didn't look like an Indian to me. So I didn't really ask any questions. Oh, I must be at the wrong place. I went back on the bus and went back to town. And I asked, "Are you sure that's an Indian school?" He said, "Yes, that's it." "Well, how come there's a lot of Anglos over there?" He said, "They are Indians too." I said, "How come they're Anglos and yet they're Indians?" I couldn't believe it. So I went back over there. This time I got off. And then one of the men came. His name was Lindley Topaz. He looked like he was a half-breed though, Indian and white. And I asked him, "Where are you from?" He said, "Topeka, Kansas." "Is there an Indian Reservation there?" " Not in Topeka. A little ways from there, they call the Holton." He said, "There are two reservations there." He said the one he comes from was a Potawatomi Indian Reservation. "What's the other one?" And he said "Kickapoo." "What's Kickapoo?" I thought. I only hear that in comic books [laughs]. He says, "Yeah, there's a Kickapoo tribe there." So that's where I started going to school, and I took up house wiring and refrigeration mechanics. With either one, I could get a job easily.

So I stayed there, that was in 1947. That's where I met my wife. She was going to school there. And I didn't know there were Navajos there. There were all different tribes. I met Kickapoo boys, Potawatomis, and some from Oklahoma. They don't speak Navajo, so I just start talking English all the time. On my second year over there, there was a guy that came in from Alaska, took up refrigeration mechanics and house wiring. He came in and he used to watch me work on refrigeration. Our instructor told us to build one. I found out that he is from Alaska. I thought, "You took up refrigeration and you're from Alaska?" I thought Alaska is always wintertime. And then he told me he is a fisherman. "We go out and fish just for the day and bring it in and sell it to the cannery." But what he wanted to do was to learn refrigeration, to build coolers, freezers. On the ship, when they go out, they can stay out there almost a month. Fill up the fish and keep it cool all the time and then take it to Seattle. He said that's where you make a lot of money. So we plan to go back up there and we'll build all this refrigeration in our ship. Oh man! That guy has money all the time. He just throws money around. "Where did you get all that?" "From the fish," he said.

So it's time for me to leave there and then I found out I have to get a job at Chemawa, Oregon. Close to Salem, Oregon, there's an Indian school there. I started working there as an electrician's helper. They had an old-type freezer. That freezer is very dangerous, because it could explode. When I got there, I found out [they were looking for] somebody who knew how to change over from this old freezer to the new ones. And they asked me about that. "Oh yes, I can build it," I said. So I was assigned to do that, build a walk-in freezer. They had dairy cattle, instead of buying cattle from outside. They raised their own there and fed the students with it. He said, "Can you handle it?" "Hey, no problem," I said. "So, well, let's see your work on paper." So I designed it. And then they wanted to take it to the Salem Refrigeration Company for them to check it. I said, "You don't need to do that; I'll take it over there myself. I'll sit down and talk with the men there." So we all went down there and checked it out and everything was fine. But the only thing I said was, "I want all the electrical wiring separate from house wiring and the other circuit on machine. And we need to change the transformer." He asked, "Why?" "Because when we put those things on that it won't carry it." And then later on they said, "I guess you know what you are doing." I said, "Yeah, that's what I learned."

I kept watching the date. That guy from Alaska, he was supposed to stop by and pick me up and go to Alaska. I found out that he never showed up. And I called back to school. He said, "Oh, you mean Freddy?" I said, "Yeah." He said, "They left in the middle of the winter." "They left?" "Who are 'they'?" And then I found out that there was a young Cherokee lady, we used to call her Kissy. She's Cherokee with sort of reddish hair. They just took off and went up to Alaska and left me stranded over there in Chemawa.

But I worked there in Chemawa for at least two years. I changed that refrigeration completely over. When I changed it, the engineers didn't have to check it. It was all automatic. The refrigerant wouldn't explode. The refrigerant had two machines on it. I had to design the switch myself. "You mean you designed this?" "You go over to the bid electric shop and they show you over there. That's where I get my ideas," I said. After working there for two years, I was the electrician's helper. All of a sudden, the head electrician decided to transfer down to Panama. He moved over there, and here I was left alone. So I ran the whole shop there. We got some young men who want to learn how to do electrical wiring. They said, "Can you teach it?" I can teach it, but I don't have a degree. "Keep them busy," they said. So I did. I taught them how to do wiring, different sizes and all of that.

That summer, they had a workshop over at Intermountain School. "You all go over there and take classes over there," they said. So I went over there. Who do I find over there? My wife, she was there. That's where we got reacquainted, and that September, I quit over at Chemawa and transferred over to Intermountain School. By that time, there were two other guys after her. I was the third one. So instead of the other guys having their way, I bought an engagement ring and gave it to her. "Here, if you want it, you can have it. If not, I'll be on my way," I said. And then I found out I was the one that was chosen. There was one guy; his last name was Husket. Man, he could have been a movie star. He was a real handsome young man. Why she chose me instead of him is beyond me.

Anyway, that's where I started my family. I transferred over there as a teacher's aide. I worked in the classroom and helped the teacher. I only worked until that fall, about two and a half months. I got laid off. I tried to find a job, but no. So the only thing I could do was to go on back to school.

Whether I was ready or not, I was just determined to tackle it. I decided to go to Utah State University. I went over there, took the entrance test, and when the test results came in, they put it on a bulletin board. You can go over there and look for your name. So I went over there and looked at the top group to see if my name is up there . . . no . . . second page . . . no . . . third page . . . none. From then on, it's just blank. So I went over to the dean's office and I asked him, "How come my name is not on there? He said, "It's on there, go back and check." I went back and checked. Still not there. I went back and told him, "I can't find it." And then he said, "Did you take a look at all the pages?" It kind of stung me. So I went back and looked at all the pages. Almost toward the last page and there was my name. And then I asked, "Would they still take me?" "If you catch up."

So I started going there and about a week later, I got into an argument with one of the professors. His name was Professor Hardy. He just chased me out. "How dare you come into my classroom, almost a month late. What do you think you're going to accomplish?" I just stood there, dumbfounded. "Now you go on out and don't come back." So I just left. Walking down the hallway, I thought about it. All of a sudden, I don't know what made me feel my pocketbook. Oh yeah, they have to work for money too. So I turned right around, went back into his office, took out my pocketbook, and just put it on his desk. "You need this money and you're going to teach me and you're going to earn it." So with that, I left and the next day I was in his classroom. He just kept giving me a mean look.

I think either it was a month later or sometime, we took our first test and I had a struggle. I was the last one out of that classroom. I turned in my paper, walked down the hallway and down the steps. Right at the end of the steps, there's a seismograph sitting there. As I walk down and passed by that seismograph, I noticed the seismograph is making a strong recording, so I ran back up and told Professor Hardy. "Dr. Hardy, the seismograph is recording something strong." He just cleared his desk and ran down there and took a look at it. He phoned into Salt Lake City. He got the credit for calling in, the first one. From then on, we became buddies.

My major was elementary education. But I took geology because there's a lot of young kids who need to learn all these rocks and stuff. That was the reason why I took that and it really helped. When they put you on teaching practice, the kids they are really curious. We go out on a field trip and they pick up rocks. "What's this?" So I had to name all of them for them. And out of something like sixty-four students taking that test in geology I was surprised I had an "A." So that was very encouraging.

I got my high school diploma from Fort Wingate, New Mexico, in 1942, sometime in the latter part of May. They sent me out to Fort Wingate High School. Usually Navajo students go home during the summer. I never did. My parents were so poor that they couldn't come and pick me up. So I just stayed out there for four straight years. When I was a senior at Fort Wingate High School, that's when the Japanese bombed Pearl Harbor, December 7, 1941. The following Monday, all the boys in my classroom didn't show up because they can get around, they have a little money. Me, I couldn't. So me and another guy, he's smaller than I am, they just put us over at the power plant. They just put us to work there at night. Shovel coal in the boiler all night long. In the morning, they released us and we went to sleep until noontime. In the afternoon we went to school. All those young men that used to be in my class, somehow, they joined the service. Some of them joined the army, some joined the navy, and some joined the Marine Corps. The ones that joined the Marine Corps, they became the First 29 [Code Talkers]. They were right out of my classroom. I stayed until that year in '42 in May. I thought the Federal Government would take me home. They never did. They just told me that there is a road down that way; there are jobs along the way. I didn't know what to do, where to go. I just took my suitcase and went down the road to the main highway. The bad thing about it is I didn't even have a dime in my pocket, just sent out. I thought that little suitcase I had, I'll take it to the highway. About a mile and a half down the road, that thing got so heavy I can't carry it. I have to go along the fence line looking for baling wire. I found some, fashioned it, hooked it to the suitcase, put it over my bag and the wire over my shoulder. And I had to take my jacket out and pad it underneath it and I start walking. I don't know how long I walked, but I stopped and rested until I got to the main highway. I didn't know which way to turn, to the right or to the left. But that suitcase is in my way. So I just took my suitcase, went across the main highway, across the railroad, and I went to find an arroyo and I left my suitcase there, hoping that I will come back and pick it up. That was 1942, sometime in May, and that suitcase is still there.

I finally got my elementary education degree sometime in the first week in September. The following Monday, I was hired at Intermountain School as a teacher. What I really wanted was to come back down here to Many Farms; that's my home area. I used to herd sheep around that area and that's where I wanted to go back. So I told Many Farms that I got a job over there and then Many Farms said, "No, you come over here, we'll give you a higher pay." So I went back and told Intermountain School that Many Farms is going to hire me with a higher pay than what you gave me. They said, "No, no, no you stay. We'll give you better than that." So I called back over there and said they're going to hire me; they want me there. They said, "No, no you come here. You speak Navajo and you speak English; we need you." So now my education was really in demand. I had to use one another against each other. Finally, Intermountain School won out because instead of starting with a GS 6,[1] they started me with a GS 7. So I started teaching there. I taught there for two years in lower grades.

The third year, they found out our students over there were being released to work. They had a very low mathematical ability and they asked me, "Can you do something about it?" "How would that be?" "You will teach math only." I said, "Okay, I'll see what I can do." So they started math classes, but I found out that I needed help. What kind of mathematics do they teach over there? We developed a different curriculum for the kids. We examined the curriculum from a school in San Diego, Albuquerque Menaul High School, Phoenix Union High School, and Denver. We examined all of their math programs. We took some out from here and there and put it together and built it. And then kids asked me, "What's this thing for?" "Well kids, when you go out working on housing projects, someday some of you kids might become foremen. When you become foreman you can't be standing at the project area, figuring out. You got to have it up here [points to head] when you go up there and lead your men." "Is that right?" So I started on my math program and sure enough, the kids started to improve. And then I was working in the math and science department.

The teachers didn't really go along with what the head of the science and math department was doing. So they all got together and signed a petition to

---

[1] General Schedule pay scale rating used for federal employees

remove him. They gave me the petition. Nope, I'm not signing. He is a good man and all you need to do is work with him. Oh, the rest of the teachers didn't like me from then on. They finally got rid of him. He recommended me to be the department head. That's how I got my promotion. I ran that math and science department for two years and then I quit. I transferred to this little school here, Lukachukai Community School. I became teacher supervisor there. And then I found out that the kids were really struggling. "They keep speaking too much Navajo." "Oh, I don't know about that," I said. "I speak Navajo and they are learning English. Other people speak three different languages. Why can't you and I speak two languages?" It can be done. It's being done, and a lot of people are very successful. I kept driving that and driving that until I think they understood.

Frank Chee Willeto

April 23, 2010, Crownpoint, New Mexico

on a Friday evening. We had finished the last Code Talker interview with Frank Chee Willeto. It had been another creative search. I didn't have a map this time, only oral instructions. We were in the eastern part of the rez in New Mexico where landmarks are few. Fences ran parallel to the highway and were punctuated by cattle guards that opened to dirt roads that led towards hogans, houses, and sheep corrals. We hurrayed when we found the cattle guard where we were to turn in. The dog was the only one home to greet me when I opened the gate. The wind blew fiercely across the windswept land on this spring afternoon in April. For miles, there was only the dry earth and the wind blowing east. Outside the Bashas' grocery store in Crownpoint, a sign read *"T'iis tsozí,"* the land of the skinny trees. It was easy to see why it was named this because there were very few trees, and the ones that survived the wind stood almost denuded of leaves. There was no cellular service in this part of the rez to call Mr. Willeto, so all we could do was wait and hope he would arrive soon. Once again, we were doing research "old school," as my sons would say. One had to be patient and wait, regardless of the appointment time. We waited for nearly an hour before the Willetos drove up. He explained that he had been detained by an appointment that ran late in Grants.

Mr. Willeto's working life has been colorful and dynamic. Like many of the Code Talkers, he continues to travel and give talks to audiences throughout the country. Much of his life has been devoted to community service, having served as a Navajo Nation Council Delegate for fifteen years for the Pueblo Pintado chapter of the Eastern Navajo Agency. Most notably, he served as the Navajo Nation Vice President in 1998, despite attaining only an eighth-grade education.

177

Nevertheless, he strongly advocates the value of an education for the younger generation of Navajos.

While he built the hogan for his family to hold Navajo ceremonies, he simultaneously believes in the stories and teachings of Mormonism. In his studies, he finds that Navajo traditional stories intersect Mormon mythology. When we concluded this session, Mr. Willeto left me with the impression that he deeply appreciates everything he has worked for throughout his life. He had been married forty-eight years when his first wife passed. His current wife sat nearby and photographs of his family decorated the walls in the kitchen. "I'm hoping to live long enough to see the fourth generation," he said.

■ ■ ■

Shiéíya Frank Chee Willeto yinishyé. Áádóó Bit'áhnii 'ééya nishlí. Áádóó "Tóhdich'iinii 'éíya danízhé'í shidoo'niid. Naakaii Dine'é daninaalí. Ta'neeszahnii 'éí danicheii." That's what I was told.

■ ■ ■

I am called Frank Chee Willeto. And I am Within His Cover People clan. And then I was told the "Bitter Water People clan are your fathers; the Mexican People clan are your paternal grandfathers; the Tangle People clan are your maternal grandfathers." That's what I was told.

■ ■ ■

I noticed that the older boys were leaving, but I also noticed that there was a marine, a Navajo marine. Oh, he really looked sharp. He visited our school. They didn't say anything about where they were going, but I guess they asked for volunteers, anybody over eighteen or just becoming. I was not that age. I finished the eighth grade in 1943. After graduating, there were, of course, no jobs for anyone under eighteen. I was still herding sheep. I had a grandfather who was transporting people to somewhere in Arizona. He asked me, "Why can't you go along with us and get a job over there?" So I went and got into the three-quarter-ton flatbed truck. We started in the afternoon from Crownpoint with about ten other people, and we drove west and then south. We traveled all night and in the morning we got to the place they call Clifton, Arizona. Everybody in the group got in line to get jobs. When it came my turn, this lady asked me how old I was. And without thinking I said, "I'll be eighteen in three days," which was not true. She said come back in three days and you'll get a job. So I stayed around there and my dad was working there. He was working at the smelter plant in Morenci, Arizona. Three days later, I went back and the lady smiled and said, "You finally became eighteen, huh? Where's your draft card?" I got a job just like that. My first day was on the railroad between the smelter plant and all the way down to the mine. By the end of my first day, my foreman said, "You don't belong here." I figured, well, I got fired right away. He said to come back in the morning. From there, they put me in the smelter plant. I can talk English and Navajo. Of course, Navajo is my first language. I would work there for one week and then they would put me on another job. Pretty soon, I had been in about a dozen different jobs. One morning, there were two Navajos that had come off the reservation. I'm sure because they were not one of the eastern people. They had a [hair] knot and a straight hat and they only talk Navajo. That foreman said, "Take these guys and go over to that job that you already learned and tell them how to do that job." I did not know that I was an instructor. They needed to get people from the outside and put them to work. They called me. They said, "Here are two more guys, go show them the job." I was working seven days a week, sometimes sixteen hours. It was really interesting to me because I met more people.

Before I knew it, I got my draft card. That was somewhere in November. And then I told my foreman. "Look, I got my draft card. I got to go in for a physical." He said, "You don't have to go. We can ask for a waiver because you are working in a defense plant. We need you here." All the talk he gave me, it didn't work on me. I said, "I got to go." So I went and got my physical in Santa Fe. When I was in line for my physical, in comes a marine coming down the line. He stopped by me and asked, "Are you a Navajo?" I said, "Yes sir." I learned to say "Yes, sir" in school. He said, "Come with me." He grabbed me by the arm and we went to a navy doctor. That navy doctor asked me five questions, if I had broken bones or if I had anything wrong with me and, of course, I had nothing wrong with me. That doctor said, "Son, you just passed your physical." He didn't even look in my ear or anything. That's how I came into the Marine Corps. I told my mom that I was going into the service. She said, "You know you're not old enough." "Yes," I said. "I know that." That's all she said.

Ten days later, I was in San Diego. We got there by train and then by bus to San Diego. I thought, they are going to let us sleep. We had been traveling all night, but I was wrong. They asked me how I like my hair cut. I would like to have a flat top. That flat top that he gave me was completely bald. By six o'clock,

I had a bucket of water, a toothbrush, shaving gear, and whatever I needed, and some clothes that were thrown to me. I started wearing marine dungarees. I knew only one other Navajo marine. His name was Benally from Red Valley. It seemed like we were the only ones that came in first in almost everything. We ran and did exercise and all of that. We didn't have a problem. We graduated eight weeks later. They put me in line for swimming. They just push you in and see if you can start swimming. Some guys just go down and come up. I learned to swim in my backyard here at the windmill, at the sheep water pond. It was maybe about fifty yards that you have to swim down there and come back. I qualified. At the rifle range, I had my old .22 single shot here. I didn't have any problem. But I did not become an expert. I was kind of holding back some of the things. I guess I could have been a much better marine. By the time eight weeks came, we graduated from there, and both of us were sent to Camp Pendleton. To our surprise, there were more Navajos there, about thirty of them. Then I was back to school using our own language. Planes, all of our birds, and all our fish became military equipment. We had to have names for [everything] from PFC to four-star general. I forgot most of it now. I believe that there were about four weeks of courses and that's all.

Then they sent us to the South Pacific. The only island I remember was Pearl Harbor. The ships were still sticking out of the harbor, the ones that sunk. We spent a day and a half there. I don't know why they call it the South Pacific. I always thought I was going north. I guess I was off direction. Transports, cruisers, battleships were all out there. We were more or less in the middle. Almost everyday we start going zigzagging. When we came back I [found out] that Japanese submarines were sighted and they had to do that. But all of this is just an adventure to me, something that I never had. It was something childish, that's the way I looked at it. We came to Tinian, a small island. We just bypassed it and went to Saipan, where we landed. We were given tents to live in. I heard it was just secured one week before. But every night, there was always somebody getting killed in that area. So I was just one of the marines; I was the communication person.

I was carrying an air-cooled machine gun. Two other non-Navajos carried a machine gun and the other carried the tripods. We had to go up the mountain. There were a lot of caves there. We had an interpreter, a demolition man, and a flamethrower with us. I was carrying a machine gun. And this interpreter would

yell into the cave and say, "Come out." If no answer, I was supposed to get out there and give them a blast from my machine gun. Then I would go back and then this guy would yell again, and if nothing happens then your flamethrower person, he gives them a shot all the way into the hole. It was a big flame. The interpreter yells again. Then if nothing happens, your dynamite people go in there and set up their dynamite. We have to go back quite a ways and then they close the caves and the dynamite blows it up. That's what we were doing for about two weeks.

The most scary thing was when I was put on guard [duty], guarding the kitchen. That's where the enemy, or the Japanese, tried to get food. It was so dark. There was no moon. You can't even see your hand. How do they expect us to make rounds around the kitchen? I just stood in one place. I didn't move until about six in the morning. But we went and had more training. I was being used as a scout between our own forces. And then all at once, we were told to get our gear ready and we started moving. About two months after I had been on Saipan, maybe three, we got on the ship and started going north again.

The third or fourth day we were still coming in and our planes came in and pretty soon you could hear the guns landing. They were bombarding the island of Okinawa. There were battleships. You could see sixteen shells leave the gun. There was so much confusion. When I got into the landing barge, I was given only one clip, that's only four shots. I didn't ask, "How come I only got four shots?" I went into the landing barge and there were only ten of us in there, and there was supposed to be thirty. We started going north again. Oh, there was so much shooting. The water got rough. Our boat went up and down and pretty soon we almost ran into a battleship. Somehow or another there was a signal given. That was what they call a smoke screen. We came out into daylight as clear as can be and land was not even two hundred yards away. A signal was given and we turned around. How we found our ship, I don't know. Somebody thought it was a fake landing. That's what I was in, a fake landing, April 1. And that's April Fool's Day. The main force that landed there, came in from the west side and went across the island and the airport. They went across Okinawa and cut off the Japanese. The American ships were all the way around. That's where they had another Iwo Jima type, real bad fighting. As for me, we floated out there for two weeks. I guess we were the reserve. Then we went back to Saipan.

By that time, my ankle got stuck on both sides and it didn't move this way or that way. I was walking like a baby, just starting to walk. I ended up in the hospital. They told me that I had some kind of acute arthritis. I was given a shot every three hours, twenty-four hours a day. While I was still there in the hospital, one day the horns [blew]. Someone came in and he said, "The war is over!" My boys and my platoon were loading up into another ship. I thought they were going home, instead we loaded up on the aircraft carrier. It was an aircraft carrier that had been converted into a medical ship. I got on that one and the other guys, I saw them go on to the other ship. They were going on to Japan and China. I came back to the States. When I left the United States I was 135 pounds strong and when I came back I was only 90 pounds. They asked me if I was a prisoner of war and I said no. It was the pain of the arthritis that wore me down. I stayed in a hospital again for quite a while. Then I went back and I was given a Jeep and I was to carry a messenger. Again, I don't know how long. Some of the people were getting out on points. I didn't have enough, but I did ask about medical discharge. They checked my medical record and it was lost on Saipan. So they said we can't do anything about it.

I got to San Diego in 1944 and in June 1946 I finally got discharged in May. That Lieutenant who gave me the discharge papers said, "Here Son, go back home and forget everything you have learned in the Marine Corps and start off where you left off." That's what I was told. I didn't know that we did something special. I didn't know that we were a special weapon and all of that. Until 1968, I believe, President Reagan took office and he asked the Navajo Nation and the Marine Corps to have the Navajo Code Talkers at his inauguration in Washington. [Perhaps Mr. Willeto mixed up the dates. It was Ronald Reagan who officially made August 14 Navajo Code Talker Day.] The Navajo Tribe had to look for who were the Navajo Code Talkers. They finally got a list from the United States Marine Corps. They found about thirty of us. One day, I was over at Pueblo Pintado and a policeman came up and asked me if I was a Navajo Code Talker. I said, "I don't know." He asked, "Were you in the service?" "Yes." "Did you use Navajo language?" "Yes." "Okay, you're a Navajo Code Talker. Be in Window Rock and you're going to go to Washington." Just like that. That's the first time I had ever heard about Navajo Code Talker, twenty-five years after the war in 1945. We didn't say nothing, we just went home and started herding sheep again or got a job somewhere. I did not go back to school. I was supposed to. I didn't even finish my high school.

I graduated from eighth grade in Crownpoint. That's the only education I had. I went to work in June—the same month I got discharged. I worked for the road department and the rest all in education. I was a bus driver, a maintenance man, and supply man. All I have to do at the school was build a fire at six o'clock in the morning everyday, five days a week. Today I'm a chapter official. I have been a Council Delegate for fifteen years. I have been a Navajo Nation Vice President. I have done just about everything and a little more than an average person I think. I have been with the Pueblo Pintado Chapter since 1950. When I was serving in the council it was just common sense. I didn't have to read up on it. I didn't have to know anything about it, but when you start talking about something, you use common sense and thinking. Vice President is a real easy job. You have people running around for you. All you do is tell them what to do, what you want, and that's it.

On June 6 I'll be eighty-four. I was born in 1926, but I went back one year on my record because that's when I got that job. Without thinking I went ahead and said I'll be eighteen in three days. It says June 6, 1925, on my record now. Whoever my maker is, I guess He is guiding me around or whatever. But again, I still say that the guys that went before me, they really got into it. I knew a lot of them that left school when I was still going to school. The only guy that I work with nowadays is Bill Toledo from Laguna. We make presentations in the United States. I don't brag about it and I don't add on anything. I know one guy said that he jumped up and got mad and shot all the Japanese and that's not true [laughs].

To our young people, I keep saying in my presentations, you can be whatever you want to be. All you need is hard work. Learn, learn, learn the *Bilagáana* way. If you decide to come back with your education, you can help our elders and our young people. That's what I keep telling those [kids], wherever I make a presentation at a school. It's hard, but the harder you work, the easier life can be. And I try to tell that to the parents—keep your children in school. Take them to school. Nowadays, it seems like our children are the boss of the families. That's not the way it was. My grandparents taught me some things and I taught that to my kids. My children did not pass it on to their children and now the old teaching is out of hand. They go as far as eighth grade and then they drop out. Most of the time they don't learn the job they can make a living on. And that's where I keep trying to tell the parents. Put your children in school and let them stay and let them finish high school. We got all kinds of colleges close. Let them go there, but somehow or another their parents are not doing that. Very few parents keep their children in school. That's why we got night people. Young people sleep during the day and go out in the middle of the night. That's not right.

The hogan that we have out here, we built that to have gatherings with our family. I used to do most of the talking, but now my children are running the program. I'll just sit back and say a few things. You won't believe it; I have great-grandchildren, that's how far I am. I'm hoping that I will live long enough to see a fourth generation. I had thirteen children. I had a wife from 1941 all the way to 1989 when she passed away from diabetes. I thank my maker for a lot of the things that are happening to me. In the morning, I say my prayer. In the evening, I say thanks for the blessing. I'm not a missionary, but I used to read the Bible and then I joined the Mormon Church. I used to read their Mormon book also. Their story and our traditional stories crisscross each other. I get along with what I got. I'm not a medicine man or anything.

The Descendants Speak

Mother, Grandfather, I return
I return from the enemy
By means of sacred prayer,
I am cleansed of war
I am renewed with the four directions
I am restored in a sacred manner

Shimá saní, shicheii, nánísdzá
Nayéé' bits'ą́ą́dóó nánísdzá
Tsodizin bee
anaa' shąąh náá'éél
T'áá dį́į́'góó bee náhosésdlį́į́'
Hózhǫ́ǫ́go náhosésdlį́į́'

—LAURA TOHE
from *Enemy Slayer: A Navajo Oratorio*

185

Frank and
Francine Brown
Son and Granddaughter
of John Brown, Jr.
April 24, 2010, Window Rock, Arizona

AROUND THE AGE OF EIGHTEEN JOHN BROWN, JR. ENLISTED and was sent directly to boot camp in California. He and twenty-nine others made the first all-Navajo platoon. Later, one dropped out for inconclusive reasons making it twenty-nine. He and the remaining young Navajo men were charged with devising the code under strict secrecy, a code that would be used until the war ended. He fought in at least four of the bloodiest battles before he contracted malaria and was sent to a naval hospital to recover. After his discharge he served as a council delegate for the Navajo Nation from 1962 to 1982 for the Crystal, New Mexico, chapter. I grew up in that little community and I often heard his name mentioned by my parents and other adults. Not until I started this project did I realize that he was one of the original twenty-nine Code Talkers. While conducting these interviews whenever his name was mentioned he was always spoken of with great respect. It seemed a great deal of people knew him.

It had been difficult enough to locate any of the Code Talkers, let alone finding one of the original Code Talkers. Fortunately, I met Frank Brown at one of the monthly Code Talker meetings and he agreed to an interview along with his daughter, Francine, who told inspirational stories about her grandfather. Mr. Brown passed on May 20, 2009, at his home in Crystal, New Mexico, with his wife at his side. His legacy lives on in the great breadth of service he gave to the military, the United States, the Navajo Nation, and in the stories his son and granddaughter tell. John Brown, Jr. received a Congressional Gold Medal from President George W. Bush in 2001 at which time he spoke on behalf of the Navajo Code Talkers.

■ ■ ■

My name is Frank Brown. My clan is the *Ta'neeszahnii,* that's the Tangle People clan. I'm born for the *Ma'ii deeshgiizhinii* which is Coyote Pass People clan. I am originally from Crystal, New Mexico. I'm employed with the white collar crime unit for the Navajo Nation.

My late father John Brown Jr. was well respected and a popular figure on this portion of this reservation. My father lived a very hard life ever since he was little until his service and all the way up to his death. My father was born in the traditional Navajo way somewhere on the rim of Canyon De Chelly, near Chinle, Arizona. He was born in one of those pitchfork-type shelters. His mother had considerable difficulty giving birth to him where she had to be tied up to a post set up in the middle of the hogan, where I believe there was a medicine man in attendance and a midwife. Shortly after my father was born, a medicine man, maybe that medicine man, did a prayer for him and asked, "I want this baby to be a leader; I want this baby to grow up strong," because my dad had had a difficult birth coming into the world. He was born in a real harsh time of the year on December 25th. My father was born to Nanabah Begay and his father was John Brown Sr. He had a Navajo name but he was widely known as John Brown, Jr. His paternal grandfather was Laughing Lefty. He had a great influence in my father's upbringing. He remembered staying in the hogan with his mother and his aunt and from time to time his grandpa would visit his grandma.

He always remembered his grandfathers, especially Laughing Lefty. He wouldn't give my father any rest. Early in the morning when it was still dark he would make sure that my dad got tossed out the front door of the hogan and made to run a considerable distance away from the home. I guess it was really hard on a young child. He hated having to do that, and he got to where he would run only a short distance and wait for a while, and then run back home. So one time his grandpa got suspicious. He followed him out there and saw what he was doing. He was really angry with him. "Doggone it! These children, the first thing they learn is how to be sneaky." One time his grandfather made him go out and it was snowing and cold out there. He was crying and kind of scratched on the door to let the people know that he wanted to come in. His mother and grandmother were inside feeling sorry for him, trying to appeal to the grandfather for him, saying, "Why don't you just let him in? It's so cold and he's so little." I guess he was a real authoritarian type of guy. He told them, "He's growing up into a very harsh world. He needs to be tough. He needs to be strong. He needs to get prepared for this world." That was my father's upbringing. He also remembered the old days when his mother and father would be coming back from the trading post. It was usually an all-day trip. It was actually only a few miles to the trading post. He always heard the wagon coming back. He could hear the Crackerjacks[1] making a little noise as they were bumping along, and he would know that they would be bringing him Crackerjacks.

In high school Dad was pretty athletic. He loved playing baseball, basketball, and football. He played for one of the schools in Chinle. When they would have an away game they would have to travel all night long over the summit to Fort Defiance to play in the softball tournament. They had to camp out somewhere in the mountain, riding on the back of a wagon. For his high school years, he ended up at the Albuquerque Indian School. Dad graduated from Albuquerque High School. He remembered playing basketball the day that they heard that Pearl Harbor had been bombed, maybe a few days earlier. He used to stress that back then there were no means of communication, telephone lines; everything had to be done overseas via telegraph. News didn't hit the mainland for at least a day or two and even longer for guys like my father and his friends. But they heard about Pearl Harbor and they knew that it was a pretty serious thing that happened and eminent war was just right around the corner.

Not long after that, his high school was visited by a number of recruiters from the Marine Corps. They were particularly interested in the Navajo boys. He remembered them talking to them and he was kind of skeptical but listened. They told him, "Hey John, where you're going there's a lot of pretty girls out there on the islands," and so forth. Anyway my dad decided to join up. They were told to report to the military base at Fort Wingate, New Mexico. When they reported there, they were given their physical examination and probably their military exam. They were sworn in right there that same day. That same day they were also bussed out and sent straight to basic training in California. He was around eighteen years old. Normally everything takes about two or three months to go through the process. You make arrangements and get everything in order and let your family know that "Hey, I'm leaving for the Marine Corps." Dad's mother never knew. He got sent straight to Camp Pendleton with all these other Navajo boys.

---

[1] Caramel popcorn that was a treat for Navajo children

I believe that there might have been thirty of them [original Code Talkers]. And somewhere along the line, one of them either failed or for some reason he was excluded, so that's where they came up with the "twenty-nine." The "twenty-nine" were all in the same platoon. Normally a platoon like that you have people from all over the United States in the same platoon. There might be about one or two Navajo guys in there. This one was an all-Navajo platoon. Not long after their training everybody was taken into one large room and the doors were locked and everything was top secret. They were told, "You Navajo boys are here for a reason. You are here to devise a code. The enemy, the Japanese, they are breaking all of the codes, decrypting all of the secret encryption that we are using out there." A lot of the Japanese were graduates from universities from America and they knew the English language very well and they were easily able to decrypt all the codes. So Dad and all these young guys really didn't know what they were doing but they said, "All right, we will do it as simply as we can." They would create words based on letters.

You know Navajo words don't correspond with the American alphabet and all the different dialects from the reservation, different ways of describing things. I don't know how long it took them to come up with this code. They had to talk about things like tanks and amphibious warships and airplanes and so forth and different types of artillery and big guns and so forth, and troop movements. So they devised all of this stuff over what I think was a really short period of time. Again without being able to tell anyone where they were or what they were doing. Their training ended and they were loaded onto an old cattle ship. It's a ship that had been used to haul cattle with. I'm not sure where their first stop was, but almost immediately they were sent directly into combat.

He would describe approaching an island and how awful to see all of the smoke. They would see all hell going on over there and they knew that's where they would land. At least three different waves would hit the shore. The first wave was usually always wiped out completely and the second wave would usually secure the island. He was almost always in the third wave. He did at least four of the major battles: Tinian, Saipan, Guadalcanal, and Tarawa. Every time they would hit these islands they knew ahead of time. The commandant would line them up and tell them, "You guys, I want you to think about what you're doing, where you're going. A lot of you are not going to make it. You're going to die. So however way you know how to do it, you pray for yourselves." And they would do so.

It wasn't until later years that Dad would open up and describe some of these things—the sights and sounds and seeing his friends laying there on the beach as they landed, and how they secured the island, and dealt with all of the snipers, and other war elements that were going on. About eight years ago we were in Chicago and Dad was giving a presentation at a large inner-city high school. I think they had about 5,000 students there. Some of the kids asked, "What were some of your memories, anything that comes to mind that you can share with us?" He said, "Yeah, I remember watching those Japanese Zero planes and United States fighter pilots having it out up there in the air." He said, "Man, that is one thing that I will never forget. It was really scary watching, fighting up there in the air, from the foxholes."

He enlisted around 1941 and may have gotten out in '44. Towards the end he contracted malaria. It nearly killed him on the battlefield. He ended up on a naval hospital battleship for about six months somewhere near Hawaii. By the time he was ready to go back he was seeing all of these soldiers coming in by the hundreds all torn up and still alive. It scared him. He talked to one of his commanders. "Can I get discharged? I have enough points to get out of the service." Back then they used to have some kind of points system. If you were in there long enough you could get out of the service or stay in there if you wanted to. So he and the late Carl Gorman, one of our very close relatives, they got out on leave and came back here to the United States. They spent some time in the Los Angeles area when the war had ended. Before they were discharged they were told, "Don't you ever give out this secret to anyone. Forget about what you did."

He met my mother somewhere along they way and they eventually married into the Mormon Church in a temple wedding ceremony in Manti, Utah. I'm not sure when my father became a Mormon. When he first got out of the military he was struggling to find a job out here. There was basically nothing, having to walk all day to get back and forth. He worked for some of the churches around here as a Navajo interpreter. During that time he learned about the Bible and the different philosophies of these different churches. One that he always remembered was the Pentecostal Church. He was working with the minister. That minister was always telling him, "You got to get rid of that *tádidíín*, your corn pollen bag. I want you to destroy all of that. Leave that life. That's not the right way. You go with the church and church only. What you are doing and what you believe in is not the right thing." Dad had grown up with traditional beliefs, so that he knew about all of those things.

His mother, Nanabah Begay, was somewhat proficient in Navajo beliefs. When the family finally found out that he was in that terrible war, I guess his mother cried inconsolably for several days. And at some point, old Laughing Lefty came to visit and saw her crying and always being depressed. He asked, "What are you crying about?" She told him about her son over in that terrible war and she just knew that he was going to get killed. So Laughing Lefty told her "You got to stop doing that. What you need to do is say this prayer." He taught her a prayer and gave her a couple of arrowheads and Dad remembers one of them as obsidian. "Take John's shoes and take them over to this hill." There's kind of a sacred hill not far from where she lived and not far from where he was born. He said, "You take these over there over to that hill. Every day you pray for him while he's over there. He will be okay."

Dad remembers several times when he came really close to being killed, one time when they were trying to triangulate the position of a sniper and those Japanese snipers were some of the best in the world. They were trying to find him. At one point he was behind a tree in the jungle and he just moved his head over a little to try and get a view, and a gunshot went off. The bullet hit just above his head. It hit the bark of the tree and sent bark splattering all over him. He came probably just centimeters from being hit in the head. There were other times in combat that he just couldn't believe it that he came through unscathed when everybody was going down around him. So he knew that there was something to this Navajo religion that he had been reared up on all his life. He always had resentment for these ministers that told him to destroy your way of life; it's not the right way. Dad in his heart and mind knew that there was a connection between what these ministers and religious people preached in the Bible and even in the Book of Mormon. There is direct correlation with the Navajo beliefs where they are almost like one and the same. He always stressed that to me.

Ever since I was little I was raised to have great respect for the traditional herbal medicine men and the way that they do their things: the sand paintings, the Yeibicheii, and the Blessing Way ceremonies. I experienced a lot of those when we were growing up. My family has always had a strong connection with the Mormon Church too. My father was with the church in St. Michaels, Arizona, called Lee's Chapel at the time. I think he was Second Councilor there and I used to see him sitting up there with his suit on during Sunday services. We moved to Crystal, New Mexico, around 1965. They had a small ranch in Fort Defiance just across from that old Thriftway store where he had a number of corrals. My father was always a horseman. When I was little he had some of the finest quarter horses in the area. People would come around to borrow his horses for parades and so forth. This included the chairman's office and tribal rangers. Even when we moved up to Crystal where my mom still lives, he had quarter horses.

We knew he had been in the war. It wasn't until, I'd say, about '77 I found out he had been a Code Talker. One time there was a group of his Code Talker comrades sitting underneath the juniper and oak trees. My dad had this little place where he had about three different species of trees all growing together and they would always sit underneath that tree and talk all afternoon. Kenji Kawano, the photographer, would be real quiet and taking pictures. That was about 30 years ago. Slowly I started educating myself on the Code Talkers. By then there were at least two major books published about them and I read them and started getting a little bit more curious. Dad was real tight-lipped. He didn't like to talk about the war; it obviously made him feel real bad.

■ ■ ■

My name is Francine Brown. I am *Chíshí Dine'é,* Chiricahua Apache People, born for the *Ta'neeszahnii,* Tangle People clan. *Deeshchii'nii,* Start of the Red Streak People clan are my maternal grandfather clan and *Ma'ii deeshgiizhinii,* Coyote Pass People clan are my paternal grandfather clan.

My mother and my oldest sister were going to school at NAU (Northern Arizona University) when I first started to know more about who the Navajo Code Talkers were and from the sculpture R.C. Gorman made of his father, Carl Gorman. I believe it is at NAU campus. I got to spend a lot of time with my grandpa. Those are some of the best times. When we would drive around he always told me a traditional story about a certain mountain or hill. Behind their house at Crystal, they have a little creek. He would lay there and fall asleep. He was always so peaceful that it made me feel comfortable around him. I would also describe him as strong and inspirational. He was one of my grandfathers that I really looked up to.

John Brown, Jr., speaks at the 2001 ceremony where he was awarded
the Congressional Gold Medal by President George W. Bush.
PHOTO BY DOUGLAS GRAHAM, COURTESY GETTY IMAGES.

I was in Alaska a couple years ago and I was in a place called Dutch Harbor, way out there on one of the islands. It is really hard getting off the island. My flight kept getting delayed and I was really missing home. I remember talking to my grandpa on the phone. I didn't tell him that I was sad. He was telling me what certain animals, like the eagle, meant in Navajo. We were talking a lot about that, and he was giving me all these names for animals and what not. I remember being in the room and scanning the channels when I came across the History channel. It had to do with the Navajo Code Talkers. My grandpa was talking and my grandma was sitting in the background. So that's what it showed me, how powerful he was in his prayers. With me and my two sisters he was always just one call away if we had a bad dream or if we felt unsafe about something. He was a part of the Navajo Code Talker Association. Being in parades is something I always remember about him. He would always be waving. That's how I remember him mostly. Children would come up to him and hug him. He would always reach his arms out in everything.

Larry P. Foster
Son of Harold Yazzie Foster
August 24, 2010, Gallup, New Mexico

LARRY P. FOSTER, son of Margaret Blackgoat and the late Harold Yazzie Foster, possesses a quiet, intense intelligence. He is well versed in the history and contributions of the Code Talkers from his own extensive research and from the many stories his father told. I met him at one of the Code Talker meetings where he usually watched the proceedings and made mental notes, it seemed. Larry gave many details about the oral history of the Code Talkers, which added to the larger story of them. He is married to Mattie Y. Tsosie, a gracious host, who welcomed me to their home. Larry works for the Gallup Indian Health Service as the supervisor for the disease section on sexually transmitted diseases and is the epidemiology officer for the Four Corners states.

He spoke at length, sometimes poetically, about his father, who taught him and his siblings *Diné* values about being a warrior for his community and to respect all that is sacred in the natural world. The Foster family is a well-known family in social and community activism on the Navajo homeland. Since the Nixon administration, Larry participated in a number of long-distance walks that moved across the country and culminated in Washington, D.C. The Foster brothers' activism resulted in bringing sweat lodges to prisons with Indigenous American inmates.

After his father returned home, he remained in the Marine Reserve for fourteen years. "He was still government property, even though he was working for Fort Defiance hospital," Larry says. It is said that when an individual knows more than one language, that ability makes a person powerful. This was the case for the elder Mr. Foster. Like many of the Code Talkers, Mr. Foster worked for more than thirty-nine years in community service, for the Navajo Nation as a chauffeur, for the Indian Health Service, and interpreter for the community health nurses, before retiring in 1981 after thirty-nine years of service. Larry attributes his father's long work record to his fluency in Navajo and English. Mr. Foster drove the nurses on narrow, primitive roads so they could give immunizations and healthcare to families living in remote areas. In addition to his driving responsibilities, he continued to work as an interpreter of the Navajo language—teaching Navajo terminology in anatomy and physiology, and Navajo language to the health workers.

Many of the Code Talkers participated in sports and athletics while in high school. Some had exceptional talent in baseball, basketball, football, and even boxing. During his R & Rs in Hawaii, Mr. Foster passed the time boxing, a sport that Larry eventually took up and went on to earn a boxing scholarship. More notably, Larry says his father was the only Navajo who played for the USMC Division League with the extraordinary "Duke" Snider, who later played professionally for the Los Angeles Dodgers. Back at home, veterans like Mr. Foster formed local baseball teams in Fort Defiance. After his retirement, Mr. Foster was in demand to give talks about the Code Talkers to local schools and organizations throughout the country. It was during one of these trips that he suddenly passed, just before his 70th birthday in May 1995.

■ ■ ■

My name is Larry Foster. Kinyaa'áánii éí nishłį́ dóó Dził Tł'ahnii éí báshíshchíín. Áádóó éí Tábąąhí dashicheii ádaat'é. Áádóó Kinłichíí'nii éí dashinálí danilį́. I'm the second son of the late Harold Yazzie Foster, Sr. Ako éí shizhé'é nilį́ n̈t'ę́ę́'. Éí Dził Tł'ahnii nilį́. Áádóó Kinłichíí'nii éí bizhé'é. Ako, éí shinálí ádaat'é. Áádóó bízhi' t'áá Diné k'ehjí éí Hastiin Yázhí Biye'. Bízhi'ígíí éí siláojí éí bízhi' éí Harold Yazzie.

■ ■ ■

My name is Larry Foster. I am Towering House and Mountain Ridge People clan are my fathers. And Near the Water People clan are my maternal grandfathers. Red House People clan are my paternal grandfathers. I am the second son of the late Harold Yazzie Foster, Sr. He was my father. Mountain Ridge was his clan. Red House clan were his fathers. So, they are my paternal grandfathers. And his Navajo name was Son of Short Man. His military name was Harold Yazzie.

■ ■ ■

But the military took it as Hastiin Yazzie. They wrote it up that way. Actually, his father's name was Sam Foster. There's a discrepancy on that. *Áádóó shinálí adzání éí,* my paternal grandmother, her name is Ann Foster. *Áko éí Dził Tł'ahnii dóó Tsélání éí yáshchį.* So Mountain Ridge and Many Rocks are her fathers. Harold Yazzie Foster grew up between Newcomb, Sheep Springs, and Two Grey Hills in New Mexico.

The way my father talked about how they were recruited, stations were set up after the tribal resolution was passed in Window Rock, that it was okay to recruit and have young Navajo men inducted into the armed forces during World War II. It gave the authority for the United States armed forces, in this case the United States Marines Corps, to come into Navajoland and the border towns—Flagstaff, Gallup, Albuquerque, Phoenix, and to the boarding schools sites like Fort Defiance, Shiprock, and, I think, Navajo Mission. John Benally and some other recruiters came to Fort Wingate High School, where the first induction occurred. My father was sixteen years old then, and he was very interested. He used to tell us that the uniform attracted him—the colors, the way it looked sharp, outstanding. At that time, he was only in tenth grade. So that following summer, his brother, Daniel Yazzie, went and joined and was put in the Second Platoon. That really inspired my dad. *Díkwíí shįį ákódaadzaa dó' nááná.* A number of them experienced that too. He didn't complete his education in high school. He went as far as eleventh grade. Then he went back to the Newcomb/Sheep Springs area. He really wanted to join. He talked to his mother and father, Mr. and Mrs. Sam Foster. The traders up there had a big role in my father's decision. The trader was the clearinghouse. He wrote and read letters for my grandparents. There's a couple of men, Richard Nez and Fred Stevens, Sr., they were Navajos, and they knew how to write their names. When my father wanted to join, they had the pastor there, those two men, the trader, and my grandparents—Mr. and Mr. Sam Foster. My grandparents just thumbprinted the document. Richard Nez and Fred Stevens signed, saying they were the witnesses. The pastor and the trader said it was okay for my dad to join the military.

So October 5, 1943, that's when it all began. My dad was an expert with the .45 caliber. He got the expert badge. He was also an expert combat swimmer and outstanding with the USMC KA-BAR knife. Those were his specialties. Then they asked him if he was Navajo. He said, "Yes." They said, "We're going to give you some assignments after you complete your boot camp." He completed his boot camp, which he said was very easy. I guess what he meant is that they did drills in boarding school, like marching and walking early in the morning and doing certain chores before the sun comes up, things like that, and running, and following orders. It was kind of difficult for the Anglo young men. But my dad and these Navajo young men, they're used to rugged and rigorous types of lifestyles, so they adjusted very quickly to boot camp.

The other area he used to talk about is how recruits were chosen based on their features. They were asked if they were Navajos. They said, "Yes, we're Navajos." So they were told, "We're going to give you an assignment." Later, when they completed their boot camp, they were instructed that they were not going home. They were sent directly to a place called Camp Elliott. That was the place where they had to learn the codes. I have his papers here that describe that. It's called Code Talker and 642. That's the code that was used for his assignment. Some of the people he was with were recruited together, but when you look at the serial number, they're kind of different here, just like a man called Benson Tohe. My father's serial number was pretty close to his. So they must have been together during the same time period when they went to boot camp. Other Code Talkers that he went to training with were Freeland Nez, John Augustine, Milton Gishal, Peter Johnson, Paul Kinlahcheeny, Matthew Martin, Willie Notah, Chester Tso, Deswood Etsitty, and Bobby Burke. These are the young men that learned the code language, and after that, they were deployed into their respective areas.

But according to the documents that I received and researched, my father, after he finished his boot camp, was sent in with the Second Marine Division. Within thirteen days during that time period, he was sent into combat. And that fighting that they did at that place was a very difficult area to fight in. It's called Tarawa. I think there were a lot of marines lost over there, but my research says there's eleven Navajo men that served over there. The code wasn't really used for some reason. These guys were there—King Mike, Johnny Alfred, Willard Oliver, Fleming Begaye, Frank Thompson, Jerry Begay, William Dean Wilson (he was Yazzie at the time), Howard Billiman (who was one of the instructors), John Brown, and Carl Gorman. The guy named Wilsie Bitsie was stationed in Wellington; that's in New Zealand, not too far from the Gilbert Islands. There was one [Code Talker] shot there, I understand. He was mistaken for a Japanese soldier. Some of the Code Talkers were reassigned into different divisions. My father was with the Second Marine Division at the Gilbert Islands.

When they went back to Hawaii, they activated the Fifth Marine Division, and he was reassigned into it. So during the war, the Third, Fourth, and Fifth Marine Divisions were new and activated. The First, Second, and Third have always have been part of the Marine Corps. So once that Fifth Marine Division was activated, they brought in all these hard-core veterans, marines who fought in different campaigns. They fought at Iwo Jima. My father was part of the Fifth Marine Division Signal Company. He was assigned to the Third Battalion with the Twenty-Seventh Marines. So when they landed in Iwo Jima, his ship came in on the second wave. The first wave of marines were just like targets when they came in. A lot of marines were lost on the first wave. The second was not as bad as the first wave.

They brought in the radios. A lot of the Code Talkers that served on Iwo Jima were assigned the long-range TBX radios. They communicated from the ship to the beach. Then once the radios were brought into the combat area, they set up their network. When there was a message sent from combat, it went to the beach area, then to the ship, then back from the ship, back to the beach, then back to the combat zone. All those were under strict orders of commanding officers. They sent dummy messages in Morse code too, so they would knock the intelligence of the Japanese. He told me this is how the system worked. There weren't any messages that were missed. In fact, some of the books that we read said there were over eight hundred messages that were sent out, and there were no errors. So that's a perfect language system.

My dad told us there were three cultures that came together—the Navajo, the United States Marines, and the Japanese. They had a different sense. This other Code Talker told me that when they were coming in on the half tracks. They saw Mount Suribachi, and it looked like a hogan. I think that spirit of *Hózhǫ́ǫ́jí,* Blessing Way, and Protection protected them. They had that extra sense to feel some of this spirituality out in combat. I think that was their level of thinking at that time. It was really outstanding. I think that's what my father meant: "The stronger culture was us," he said.

Our language was like an arrowhead; it didn't stay in one place. One of the codes that they used was "*mósí, né'éshjaa'í, na'asts'oosí, shash, wóláchíí', tązhii,* cat, owl, mouse, bear, ant, turkey." That spells "combat." At the end of the message they would say, *"Gah anáálwod.* The rabbit went back." That meant "Over and out." Or, they also said, *"Bidíchííd.* Let it go." When they wanted to say, "The area is secure. *Dibé bináá' náádzíí'.* The eyes of the sheep are healed." Or, *"Łį́į' bináá' náádzíí'.* The eyes of the horse are healed." These messages were used in Iwo Jima. I don't know about other places.

That's Sam Billison's voice on the Code Talker doll. I looked in the book, and sure enough, he was on the ship to Iwo Jima. He was sending messages from headquarters over there. Every now and then, the Code Talkers would quiz each other to keep abreast of all the correct wording. My father mentioned when you sent out a code, you couldn't stay there. You had to move, because the Japanese intelligence would spot you. Because they did not understand this language, I guess they just shot at that area. Unfortunately, two Code Talkers stayed in the foxhole too long, and they got hit and passed. Once a code was sent, it was protected like in that movie, *Windtalkers.* I believe my father had a bodyguard. His name was Raymond A. Dooley. He's from Mission Viejo, California. He was still alive when they had their reunion at Camp Pendleton. I talked with this man once on the phone; he sounded like he was elderly. Those are some of the significant areas that I wanted to mention.

The weapons that they carried were short-moving machine guns. They also had to carry the marine knife. The uniforms that they used were reversible. One side was camouflage; the other side was regular green. A lot of times, they would remove their uniforms, like their leggings. They didn't care for them. Their helmets helped them get water, and they would carry their food in there. Everything was done on foot. They walked from the tip of Iwo Jima to the north side. That's what, about ten miles? They fought hand to hand all the way up. Their assignment was with the Twenty-seventh Regiment to go for the airfield. Their job was to clean that up, clean up all the resistance. But he also talked about this cave. There were dead Japanese in there and a lot of food. They opened some and it said American Red Cross. I guess Japan had an earthquake years before. That food was given to them as a donation. Somehow it ended up in the hands of the Japanese soldiers. I don't know if it made him angry. Of course, it upset a lot of people. Those are some of the things that he saw. At night they would tie strings to the next foxhole. Every now and then they would pull on it and see if that next person's okay or awake. A lot of the Japanese soldiers would counterattack. That was their preference, to attack at night. So they had to be alert during those times.

He got shrapnel on his right calf, but it was removed. He completed the duration of thirty-six days that they fought at Iwo Jima. He did receive his Purple Heart, with a bronze star on that. During those times, they would travel on ships. I think he went on that ship called USS *Karnes*. He told me a little bit about the ships. It was a crowded place. People were sleeping right next to each other, people's feet on each other. It was hot down there. People would smoke cigarettes. To catch fresh air, they went outside. The other ship that he served on was the USS *Arthur Middleton* and he was transported on the USS *Sandoval*. That ship was named after Sandoval County in the state of New Mexico. That ship took him from Hawaii to Iwo Jima. The other ship that he traveled on was the USS *Dashing Wave XAP* from April 5, 1946, to April 22, 1946. After the war at Iwo Jima, they were going back to Hawaii to reboard the ship to Japan.

This was the time of the Nagasaki and Hiroshima bombings. The Special Forces for the Imperial, in fact, are the ones who fought at Guadalcanal with the Second Marine Division. So whoever the Navajo Code Talkers were, I know Carl Gorman was one, fought against the Japanese Imperial Army. My father went to this base. In the meantime they had the bombings up north. Everybody in the U.S. Marine Corps were being shipped to Japan. He was there six months. That's a long time for a Code Talker to be in a certain area like that. My father was sent to Nagasaki; that's one of those places that got bombed. There was a lot of radiation in the air and they were breathing it. I remember my father's hair got white at an early age, like forty years old. His hair started falling out. He was a man that never went to the hospital, not even for an immunization, dental exam, or blood pressure check, even though he worked in the hospital. Some of them were like that. Their level of thinking is different from most people. The war made them that way.

My father stayed with his tradition, beginning to end. He was a traditional man. He really believed in the sweat lodge. Every Veterans Day, he would get in the sweat lodge. One thing that really bothered him, that he would always talk about, was that in order for him to survive, he had to kill another human being with a knife. He told us it was like a sheep. You get the knife and you cut here to here. That bothered him. I guess they had one significant feeling that bothered them, and that was his, the spirit of that Japanese soldier. In fact, the last time he had his ceremony, he shed his tears and told us. He brought all his sons back together. He told us, "Help each other. Don't argue in the future. Take care of your mother." Those were his exact words.

Four days later he had a severe heart attack. He had his Navajo Code Talker uniform on, and he was with Albert Smith, doing a presentation at Coconino High School at Flagstaff. I received a call that morning saying, "Your father is being taken to the hospital." That was at 7:45 in the morning. At 8:15 he passed on. So that day, my brother and I went down there, and we got all his clothes. He must've really struggled, because his uniform was soaking wet, especially his velveteen top. So that's how he passed. He died with his uniform on and with what he believed in. He believed in the language, the culture that he talked about. He always wanted his kids and grandkids to talk in Navajo language. *T'áá Diné k'ehjí háádaahdzih doo. Nihá yá'át'ééh. Jó éí nihizaad. T'áá shíí aníí nihizaad t'ahdii níléédi naaldoh in the South Pacific.* Speak Navajo. It's good for you. It's true that the spirit of our language still floats in the South Pacific. One of these days we're going to take a Navajo medicine man down there and let him talk to the spirit of the air.

> *Nítch'ihígíí bich'į' háádoodzih.*
> *Éí tsodizinígíí áájį' niidooléél.*
> *Béésists'ogii niidooléél.*
> *Áájį' shįį yá'át'ééh dooleel.*
> *Áádóó shįį éí nihizaad áádi naaldohígíí éí*
> *it's going to come back to our homeland, níí łeh ńt'ę́ę́'.*

The air will speak to them again.
He will place the prayer there.
He will place an arrowhead there.
Then it will be okay.
Then our language, that is floating there,
will come back to our homeland, he used to say.

That way, maybe these young people can relearn their language. "*Bizaadígíí biih ńdoolyééł,* They will relearn their language." That's what he said. That's his belief. I honor that. I think there's a truth to that. The

Code Talkers went back a few years ago—Guam, Saipan, Iwo Jima. I asked them, "Did you hear anything there?" "Yes." Our medicine people say it's still there. Teddy Draper is the one that would really listen. He's got that sense. Albert Smith is another man that has a traditional concept. Those guys were there, so they know.

I also have a sister, Marilyn Willie, and I have a brother, Len Foster, and another brother named Dr. Harold Chuck Foster. He's a doctor in education. And I have a brother who's a writer of sports, Oree Foster. So there are five of us— four sons, and one daughter. My father has fourteen grandkids and eleven great-grandchildren. He always said, "Try to stay within your tribe. Don't go out and marry a *Bilagáana* [Anglo] or another tribal person. During the '70s and '80s, that was difficult for my brothers and I. We went out into the world too. I have a bachelor of arts degree in sociology from the University of California, Los Angeles. My brother's got a master's degree from Colorado State University. Oree's got two master's degrees in journalism from Arizona State University. And Dr. Chuck Foster has a Ph.D. from the University of Arizona.

We grew up in Fort Defiance, a place called 7th Street. We were trained to get up at 4 o'clock in the morning. We all had assignments—clean the bathroom, clean the kitchen, pick up the trash outside, things like that. That's what we learned. And then, he always had books for us. He would never say, "Read it," or he'll buy the books. He put it there for us on the bench, so we would pick up what we wanted to read—sports books, other books that he would bring back, health books, and things like that. So we learned how to read like that. My father believed in being self-sufficient. "Go work. Don't just stay home." My brother and I started hoeing weeds when we were twelve years old for people. He took us to Long Beach to this batting cage. He hit so many home runs, he won a hundred dollars. That's the kind of man he was all the time. He was determined.

He told us that he used to box and he played second base for the USMC Division League in 1944–45. He played with a guy named Duke Snider, who later played for the Los Angeles Dodgers. When they came back after the war they formed their own teams in the Fort Defiance area. Ralph Bennet, Barry Lincoln, Eddie Lincoln, Ned Showalter, those guys formed a baseball team called "Navajo Servicemen." They went all over—McNary, Flagstaff, Winslow, Holbrook. They used to pile into this old ambulance from Fort Defiance. A guy named Ken Dyer used to call the ambulance the Green Hornet.

I saw his uniform in the closet. He had pictures he used to look through, all these Japanese that are dead. I don't know why he had those pictures. We didn't know he was a Code Talker. On July 7, 1971, they had a reunion at the Window Rock fairgrounds at the museum. Martin Link coordinated that one with a guy named Lee Cannon. And they brought all the Code Talkers. Today the reunion people are still with the association—Keith Little, Teddy Draper, Samuel Tso, Jessie Smith, Sam Smith—their pictures are in there. My father got his medallion. Jimmy King sent out a code. "May the Creator God Bless the Land Here." That was the code they sent out. They called it C Ration Hill. They all camped up there, the tents, the radios. I was a teenager then. The first officers were selected—John Benally, Carl Gorman, James Nahkai. Fort Defiance had the largest Navajo Code Talker population. The reason why is the jobs. Some of them worked at the trading posts, schools, hospital; some worked for the BIA. Bill Cadman was a butcher up there at Earl's Ashcroft Trading Post. John Benally worked for the BIA. Sam Billison worked for education at the BIA in Fort Defiance. My father was working in Fort Defiance at the Indian hospital. Rex Kontz was the postmaster there. I believe when the Code Talkers came back, they made something of themselves. They're the ones that built the government. John Brown, James Nahkai, and George Kirk became council delegates. Of course, Peter McDonald was the Chairman at one time. There's others. They had a big role in the development of the foundation of our nation. That was because of their ability to speak Navajo and English. That's how far it took them.

I do presentations myself. I gave a presentation not too long ago at the Phoenix Indian Center. Some of the students from Arizona State University, the history students, the Navajo students were there. I research all this stuff. I look through archives, talk to people. I get all my information together. One time, I had a chance to go to Washington, D.C., but I didn't get to the Marine Corps up there at the Pentagon. A lot of this is up there, too.

We are going to write our own book, my brothers and I. There are a lot of things in there that you asked me to speak about, about being an activist. We had our roles in the political arena. My father supported what we did. My older brother was a participant in the occupation at Wounded Knee [II]. He was a bodyguard to Dennis Banks. They wrote an introduction to a book. It talks about how my brother led Dennis Banks out of the village there. And now he works with corrections in federal and state prisons throughout the country. He represents at parole hearings, probation hearings, and writes letters of recommendation to judges of the people that are going to be sentenced. I was an activist from 1972 through 1978. I went on a number of campaigns myself—Trail of Broken Treaties, across the country to Washington, D.C., during the Nixon administration. I did the Longest Walk across America. I joined in Pueblo, Colorado, in February during the winter and walked all the way to Washington, D.C. And the most recent one, two years ago, the Longest Walk from Alcatraz to Navajoland. My brothers and I became community activists. We did a lot of things people wouldn't do, like medicine man services, legislations, requesting from our state legislators. The Code Talkers assisted us to get legislation for sweat lodges in prisons. We all worked together on these, and now it's a federal law. Some of the medicine men services are state laws now. So those are some of the areas in which my late father supported us. My grandfather supported us when he was still alive.

In our genes, in our DNA, my grandparents both lived to be over ninety-five years old. We have that gene on our mother's side. On my dad's side, *shinali,* paternal grandfather, lived to be ninety-seven. And Grandpa went to ninety-nine, I believe. But my dad passed when he was just going to turn seventy, May 12, 1995. He was born May 15, 1925. So he was a few days short of being seventy. It's our turn to be in the forefront with the Code Talkers. I also did presentations in Los Angeles, Long Beach, and then the Albuquerque Indian Center. When I did that, I did run into some other descendants from other tribal Code Talkers. There was a guy from Oklahoma who said, "My grandpa, he was a Code Talker with the Comanches." They're proud of it too. I always propose to the *Native America Calling* show to have the Code Talkers and descendants on the radio show to expose it throughout the world.

In closing, I just wanted to mention a few things about traditional rights and traditional medicine that my father used to believe in. He had foresight that my brother, Dr. Chuck Foster, would be a long distance runner, so they trained him. Some of the medicine he believed is how you can use certain elements from a hummingbird, in this case. *Tádídíín bąąh ájiiłʼįįh nóo.* You put corn pollen on it, he used to say. He rubbed it on my brother's leg when he was just a little child.

He grew up that way, so he had the ability through that prayer. My father used to take us to hunt squirrels, prairie dogs, rabbits, but he never took us on a deer hunt. He always said, "*Éí baahasti'*. That's dangerous. I don't want to take you guys over there." You got to purify in certain ways and act in certain ways or you can get spiritually hurt from a deer.

We're descendants of our great *nali,* Narbona Tso. He had five sons and three daughters. The fourth generation, that's my *nali,* Sam Foster. We come from that line. One of the daughters married Manuelito. Gladys Manuelito is the famous rug weaver. The medicine man taught the ladies to weave ceremonial designs on the rugs. They came from *Hastiin Tł'ahí,* the medicine man. Wheelwright Museum in Santa Fe has all the paraphernalia of *Hastiin Tł'ahí.* They want to give it back to the family. They said, "*T'óó wáhádzoo nida'ałch'íízh tł'éé'go.* They make loud noises at night." There was a fire started that burned half of that building. I think it's because of that. I guess the spirits in there are getting unsettled; it's not resting. They want to go back to their home, back to the mountains. And that's the family tree of my grandparents. Notice their names and their clans. *Asdzą́ą́ Bich'ah Ditł'oí,* Woman with the Fuzzy Hat, my grandma. My other uncle, Carl Todacheene, is a Code Talker and he was a councilman too.

What I was told was *Kinyaa'áanii Dine'é,* Towering House People clan, originated from *Dinétahí* up there at *Dził Ná'oodiłí. Kin yii' dabighan ńt'ę́ę́'. Diyin Dine'é danilį́i ńt'ę́ę́' jiní. Éí bits'ą́ą́dę́ę́'ígíí.* They used to live in a house. They were Holy People, they said. After that a lot of *Kinyaa'áaniis* intermarried with mainly the Pueblos, maybe the Hopis and the Zunis. My uncle told me, "Hey, nephew, you have relatives in Mexico." One of our relatives went into Mexico and had a big family. That man passed away, and they brought his body back and buried him over here. That generation are part Navajos now. You know the history of how the Navajos fought for land rights, fought against the Spaniards, and the Mexicans.

As far as contributing to opening up the [Code Talker] museum, I'd like to see it fully developed. Not to argue about it, but the land that Chevron gave us is nothing but hard rock, hard even for plumbing. They're going to have to figure that one out. So it's going to be a lot of work ahead. When I retire, I'd like to be the manager up there. I know most of the Code Talkers now. I've met almost all of them. I saw your dad's name in here too.

I want to clarify my dad's congressional medal. There was some confusion. His name during the war was Harold Yazzie. Because like I said, my grandfather's Navajo name was *Hastiin Yázhí.* The traders or pastors or military people transformed that to Hastiin Yazzie when actually his name was Sam Foster. [It was customary to have a Navajo name and an American name during this time.] They confused the names, so when my father went into the service his name was Harold Yazzie. But when he came back, October 25, 1962, he changed his name back to Foster. In closing, I just want to say that the late Harold Yazzie Foster, Sr. was promoted to Sergeant, April 6, 1946, and then to Sergeant Major on February 19, 1988. That's an honorary field promotion. Only eleven were selected.

*Herb and Joanne Goodluck at the
Window Rock Veteran's Memorial.*

Herb, Clara, and Joanne Goodluck
Children of John V. Goodluck
February 4–5, 2012, Window Rock, Arizona

JOHN VELASQUEZ GOODLUCK WAS BORN FEBRUARY 20, 1922, in Lukachukai, Arizona. He was *Tó'aheedlíinii*, Water Flows Together People clan and born for *Dibé Łizhíní*, Black Sheep People clan. His maternal grandfather clan was *Táchii'nii*, Red Running Into Water People clan and his paternal grandfather clan was *Kinłichii'nii*, Red House People clan. During Mr. Goodluck's youth families often arranged marriages for their children, as was Navajo tradition. His arranged marriage to Rita Leonard lasted more than forty-five years and together they raised four daughters and four sons.

Born into a family of fifteen children, he herded sheep with his grandmother and was not allowed to attend school. When his parents could not care for all of their children, the aunts and uncles stepped in to raise them. John wanted an education, so he ran away from home and enrolled himself at St. Michaels Indian School at St. Michaels, Arizona. During the era of assimilation when John attended school, students who spoke their native language at school were punished with ruler slaps on their hands or their mouths were washed with soap. John received such harsh treatment. While still in high school at Santa Fe Indian School, he enlisted at Fort Wingate, New Mexico, in 1943. He was discharged in 1945 as private first class (PFC) in the Third Marine Division. He was also the brother to one of the first Navajo linguists, the late Dr. Alise Goodluck Neundorf, who helped write a Navajo/English children's bilingual dictionary. Mr. Goodluck passed in 2000 at the age of seventy-nine.

Herb, Clara, and Joanne Goodluck, brother and sisters, are *Tótsohnii*, Big Water People clan, and born for the *Tó aheedlíinii*, Water Flows Together People clan. Their maternal grandfathers are *Kinłichii'nii*, Red House People clan, and their paternal grandfathers are *Dibé lizhin,* Black Sheep People clan. Herb said he once introduced himself as H_2O to the second power. "I'm really powerful. In a way you guys need me everyday," he joked. It wasn't until after the Navajo code was declassified in 1968 that the siblings heard their father's stories as they chauffeured him to meetings and events. But he chose not to tell them stories about the atrocities of war and instead spoke of events and people that were more positive. In this way they feel their father protected them, because *Diné* believe that telling such stories can be harmful, especially to the young. Herb finds tremendous enjoyment in carrying on his father's role as a radio man. He holds an amateur ham radio operator license to communicate with other ham operators throughout the world. As part of his tribute to his father and the Navajo Code Talkers, Herb sets up his radio equipment that brings him into radio communication with other radio operators all over the world at the annual Navajo Code Talker day celebration in August. Herb, Clara, and Joanne are deeply dedicated to honoring their father's and the Navajo Code Talkers' legacy and teaching it to the next generation. Clara teaches at Window Rock Elementary School where, after showing her students a documentary film on the Code Talkers, the children were so moved that they stood and applauded. The education that was formerly denied her father influenced Clara to earn several degrees and she is now working on her doctorate in administration.

■ ■ ■

I think he said he was about ten years old when he ran away from home and enrolled himself in school. His older brother was already going to school, and when he came home he taught my father English words. "Hey, *díí kolyé.* This is called [a spoon]. This is called a fork." By then he didn't want to live the life that his father and his aunts did. The natural parents couldn't provide for all, so they gave them away to the aunts and uncles to help with herding sheep and doing chores. He wanted to learn more rather than just the Navajo way. I think he was really fortunate that he did that for himself. My mother never attended school but she always used to say, *"Da'iinołta'. Shídah shinołí.* Go to school. Look at me. I don't even know what English is. I could have been something else instead of me just being a weaver. *Éí biniinaa ahó nihidish ní.* For this reason I'm telling all of you this." We used to sit around the table and, if we didn't want her to listen to us, we would talk in English but she would figure it out. She was a very smart woman, my mother. *Niléí dahiistł'ó,* a textile weaving, uses geometry or calculus. One side *łahó anolnin,* looks different, and the other side has a different design. *Iimás dah daalyé ya'.* They are also described as textiles that can be rolled up. That all comes from geometry. So I think she could have been somewhere else like in an office, but she never went to school.

The way I was raised was military like. It seems like everything had to be square. Your shoes had to be in the correct place; the towels had to be stacked like a square. That's how he taught us. He went to St. Michaels Catholic Indian School and then Santa Fe Indian School. One time he checked on his younger sisters on the playground to make sure they were okay. Then he bought them jackets.

He was in high school at Santa Fe Indian School when he heard about the bombing of Pearl Harbor. He told me you see all these posters, you know, about the marines standing there, proud. The marine blues really appealed to him when he joined the Marine Corps. Those were the people that carry on a tradition. I guess that's what he had in mind. Secondly, he wanted to protect his own land. That was fortunate that we have this land or otherwise we probably could have been sent to Mexico or somewhere, he said.

After his time in the South Pacific he went to Chilocco Indian School in Oklahoma to finish high school. The military had the G.I. Bill back then too. He went into auto mechanics in high school. Maybe it was in 1946 when he rebuilt a vehicle. He had to stay after school ended, maybe a couple of weeks or months; and then he drove the vehicle back. At that time he said he was the only one that had a vehicle. You had to be rich to own one back then. And then everybody used to come in and want a ride from here to there.

Most of the time he stayed with his aunt and uncle who raised him. Maybe that's the reason why he wanted to run away and learn the English way. But when he was raising us he still had the traditional within him. We also had to go to Catholic church and wear black slacks and white shirts. But he was a pretty interesting person. He never really talked about what he experienced, only the good times. Being that way is the traditional way, like when you go hunting. *Doo ts'ídá t'áá ńt'ę́ę́' baa hane'da, daaní. Kojí nijibaaho shį́į́ t'áá' ákót'é.* They say one doesn't tell everything. It's the same as when one goes to war. You don't really go into depth. We went to Colorado and this lady was interviewing the Code Talkers. She was asking, "What actually was going through your mind? When the bullets were flying how were you able to translate the incoming signal through the radio, writing it down at the same time? What was your actual feeling?" That kind of thing. There were two of them being interviewed. They wouldn't really hit right on what she wanted. *Bahasti' daats'í biniinaa.* There is danger placed on it. They told only half of the whole thing. So that's what I noticed.

He said growing up on the reservation we can withstand just about anything. We know how to hunt. We know how to survive without electricity and running water. We're used to it. We had our Navajo language too. We had that advantage the Japanese couldn't overcome. The Japanese people had empires *niléí hadą́ą́'shį́į́ yę́ędą́ą́'* sometime during the 15th century. It amazed him. *Nihizaad nihí chódeisiil'į́įd. Ayóo nisídaakees. Nidi nihizaad ch'éé ádajiiłį́įd.* And we had awareness of our language. The [Japanese] have a strong intelligent mind. Even so, they couldn't decipher our language. He always said, "Don't ever lose our language. *Niha 'ałchíní Diné bizaad bínidanołtin."* Ádanihi' di'níi nidi doo ádeit'į́į da.* Teach your children the *Diné* language." They tell us that but we don't do it.

My dad and John Kinsel experienced the Great Depression. They were in downtown Gallup when they saw white people standing in the soup line with just a little bowl. Someone comes around and gives them soup. John said, "*Háahgóóshį́į́ Diné biwók'iz nida'atsigo háágóóshį́į́ nidaazį́į́ łeh. The Diné* would be picking their teeth as they stood around." The Depression was nothing to them. They already lived that life; they were living that life. It didn't faze them is what both of them said. If you wanted something, you had to go after it and get off the reservation. Go find something and, hopefully, you come back. There's a lot of difference to how it is right now. "We lived through all the punishments. I think it was good," he said. He compared it to the Anglo during the war. He saw white guys who couldn't take it anymore in the foxhole. "They just stand up and get shot. It's the easy way out," he said. "But I'm thankful that I had lived a hard life, that I grew up on the reservation, and the outside world makes it so easy," my dad said. *Éí t'áá 'íídą́ą́' nihídaneeztą́ą́', t'ą́ą́'ałtsoní. Dichin, dikos, ádaat'éi t'áá' íídą́ą́' bii'nisiikai; áko dibáá'da, haashíí nízáád. Níléígóó dighádílyeed danihi'di'nįi łeh.* [The hard life] already taught us. We already experienced things like hunger and coughing sickness; we have already known thirst for some time. They used to tell us to walk among other places. That makes us strong, you know. *Shimá sání shí t'áá ákóshidoo'niid.* My grandmother told me this. But you know what? I haven't passed it down to my kids yet. *T'áá iidą́ą́' daneeyá.* They're already grown up. I should have. They just do their own thing.

He told us about this one white guy and him were going to make a little patrol. The white guy wrote a note. He handed it to someone else and said, "Okay, if I don't come back send this home for me." Then went on patrol. "All of a sudden across the way there were a couple of Japanese shooting at us. And this particular guy, I don't how he knew he was going to die that day. He got shot just above his eyes. Killed him instantly." And they were just scouting out there. He couldn't believe it. He was a close friend too. I know that's the only one that he mentioned. That's why he didn't like to make friends because they might die the next day. Another story he told was during one night when he was in a foxhole. It's just big enough for one or two people. Everything was done in that little hole, even going to the bathroom, because once you got up you got shot. He thought the Anglo people are not that patient. They get frustrated so easy and then they just stand up, and the Japanese shoot them during the night.

In the marines, most of the time, he was with the top brass, like the captains and the majors. When the incoming signal comes in he would have a general standing behind him. Word for word he wrote the message down. They start getting the artillery ready. I forgot what battleship he was on. He used to be there too transmitting to the island. The messages went back and forth. The TBY and TBX radios covered only a certain range, maybe a good two or three miles. Once you go over something like a hill, it blocks the message. "*Ákót'éé ńt'ę́ę́' ní.* It was like that," he said. One time they had fun playing around with Rex Kontz, the Code Talker. It was quiet. Nothing going on, so they sent a message to Rex. They said "*Deinésts'aa'bináá' ałná'asdzoh.* The ram's eye is [criss-] crossed." The r is for ram, the e is for eye, and x is for [criss] cross. They actually spelled out Rex's name.

One night my dad was talking about, I think it was Guadalcanal, when they were camped out. A barbed wire strung with cans surrounded the camp. I guess there was a movement among those wires. They shot rapid fire at that area. All of a sudden it died out and it's calm the rest of the night. The next day they went to investigate and there was a wild pig there. That's the story that he used to tell us. *Éí t'éí yaa halne'*. He only told that part. He told us things like how he enjoyed the navy and the marine mess halls. *"T'óó báhádzidgo nizhónígó nída 'iidį́į́ nt'ę́ę́'*. We had plenty of food to eat."

Another time when the war was over he was on the ship and they met this Navajo guy. *Hashįį wolyé níine'*. I forgot what he said his name was. He was in a jumpsuit, just a plain guy. He said he was with the air corps. *"Nihí éíyá PFC daniidlí," ní. "Hááhgóóshįį bił naháatą bił nidahwiilne'*. We told him we were all PFCs," he was saying. "We sat with him and enthusiastically told stories to each other. When we sailed back to San Francisco and we docked, boy! He came out, and he had a lot of stripes. *"Doo chohoo'įįgóó hadiidzaa," ní*. "He dressed out in his finest," he said. "He was staff sergeant, maybe even better." My father said he should have gone into the air corps rather than the marines. "They just put us in the grunt and you go into infantry. There's just one guy that I knew was higher in rank than us. He was a daredevil and was the only corporal I knew back then. They don't hand out ranks, you know. You have to be real good, really smart to get to corporal or to get to the next step. I was ranked as PFC when I got out. They didn't want to give me anything. PFC, that's what they gave me," he said. Later on, those that were doing communications were supposed to be at staff sergeant rank. So finally they gave it to them. But, you know, it was too late. The war had ended 40 or 50 years ago. *'Áadi 'índída*. It wasn't until then. But I guess minorities don't have a say. It seems that way everywhere we go, unless we really push for it. *T'áá nihí*. It's up to us.

Once my father married my mother he started looking a job. He worked for the U.S. Public Health Service in Fort Wingate as a driver and interpreter for field nurses, who were mostly Anglos. Some of the things that the nurses did was to check up on people that had tuberculosis. One year he would be a maintenance worker and then another time he'd go back to the motor vehicle and then a couple of years he was the ambulance driver. I think it was July 1982 he retired from the Public Health Service. They moved back to Lukachukai, the homestead.

He went to school at Diné College. He studied auto mechanics and got his AA (Associate of Arts) from there. Unfortunately, he didn't use the G.I. Bill. I guess it runs out after a certain amount of time. So that was already gone. Most of it came from the Pell Grant and Navajo Scholarship. When I used to go home he would be sitting at the table, his books all out. He would be studying, getting frustrated. *Díí shį́į́ ha'at'íí ní?* What is this saying? And then he throws his glasses down, picks them back up. But I think he had good grades though. He said everybody calls him *cheii,* grandfather. "You better stop calling me *cheii* around here," he joked. He was probably the oldest student. He was always joking around. That's how people knew him. But once he got home he turned different, military style. He never did become a mechanic. I think part of the reason is that he was limited in that his retirement just gave him so much. He tried to become a farmer too. He had a tractor and baler and grew hay, alfalfa, corn, and squash. He didn't just want a certificate from school; he wanted to prove himself. He was that type of person that had a goal. I think that's what it was about for him going to Diné College.

My father was seventy-nine when he passed away from heart disease on April 1, 2000. At his funeral one of the veterans said about my father: "*Ei doo náhinilyéesda, t'áadoo le'é nihaadíí'áál bijiniihgo.* [John] is not afraid, if you ask him to bring it. If you go to John he'll bring it for sure; he'll be there." My mother turned seventy-nine the following year. I think they had seven months between their deaths. It seems there was nothing wrong with my mother, just her arthritis. She couldn't walk. I think what took her life was that she was so devastated when my father passed. *'Ayóó 'áhi'dó'níí ńt'ę́ę́', t'áá'áłah.* They loved each other very much. That is what took her life, I thought. She died of a broken heart. They had an arranged marriage. *Shizhé'é bá'í'déékid.* My father was asked for in marriage. My dad lived less than five miles away, yet they never knew one another. My mother used to say, "Right now you guys have it so easy where you can go out there and pick who you want to marry. *Nihí 'éí ałk'idą́ą́' doo 'ákót'ée da ńt'ę́ę́', azhą́ shį́į́ hastiin doo jinízin da ndi; t'óó baa 'iih jinízin ndi. K'ad éí nihí 'ákódaniit'éé le 'ígí 'át'éego, t'áá'ako ałts'ą́ąjį'dahidookah łeh. You give up. Nihí 'éiyá naadą́ą́'nihá siikéego kónízahgóó ahoolzhiizh.* You give up. A long time ago it wasn't like that for us, even though one might not want a man; he's ugly one might think. Would that this was the case now, but couples always end up separating. You give up. As for us, corn is our strength thus far." My parents never used really strong words that are negative, even though you could feel the tension between them sometimes. But in their own way they settled it. *Ákót'éé ńt'ę́ę́'*. It was like that.

From what my dad did I got drawn into two-way radio communication too, which is ham radio, amateur radio. My brother passed his license first. And then I thought what about me? So I passed my license and I have the highest license in two-way communication the feds can give. My call sign is N7HG. That's November 7 Hotel Golf. I talk all over the world to Europe, Japan, South America, Alaska, Russia, and Japan. I've even talked to the Philippines, just like my father used to do. I know how to do Morse code, maybe eighteen words per minute. Other countries can't talk about their financial crisis within their government, but can talk about certain things like the price of gas. As an American talking to these people, we're fortunate that we have freedom. *Nihich'ą́ą́h nidaazbaa'. Nihizhé'é danilį́, nihicheii danilį́į́ ńt'ę́ę́', nihich'ą́ą́h nidaazbaa'.* They protected us. Our fathers, our grandfathers protected us.

On August 14 I am on my radio and I talk to the whole United States. Boy! There are a lot of people that want to talk to me. This is probably my seventh or eighth year. I have been granted November 7 Charley, which is N7C. That's a special call you can use just one day. I do that on behalf of the Code Talkers and my father too. I love it! It's really wonderful to hear other people say, "Thank you. Your dad was really a Code Talker. If it wasn't for the Code Talkers, maybe we might have a Japanese flag." They also say, "Okay, if you're Navajo speak it, say something in Navajo." They greatly enjoy it. I'm trying to help keep the legacy going. Who else will keep it going? Now it's our turn, the descendants, the children, to step in to tell these stories to never let it die out. *T'óó baa danichį́'go t'éiyá t'óó háíshį́' dooleeł.* If we just hold onto it, it's just going to go by the wayside. It's going to be like our language, one day it's not going to be there anymore. That's the reason why I do this thing.

I carry on the legacy of my own family. My maternal grandmother, my maternal grandfather and also my maternal uncles, my aunts. Gone. They all died. And then the same is true on my father's side. My paternal aunts are gone. My paternal uncles are gone. My paternal grandfather too. They're all gone. I'm a baby boomer. One of my nephews came to me and said in English "Uncle, I want you to be my negotiator at Whippoorwill for my marriage." In

Navajo language he would have said, *"Shidá'í, shá 'ídídíílkił nléí Whippoorwill holyéedi."* I'm thinking I'm still young. To truly think about it, I have to carry on what was given to me and what I was told. Now I have to go up to the batter box.

People from Mexico jump the fence to come to America. And then they have to seek employment. America is something that they want to have; they want their kids to grow up in America. What about us Native American people? Why is it we don't think like that? We're already citizens. All we have to do is go after it and make something out of ourselves. Why don't we do it? It is not withheld from me, this two-way communication. They don't say, "You're Native American so we're not going to give you the highest license." If you're able to pass all these tests and give us a little bit of money in exchange for it, you can update your permit every so many years. That's how we conduct it. I think it's a wonderful place to live here in the States and especially on the Navajo Nation where there's a lot of leeway, a reservation where we don't have to pay taxes for our land. The house we still have to pay for. I work for the state so I don't get taxed because I'm working and living on the reservation. Now if I was working in Phoenix for the state, then they're going to tax me. I do pay federal tax. There's a misconception about that. A lot of people don't understand that. They say, "Oh, you guys don't pay federal tax," but we do.

There's a truck driver that used to go through Chinle, Window Rock, and Phoenix. One time he went to Kayenta to Richard Mike's Burger King and Navajo Code Talker display. He emailed me and said a busload of Japanese people came in and were talking in Japanese. He emailed me. "Hey Herb, what do you think is going through these people's minds? There's a Japanese flag on display in the middle of nowhere on an Indian reservation. How did it get here and how did this group of people get it? Maybe they think it's related to World War II." You would have all these questions going into your mind.

I was trying to think how my father's story would inspire people. I want to make it truthful, to go in-depth. *Jó badahast'éí shįį́ biniinaa t'áadoo hazhó'ó shił hóone' da.* Because of the danger placed on it is probably why he didn't tell me things in-depth. There's times when I took him to the VA hospitals and I had chances of asking him. *Haash dahoot'éé ńt'ę́ę́' íídą́ą́ nléé ndizhchį́į́ dóó hoshdę́ę'?* What was it like when you were born and when you were growing up? He said that when my oldest sister was two or three years old and was walking in the field they could just see the top of her head through that thick grass. It's not like that now. Back then it was like that. Maybe now the earth is changing.

■ ■ ■

We are going through chaotic times. Some might say I am going to give up but we are unique. Níléí háádéé̱' shį́į̱ niikai'. Diné Náhódlóonii wolyé, ą́ą́déé̱'. [1] *Sometimes the Bilagáanas say we came from Asiatic Russia and Mongolia. Sometimes I think about the Four Worlds[2] that they went through. 'Áádéé̱' tó hakéé' anol'ą́ą́ł. "Tsį́į̱łgo! Tsį́į̱łgo!" T'áá hakéé' tó anool'ą́ą́ł. [the Bering Strait] Éí daats'í yaa yádaałti'. Maybe one time the whole thing was connected. Maybe that's what they are talking about. Maybe we went through Alaska all the way to Canada. Haa'ígi shį́į̱ Diné ákót'éego nihizaadígíí áadi chodayooł'į̱́, ha'ní. Diné Náhódlóonii deiłní. 'Áádóó wóshdéé̱'. Kodi, kónízáadi níléí háádéé̱' shį́į̱ nimá sání yé̱e̱, nichó yé̱e̱ éí k'ad ánít'í.*

■ ■ ■

We are going through chaotic times. Some might say I am going to give up but we are unique. We don't know from what place we came. From there originated our ancient, northern ancestors.[1] Sometimes the *Bilagáanas* say we came from Asiatic Russia and Mongolia. Sometimes I think about the Four Worlds[2] that they went through. From that place the water rose to their feet. *"Hurry!" "Hurry!"* The water rose to their feet. Were they talking about [the Bering Strait]? Maybe one time the whole thing was connected. Maybe that's what they are talking about. Maybe we went through Alaska all the way to Canada. At some place the *Diné* used their language, it is said. They are the ancient, northern ancestors, as they are called. And then they came towards this direction. From that time on and going back to your grandmother, your great-grandmother, you are them. This is who you are. Our ancestors filtered all the way down to here. You're a stronger person because of that journey.

■ ■ ■

Just imagine, they fought all these wolves. They fought all these bears and whatever. They didn't have a gun. What did they use to fight off their enemies wherever they met them? You are now a person of those people who struggled.

---

[1] The ancient ancestors of the *Diné* people who were once one people and spoke one language. It is said that some of these people are the Athabascans and other related tribes who live in the Northwest and Canada.

[2] Navajo stories say that humans and animals emerged from the previous worlds into the present world. Some storytellers say we presently inhabit the Fourth World, while others say the Fifth World.

Ha'át'íishįį, naałniih, dikos ádaat'éí. There was some kind of coughing epidemic. They were able to survive it. *'Ákót'éego 'ádaa nitsíníkees. Áko t'áadoo bíghahígóó 'ánitéego 'ádaa nitsíníkesí.* Think of yourself in that way. Don't think carelessly about yourself. And I think that is really true. We're a people who are struggling and to this day that's who we are. We pass it down to our kids. *'Ákót'éego náás dah iildééh nahalin.* It seems that is how it goes forward. And if anything should happen I think the real people out there in the middle of nowhere are the ones who are going to survive, if there's another war. Now there's talk of another war, nuclear weapons pointed at main metropolitan areas. What if it really happens? I think the Navajos, *Bitsį Yishtłizhii danilínii,* Indigenous Peoples, have survived times of war already. *Bilagáana* introduce things to make it better, but sometimes they go in the wrong direction. But I'm glad that they're here though. Otherwise, we couldn't travel from A to B within a day. I don't really have any other words to say.

Richard Mike

Son of King Mike

July 11, 2009, Kayenta, Arizona

RICHARD MIKE IS THE SON OF THE LATE KING MIKE. Richard says his father never wanted to talk about the war. The only story his father ever told was about a fight over a rifle. Other stories came from his father's friend and from the contents of several steamer trunks that his father brought back from the war. Richard told a few stories attached to the items and how his father came to acquire them. The artifacts in these trunks are now on display in the Code Talker museum and in the fast food establishment that Richard owns in Kayenta, Arizona. Among these items are Chinese money, photographs taken during the war, his father's machine gun, a Japanese thousand-stitch belt, and a variety of objects from World War II. Some of the items raised issues with some of the local people, so Richard decided to take them down. The exhibition is a tribute to his father and to the Code Talkers, many of whom came from the local area. Tourists leave having learned about the Code Talkers, and the local *Diné* enjoy the recognition of their relatives.

King Mike was originally from Houck, Arizona. Like some of the Code Talkers, he lost his mother at age two and was raised by an older sister. He graduated in 1938 from the Phoenix Indian School, where Richard thinks he participated in football, wrestling, and boxing. The stories of his father's military service are sketchy and were filled in by friends and by other Code Talkers. Richard does know that his father fought in some of the bloodiest battles in Guam and Sugarloaf Hill in Okinawa. Such devastating battles and their outcomes can create an overwhelming reality for any soldier who has fought in war and witnessed the deaths of his comrades and enemies. How can a soldier weighed down by the atrocities of what he has seen and participated in during times of war begin to heal when he goes home? For some, the war is never over, as it wasn't for King Mike. Richard says he was wracked by survivor guilt all his life. Still, there were times when his wife's love sustained him during his R & Rs. While his father was in the marines, Richard's mother raised the children and lived near the post office so she could more quickly receive her husband's letters.

■ ■ ■

I am Bitter Water People clan, born for Big Water People clan. Many Goats People clan are my maternal grandfather clan and the Coyote Pass People are my paternal grandfathers. The Coyote Pass People are related to the Jemez Pueblo people. It must be so, because at my grandmother's house, we have rock corrals and a square rock house, which is definitely Pueblo.

My great-great grandfather was a Navajo cop back in the 1880s. It took him two days by horseback ride to get to Fort Defiance. When he first got there they told him to fill in the application. He got the job for Low Mountain. They asked him, "What is your name?" In Navajo he said something to the effect of "*Hastį́į́ Tóhńezhinii Biyé,* Son of Blackwater." They said to him, "Memorize Mike." And that was it. He only had one name. There's only one Mike family on the entire reservation with that last name, and I'm related to them.

My dad brought his machine gun back with him after World War II. He said that this Japanese fired at them and maybe hit somebody. They all hit the deck for cover. My dad said he started crawling as fast as he could on his hands and knees. He took a shot, but he was carrying a Thompson machine gun. It's not like a rifle, so he took one shot. It sprayed and I guess the steel fragments hit the Japanese's face. Then they all shot the poor guy all at once. There was a fight for the Japanese's gun as bullets whizzed by. They were right in the middle of the war and they're fighting for that stupid gun. That's the only story he ever told.

My dad never told me he was a Code Talker. He got drafted. He already had two children. I guess, you know, at the beginning of the war a lot of people joined, but then after a while, they still needed more people. So then they started drafting. They started getting down to people with one kid, then two kids, three kids. So he was drafted. My dad was truly bilingual. My dad said because he spoke perfect Navajo and English (the messages had to be relayed correctly in English) he was sent straight to the front. He said, "Damn! If I knew that I would have stuttered and spoke with an accent. I would have done anything to avoid the front lines."

Originally, my dad was with the First Provisional Brigade and they were totally wiped out on Guam. So they took the remnants, the leftovers from different divisions and regiments and created the Sixth Division. My dad got into Sixth Division and then they sent him to Okinawa and Sugar Loaf Hill. His regiment was wiped out a second time. That's where 2,666 were killed or wounded and then 1,289 went crazy. These Japanese didn't attack them. They left them to hang around for about a week. In nine days, 7,547 marines were killed. There were other hills next to Sugar Loaf where the other thousands of marines got killed. It was a jungle full of trees, but after they got through firing at it so many times, they knocked every tree out. It was just a barren hill. That was my dad's division, the Sixth Division. Both times, he came out without a scratch, and that's why I think he had this huge guilt all his life for having lived. I noticed, not only with my father, but also with Anglo marines, that they had Post Traumatic Stress Disorder. My dad had nightmares every night for years.

I didn't know he was a Code Talker, but I knew he used the language because of Husky Thorn's stories. Let me tell you a Husky Thorn story. He said they were crawling around Okinawa and you had to watch where you were crawling at night. You had to watch where you put your hands because of the bodies decaying. If you stuck your head up, it got shot. He said it was really scary. One night, they were saying they should have joined the navy. They had it made. They had their bunks, small as they were. They had their three squares [meals] a day on the ship and they sailed everywhere. They didn't have to go marching. They were bitching about their conditions and running out of water and having to pee in a foxhole. He said one time they were stuck there seven days and couldn't move. He said that morning the ocean was white and it was really weird. At first, they thought the waves were foam coming in, and so they sent a marine out to check. It was about 6,000 dead soldiers floating in from the kamikaze attacks. I don't know if it was the *Missouri,* or what ship it was. A couple of ships were totally destroyed by the kamikaze pilots, and so he said they quit bitching. Everybody was in the war. Another story that Husky Thorn told me was when they were laying on the ground, their chests would hurt because the bombs kept going off. They just kept going up and down and got sore. He told me some horrendous stories.

When you think about the Iraq war, a soldier is drafted and if he's married, generally what happens here on the reservation, about 90 percent of the time, is that the wife will move back with her mother and father, and they help raise the kids. Just like Lori Piestewa, is a good example. The kids moved in with her family; it's real typical. My mother raised us kids by herself during World War II. I asked my mother, "How come all these Navajo women moved in with their families but you had your own home?" She said, "Because Tuba City got mail three days a week, and I wanted letters from your father. Kayenta got mail only once a week." Back in those days, there were no roads. Sam Holiday [Code Talker] told me that when he and my dad got a thirty-day leave, my dad said he was going out to Blackwater to visit his wife and her family. This is before she moved to Tuba City to collect the mail. Sam said they hitchhiked out there. It took them two days to get to Blackwater. They walked most of the way.

He said when they got there, "Your grandmother invited us in and your aunts invited us to eat in the main hogan. They told your dad, 'Your wife is herding the sheep. We'll send a runner out after her.'" So they sent a runner. He said they sat there and they talked for about an hour. Finally, he got tired and he went to have a cigarette outside. Sam said, "I saw your mom get off a donkey when I was standing there. She didn't see me because I was standing behind the hogan. He said she had on a bunch of rags and had stringy black hair. She was in the sun, and she ran into the hogan. Then he went back to the main hogan and sat with my dad and talked to my grandmother and my aunts. He said, "Two hours of waiting passed with small talk." Then he said, "All of a sudden there was a knock on the door and my mother came in, and he said she was beautiful. Her hair was washed and curled. She had makeup on and was just the most beautiful woman he had ever seen." He said, "Here, just an hour ago she was full of rags and stringy hair and just the worst." The thing that got me was it took two days to get to my grandmother's place and so that's why she moved to Tuba City so she could get mail three days a week. My dad came back on an R & R to Tuba City. At that time, the highways stopped at 89 at Cameron. My sister was born when my father was still in the military. Every time he had a break, my mother got pregnant. He sent a letter to my sister before he went to Okinawa. She was just born. You could tell that he was worried about not coming back.

■ ■ ■

I remember thinking, "Where did those steamer trunks go? Where did my dad put them?" In 1990, by then the whole thing about the Code Talkers was out. I found that postcard about Okinawa. Then I read the book, *The Road to Tokyo*.

It says that 2,662 marines were killed on Okinawa from my dad's regiment, the Twenty-second Regiment. I talked to my business partner and she said, "Why don't we make a display?" At the time, people had this anti-war sentiment along with the peace movement and all. And so we thought, let's try it. So I built a little home and made a display case and put those Japanese posters and wolf cards[1] up. Some said I should have a squaw dance, Enemy Way ceremony. Just to placate them, I would say that I would. My father was Catholic.

There's a thing called a thousand-stitch belt. The Japanese have the concept of a Ghost Shirt,[2] you know, that bullets can't penetrate it. What they do is ask people to do a little stitch until they fill up the belt with stitches. And then they send it to their [soldier]. If you wear that thousand-stitch belt, you're not supposed to get killed. It's interesting, the Japanese come here and we tell them about the belt. They have all heard of them, but they have never seen them. And that's the first thing they go to, this thousand-stitch belt. I didn't know they had prayers in it. When I got it, I washed it, because it was dirty. My dad had two of them in the trunk for years. I went and laundered it, and then I discovered those prayers, paper prayers. So I took them out. And one of them has a coin in it, but you can't see the coin. I used to have it turned so you could see the coin sewed in there.

I have a postcard that says "Japanese University" on it. In World War I it was a Russian colony in China. It was real close to Peking. After the Japanese beat the Russians in World War I, they took it over, so when you read the postcards you see Japanese University or whatever, but it's in Tsingtao, China. In fact, my dad was in the occupation of China after they divided the Sixth Division. My dad had to fight a little bit more because they hadn't heard that the war ended. But my dad said towards the end of the war they started giving up. They could hear the guns and stuff getting closer and closer, so he said that the Japanese knew it was inevitable; they were losing the war. Towards the end, a lot of them just surrendered. He said when you read the books it says, "They fought to the death," but he said not at the end of the war. They wanted to come back out alive.

I got wolf cards and all they show is women with their breasts. I got the wolf cards but they're upside down. But it's interesting when I first set up those cards a couple of old Navajo ladies, rs, said, "You shouldn't have those cards in there."

---

[1] Wolf cards are playing cards showing female nudity.
[2] Ghost Shirts were worn by Native people as a form of resistance against colonization in the 19th century and as part of the Ghost Dance Movement. It was believed that the shirts were impervious to bullets.

Matter of fact, when I first set up those posters over here, the teachers came in and said, "You are teaching kids how to hate Japanese." And I said, "These are real." They said, "It doesn't matter because you're teaching our kids." So we took them down. And about those wolf cards, a couple of old Anglo marines said, "Come on, ladies. This was our entertainment during the war." They talked the ladies into leaving them up.

One thing that I noticed with the Code Talkers and with my dad and his friends, is their attitude. They just did their duty, and I can't stress that enough. They did what they had to do without moaning or groaning. A lot of Americans did what they had to do. I admire how the Code Talkers never bragged about what they did. They are very modest about it and didn't want people to know. I think in their mindset, at least when I talked to them, they couldn't see anything special about what they did any more than what other Americans did during World War II. That legacy I really like, because my god, my generation, they were taking off to Canada to stay out of the war. I can see some reason for that because, for example, minorities during World War II never got any medals. They never got any ribbons, never got any recognition. Okay, it was the Tuskegee Airmen who were black. The pilots were saying, "That guy just saved my life. Whoever is flying that plane over Germany, by god, he had better get a medal." They couldn't see he was black either. My dad had two ribbons for Guam for the 1st Provisional Brigade and for Sugar Loaf Hill. He had another ribbon, but the citation was given to the whole unit. All those medals are in the museum. He also has a high marksman medal. Man! He could shoot the eye of a bird flying.

He didn't get the medals for the occupation of China until way after the war. In my generation, during Vietnam, Americans were angry because it was an undeclared war. By then, the Blacks and the Mexicans and the Indians started to ask, "How come we're always at the front line? And how come the Anglos with college degrees are in the back? Why is that?" That's why they were going to Canada. But at least at our dinner table, the Mike dinner table, we would have fights. We would have battles because my dad didn't give a damn what you were or who you were. By god, if you were drafted, you go to war. You owed it to your country. My brother was in Vietnam in the Mekong Delta for two years sitting behind a .50 caliber machine gun. That's all he did for two years, go up and down the Mekong Delta. When he got out of the war, the first thing he did was join the Veterans against Vietnam. I was too young for Korea and too old and married for Vietnam.

I thought it would be good to continue the legacy of the Code Talkers with the descendants. Then as I thought about it, they did their thing and all the Americans did theirs. It's kind of like hanging on to Sitting Bull and Crazy Horse and to Geronimo. I don't have a problem hanging on to Sitting Bull and Geronimo. They were free, but those are our last heroes. My dad used to say, "We fought for the freedom of the white man. We don't have any freedom." We should ask the question, "How come Americans are free except Indians?" So I thought, no, maybe we won't have a legacy. I don't think that there should be a Code Talker Association.

Navajos join the military because some of them like the uniform. What are their options? I mean who are your role models? If your dad owns a gas station, you're going to go into the same field he is. We don't have businesses. And so you can become an artist and make crafts and make jewelry, or you can join the military. We don't have that many options and I think that's the main reason. Here in Kayenta alone we had, I think, 205 seniors graduate just a couple months ago. We don't have 205 new jobs this year. We have the same as last year and maybe even less than the year before. Probably half will join the military. There are not that many options and what are you going to do? Probably go to college or trade school, and then maybe a fourth go into the military.

My father died on Christmas Day, 1993, at seventy-two years of age. He died from alcoholism. But we don't know. I used to think he had post-traumatic stress disorder but don't anymore. My father went in about 1942 and stayed until the end of the war until 1945.

Michael Smith
son of Samuel Jesse Smith, Sr.
August 11, 2009, Window Rock, Arizona

MOTIVATED BY HIS FATHER, Samuel Smith, Michael joined the Marines and was placed in an all-Navajo platoon. He served with the Third Recruit Training Battalion, Kilo Company, Platoon 3043, from 1981 to 1985. Currently, he clerks for the Navajo Nation Supreme Court in Window Rock. Michael founded the annual Navajo Code Talker Day when he saw that no one was giving "a party" for the Code Talkers. On August 14, 2005, twenty-three years after President Ronald Reagan established Navajo Code Talker Day, Michael organized the first of the Navajo Code Talker day celebrations that are usually held at the Veteran's Memorial in Window Rock, where a statue of a Code Talker transmitting a message sits below the red rock with a hole in the center. The colorful event begins with a parade and a marching band followed by a prayer, drum song, speeches, awards, and a barbeque. It is a happy day for family and relatives to celebrate their fathers', grandfathers', great-grandfathers', brothers', and uncles' service. On this day, the heroes of the Navajo Nation and the United States are celebrated by everyone. The event grows larger every year and attracts over six hundred people annually.

■ ■ ■

I'm Michael Smith, Eagle Clan from the Pueblo of Acoma, and I am born for the *Naaneesht'éžhi táchii'nii*, the Charcoal Streaked Division of the Red Running Into the Water People clan. My maternal grandfather clan is the Sun Clan from the Pueblo of Acoma and my paternal grandfather clan is the *Tódích'ii'nii*, Bitter Water People clan.

I'm from Window Rock. I clerk for the Navajo Nation Supreme Court. I've been married for seventeen years and we have two boys. My father is Samuel

Jesse Smith, Sr., Navajo Code Talker. I have eight brothers and sisters and at last count we were somewhere around forty-nine grandchildren and somewhere around seventy great-grandchildren and three or four great-great-grandchildren. My father has somewhere around a little over 110 direct descendants.

I'm not sure when I realized what a Navajo Code Talker was. From pictures that my dad had, he went to the Fourth Marine Division reunion in 1969, and I was only seven then. Later, when he became active in the Navajo Code Talker Association, I found out that he was a Navajo Code Talker, and even then I still didn't realize what they did or what their role was in World War II and what they did for the Marine Corps. When I decided to join the Marine Corps and the all-Navajo Platoon is when my father started to tell me about World War II. The reason he joined the Marine Corps wasn't to become a Navajo Code Talker. He enlisted to defend our nation and to fight the Japanese because they bombed Pearl Harbor, and that was basically as much I knew. I had been asked to do certain things for the [Navajo Code Talker] Association and that's when I started to become aware of what their role was in World War II.

I think it's pretty sad on my part that I didn't retain the things I was told. Here on the reservation, we have our daily routines. Things outside of the reservation and outside of the United States were stories in far-off lands that didn't concern me, I thought, the same with World War II. We grew up during the Cold War, and always had this thing in the back of our heads that at any time somebody could push the button and nuke the world. The things that my dad grew up with and the things he had to experience [happened] even before he met my mom. I think my dad was protective on that. When you're a warrior and you go into battle, you put on things to protect yourself, and you say these prayers, and you go through these ceremonies. Then you go into battle to defend your family; you defend your country; you defend your livelihood and when you come back, you have a ceremony. And then you leave all those things where they were. So my dad didn't tell us a lot about World War II. He would say, "Yeah, I was in Saipan and Tinian and Roi-Namur and Iwo Jima," but that was just a place that was somewhere else.

I think the Marine Corps' decision to keep the code classified was a big part of [the silence]. But I think that there were also our Navajo beliefs that embraced the philosophy that you don't want to brag about it. You don't want to bring war to your home. Recently, I had the opportunity to go back to Iwo Jima with my dad. We also went to Guam, Tinian, Saipan, and Okinawa. When we were on Iwo Jima, I could see it in his face. He was very reserved. The trip took a lot of his strength. When we went to Saipan and Tinian, it was different because it wasn't as painful for him. But when we went to Iwo Jima, you could tell that he was going through a lot of things that were bringing up memories. There were times when he told me, "I had a dream about a friend of mine that was in the Marine Corps, and I hadn't thought about him for a long time." He was remembering things that he had put away for a long time. I think the suppression was part of the classification [of the code]. They were debriefed, "Don't tell anybody about this. Don't tell anybody about what you did." There were even times where they just didn't feel like what they did was something to be proud of, because it was war.

When we went to Iwo Jima, my dad said he was glad it didn't look the same. He said it was completely barren and everything was burned. It was just rock, dust, ash, and all the hills were smooth. There wasn't any life on the surface. He still had a lot of animosity about the Japanese being on Iwo Jima. The United States gave Iwo Jima back to Japan. We landed on a Japanese airbase and saw Japanese people and Japanese navy personnel on the island. All the things he had suppressed were coming out, which later on, after we left the island and were on our way back to Guam, he told me about his dreams. He didn't feel bad about it anymore, so it was actually a good thing that he saw the island. But for him to even talk about the things that happened back there, with the code being classified, it helped him to leave those things there.

We visited three islands that my father fought on: Saipan, Tinian, and Iwo Jima. It was the first time that I heard him say, "We could have transmitted over eight hundred messages in a single engagement and every one of the messages were very important, but I don't remember any of them." We were standing on Hill 500 in Saipan when my father said, "This is where the first wave landed and where the second wave landed." It was also where he landed with the third. They set up the headquarters and watched the battle ensue on Hill 500. You couldn't believe that the United States was fighting for these little itty-bitty islands out in the Pacific, and then you couldn't believe how many men were lost. To be standing there with my father, and for him to tell me this is how we were engaged and these are the movements that we made, brought those faraway lands and those faraway battles right to home, right to me, and it helped me to realize how fortunate we are—my brothers and sisters, nieces and nephews and their children. And how fortunate we are that my father was able to survive these battles and to be able to still raise us the way he did. It brought a greater appreciation of my father because he never spoke about them. The opportunity to be with him on that spot was remarkable and unforgettable.

When we landed on Iwo Jima, we drove out to the black beaches where the Fifth and Fourth Marine Divisions landed, and for my dad to actually give me a history lesson standing on that beach was amazing. We were having trouble walking in the sand, and to think that they were loaded down with their gear, radios, and equipment, and the Japanese were shooting at them all at the same time. We were standing there on that black beach and my father said, "You see this rock right here? This was the separation point. Anything on this side of that rock is where the Fifth Marines landed and advanced." It looked like a potato chip that had been stuck in the sand. Sixty years later the same rock is still standing there on the beach that is constantly moving and shifting. When the waves come in, it turns black. He said, "This is where we landed, and when we climbed the beach, it was a lot steeper and harder to climb to the top on the hill. We got stuck there because there was too much shooting coming across the airport. If you keep walking in that direction, you'll come across another airfield. The one we needed to take is right on top of this hill."

One of the stories he did tell about Iwo Jima, to set the record straight, was that the flag that they [first] raised on Mount Suribachi was smaller. The whistles and the bells and the ships sounded their horns and everybody cheered. Then later on, they took it down and set up the famous picture with the bigger flag. So that's another story my dad told me. I think about that time he was probably about eighteen. He enlisted when he was sixteen and actually went into battle when he was seventeen, that's what I figure. I think he said he earned enough points in two years to be discharged from his battle engagements.

President Ronald Reagan originally proclaimed Navajo Code Talker Day in 1982. On that particular day, Reagan asked for the state, government, and national agencies to celebrate that day. I believe I was in Okinawa that year. Three years ago, my mother passed away, and up to that time I had taken for granted my parents, that they would always be here. It was at that point that I realized that the time I spent with my dad is very precious. That was when I decided that I was going to celebrate my dad and all the Navajo Code Talkers at Window Rock. I wondered why none of the children wanted to put on a party for the Code Talkers. My idea of Navajo Code Talker Day is a party to celebrate our men, our fathers, our grandfathers, uncles, and brothers. This day is an opportunity to come out and honor the men. The Code Talkers always celebrated it on their own. The first year I approached the [Navajo Nation] president's office and I asked if there was anything they could do to help. With the president's office and various business and council delegates' help on the reservation, we were able to have a party. The following year, Councilman Larry Anderson presented a resolution to the tribal council. The legislation passed, and every August 14, we celebrate Navajo Code Talker Day.

The young marines, who we met when we were in Guam, took it upon themselves to personally take care of the Code Talkers while we were there. I mentioned Navajo Code Talker Day to them and every year they send a unit and help with fundraising, and a lot of things that I couldn't do on my own. We are celebrating Navajo Code Talker Day again at Navajo Veterans Memorial Park here in Window Rock and it's getting bigger. It's the only time that you'll ever see an exclusive Navajo Code Talker Parade. Without my boss, the chief justice supporting working on this project, it wouldn't be possible.

I think that if you look at the legacy of the Navajo Code Talkers it would be us, his children. I feel grateful that he survived those battles. Part of that legacy is to carry on the things that he taught me. I hope that I can pass that on to my children. It's unfortunate to take people for granted who are part of your history, as if they're always going to be there. Right now is the opportunity to do things for them. It's like when you put nice clothes in the drawer and moths eat them. By the time you pull them out to wear it may be too late. Preserving their legacy by building a Navajo Code Talker museum is a perfect opportunity to preserve the language and their stories in a unique way. I think that's why your book is very important. This is the time to preserve the unique stories about how the code was used in World War II.

Native Americans weren't thought of as any more than horses, property, or livestock. That is what's unfortunate, the story for minorities. These men used their language to create a code within their language and continued to add terms. My dad said, when they first started, they learned two hundred terms. By the time he was discharged, they had six hundred terms they had to memorize when they were in battle. But when they first started, they weren't used as radiomen. They weren't thought to have the intelligence to be radiomen. There were a lot of stories about them being used as point men in different squads because they had "Indian skills." They weren't relied upon to transmit a message on the radio, because another squad leader or another platoon may not have a Code Talker with them. So the Code Talker ended up running the message through enemy lines and getting shot at. My father told me that he had to hand carry messages when the lines were down. They were told it, and then they ran with it, and then they spoke it when they got there.

But it wasn't until a marine raider, who was part of the early squads, realized how vital it was to have secure communication. He had heard of the Navajo Code Talkers and requested Navajo Code Talkers in his unit on one of the islands south of Guam. He would have Code Talkers paratroop in with the unit, and when they dropped in, they called back locations of the enemy. They were basically a recon team, and they would radio back secured Japanese locations. They were able to penetrate Japanese lines on this island. That's how the Code Talkers were designed to be used, and it wasn't until that battle, that their significance was known. After that battle and the word got out, the commanders were asking for Code Talkers for their units. These are the stories that need to be preserved. These are the things that you don't read in books, and they're very hard to find because these men won't tell you what happened in battle.

I don't really have a lot of faith in the United States keeping and disseminating accurate information to the American people. I grew up on the Navajo Nation, and realized that when you open a book and you read a book about Navajo people that it's not true [laughs]. So I think that the United States has a lot to learn about preserving history and what they want the public to know. In wartime they call it propaganda, but it's something that I think the United States has to straighten out. I think the United States picks and chooses what they're going to preserve and what they're not going to preserve, and it's unfortunate because there's a lot of history that goes to the wayside.

I think that in the few years that I've been working with my dad, I have been learning from him. I've had the opportunity to meet a lot of the Code Talkers and honor them. To hear them depend on me and say, "You know, Mike, I think that we need to get this done," knowing that they believe in me and to have had the opportunity to meet a lot of these men that are now gone, that's very special. For them to share a part of themselves with me is something that I'll never forget.

Laura Tohe with her brother, Ben Tohe.

Laura Tohe
daughter of Benson Tohe
June 7, 2012, Mesa, Arizona

MY FATHER BENSON TOHE was *Tódích'íinii*, Bitter Water People clan, and born for *Tó'aheedlínii*, Water Flows Together People clan. My father spoke very little about his military service so I didn't learn he had been a Navajo Code Talker until 1983. He had just returned from Washington, D.C., where the Navajo Code Talkers had been honored. Sworn to secrecy like the other Code Talkers, my father didn't tell anyone in our family. Maybe that accounted for some of his reticence. He received eight commendations, including a Purple Heart, and a commendation for China where he was hospitalized. Like others in his generation, my father was grounded in Navajo traditional values and Navajo religion. He spoke fluent Navajo and English and was an avid reader. I am deeply grateful to both of my parents for having taught me *Diné bizaad*, The People's language. After he was discharged, my father attended college but before he could finish his studies, his father called him home to help with the Tohe Coalmine business. My parents had seven children, but they did not stay together. Two of my brothers served in the army, one in Special Forces who fought in Vietnam. Whatever it is that drives one toward extreme sport competition took hold of my father. He enjoyed the excitement and thrill of rodeos. He entered saddle-bronc competitions and sometimes won. Before he retired he was a welder. My father was born on April 16, 1926. He passed on August 2, 1994, after the public health doctors misdiagnosed his tuberculosis and gave him gall bladder surgery instead. He kept very few paper records of himself, as my brother and I found out when we took care of his personal effects. He had served in the Fifth Marine Regiment and First Marine Division and was honorably discharged at the corporal rank in April 1946. My father was posthumously awarded a silver medal on November 24, 2001, when the Navajo Nation formally recognized all of the Navajo Code Talkers at the Congressional Silver Medal Award Ceremony in Window Rock. When we cleaned out his hogan, I found his welder hats, dusty and aged, still hanging on the wall. Much of what I remember about my father is through his hats.

■ ■ ■

My father loved his hats—straw hats, felt cowboy hats, and welder caps. He liked to have his picture taken with his good going-to-town cowboy hat. *Diné* people believe in wearing their wealth. My uncle liked to have his picture taken wearing his tailor-made cowboy boots, or next to him in the photo. "Wait, wait," he's say, and he'd set his boots beside him. Only then could we snap the picture. Throughout his life, my dad kept three different kinds of hats—his good going-to-town felt cowboy hat in black or gray, a straw cowboy hat, and his welder caps. When his good going-to-town one became stained with a grease ring, he demoted it to his everyday hat. On his next trip to town, he bought a new one. In the 1970s he switched to straw cowboy hats. At home he kept his hat on the floor in the corner of the living room or in some out-of-the-way place where my brothers and I couldn't step on it.

I have a photo of my father holding his straw hat in his lap. My father didn't have many possessions during his lifetime; his hats were his pride, like jewelry is for some people. At home he wore his greased-stained hat most of the time, except for when we were having our meals. When he had to work under the car, he'd take it off and set it on the fence post or some nearby place. Years later, Jerame, my oldest son, would put his baseball cap on when he dressed. One morning when my mother was visiting he walked into the kitchen wearing his baseball cap. "You're just like your *nalí,* paternal grandfather," she said. "He used to put his hat on the first thing in the morning too."

When I was in fourth grade, one of my parents bought me a pet rabbit with a beautiful, soft, white coat. I don't remember what I called it. I kept it in a cage in the backyard and occasionally I'd bring it into the house. It was a quiet rabbit and didn't move around much, so it was easy to keep track of. One morning I brought my rabbit into the house and I must have forgotten to take it back to its cage when I left for school. When I returned home my mother's sewing machine sat on the kitchen table where she did all her sewing. She had one of those machines that could sew all kinds of fancy stitches on all kinds of fabric. Like my father's hats, the sewing machine was her pride. My mother held up my father's hat and bluntly said, "Look what your rabbit did," as she tried to stifle a laugh. My rabbit had nibbled the brim of my father's good black going-to-town hat!

The edges were scalloped where the rabbit bit into it. "*Dooládó' doodada!* What a terrible thing!" he cursed. "That was my good hat." It's not kind to laugh at others' misfortune but my mother and I couldn't help ourselves. My father didn't see the humor. "It's not funny!" he said. I think he threatened to make rabbit stew. After we stopped laughing, my mother said she could fix it. My rabbit wasn't allowed into the house after that. The next morning my father's hat sat proudly on the cushion back of the chair. Mom had cut a geometric pattern along the brim similar to the red geometric design on the Navajo rug dresses. Then she sewed the design with red thread. Mom was an excellent seamstress, so it looked almost new, except that the width of the hat was a little shorter. My father now had the most unique hat, but he still demoted it to his everyday hat that he wore to work.

We lived at Crystal, New Mexico, at this time. My mother worked at the school and my dad drove his foamy green GMC pickup truck to work in Fort Defiance, Arizona, where he worked as welder for the Navajo Tribe. A dirt road winds down the hill on the south side of the little community of Crystal. We lived almost a mile from there. In the early evening I could see my father's green GMC truck come over the hill, a small cloud of dust billowing behind. By the time I got past the cattle guard and was halfway to the trading post, I'd meet him. He'd stop and I'd get in for the one-minute ride home. Our ritual began with, "*Shitsi,'* my daughter, what did you learn in school today?" Most of the time I'd give him the same answer, "Nothing." "Nothing? Why are you going to school then?" he would ask. "I don't know," I would reply. He'd laugh. He said I should get as much out of education as I could. With that, we'd be home and parked under the Russian olive trees.

In the evenings when he took off his work boots, he had to set them outside to air out. My mother forbade him from setting his shoes inside the house. They sat at attention by the front door each night, mingling with all the outdoor smells. Our yard was fenced, so animals couldn't drag them away. In the morning he'd step back into them, eat breakfast, hat on, and off to work.

After my parents' divorce, my father returned to Coyote Canyon, New Mexico, where his family originated. They are part of my extended family, so

Benson Tohe, ca. 1945.

my brothers and I often visited or stayed with the Bitter Water side of our family that included our cousins, one male and five girls. The Tohe side had once been a wealthy family. My father's father, *shinalí hastiin*, paternal grandfather, Benny Tohe, had served in World War I in Europe and had been wounded. He had held political office as a councilman for the Mexican Springs, New Mexico, chapter. A photo once hung in the chapter house with him, his wife, Glen, my *nail asdzą́ą́,* paternal grandmother, and a group of people. I was surprised at how modern my grandmother looked in comparison to the other ladies in the photo. She wore a coat with a fur collar and a short hairstyle. I remember very little about my grandfather except that he owned the Tohe Coalmine. Much of what I know came from my mother's stories.

My father never spoke of being a Code Talker, or radioman, as they were called in the marines, and he said very little about World War II, period. Once he caught my brothers imitating the war movies we had seen. "War is nothing to play at!" he scolded. He had been hospitalized for his service injuries in Peking, China, now renamed Beijing. He said he's been to the Great Wall of China and had to wait hours for his Peking duck order to arrive. In 2010 I visited the Great Wall and thought of my father as a young man standing on one of the thousands of ancient steps that wound upward. What must he have thought seeing this sight so far away from home, so far away from *Dinétah*? Perhaps the Chinese thought he was one of theirs, as my father had Asian features. He received eight commendations, including a Purple Heart for wounds received. He gave it to my mother and she passed it on to me.

In late July 1983 I was back from the Midwest, where I was living at the time. It was a warm afternoon when we arrived to find my father sitting on a stool outside his hogan swatting flies with the Navajo homemade fly swatter, a piece of black inner tube nailed to a stick. Happy to see his grandson, he hugged him and sat him on his lap. He lived in a hogan without electricity and indoor plumbing, only a yellow gas range for his cooking that was hooked up to a butane gas tank. He wore his tan-colored straw cowboy hat. He was retired now and was a sheepherder for his sister and tended his small garden that he said the rabbits kept raiding. He had put up a fence to keep them out. This day he had many stories to tell, and it was the first time I learned that he had been a Code Talker. One of his dogs sat nearby in the shade as if he wanted to hear the stories too.

My father, with Johnson Benally, who was also a Navajo Code Talker, and my clan sister, Betty, had recently driven to Washington, D.C., for an honoring of the Navajo Code Talkers. Along the way they stopped to sightsee. When they got to Washington, they marched in a parade and each of the Code Talkers was given a silver medallion. "They gave me this," he said, and held out the silver medallion. I held it in my hand. It looked like a little shield. Had I known what the Code Talkers did during the war, I would have asked him more questions. As it was, he didn't elaborate. In 2009 when I interviewed Keith Little, his long-time friend, I said that my father didn't talk about being a Code Talker. He sensed I was looking for the pieces of my father's military life. I'll never forget his reply, "Maybe your father felt you weren't ready to understand. Maybe he was saving it for when you could." Mr. Little spoke of Navajo storytelling ethics. Stories enrich our lives and yet they can harm us if we aren't emotionally mature for them. My grandmother withheld stories from me that had sexual themes. She said, "I'll tell you after you're married." I held my father's medal in my hand and there remained so much mystery of why he received it. After my father passed, I didn't find his medal among his possessions nor did I find many records of his military service. That was the only time he spoke of being a Code Talker. Recently, I found a photo of the Navajo Code Talkers on the Museum of the American Indian website taken at the July 1983 honoring. I searched for my father's face among the Code Talkers but didn't see him. My father didn't take part in the Navajo Code Talker Association meetings and events at home.

His storytelling turned to school. He had attended Rehoboth Mission School, just outside Gallup. He said he'd been to school at St. Catherine's in Santa Fe, but it had been difficult living in a Catholic parochial school. Both of my parents attended that boarding school and had known of each other. He hated St. Catherine's. The nuns made him get on his knees and walk down the aisle to the altar. Living under rigid Catholic rules and punishments made him decide to run away when he was twelve. He told his friend, "I'm going to run away." His friend said, "I'll go with you." Together they made the more than 350-mile trek back to their homes. In those days and into the 1970s, Indian children sometimes ran away from the boarding and parochial schools where they lived for long stretches of time without seeing their families. It must have been a difficult journey because vehicles on the reservation were rare in those days. My father's parents enrolled him at Ganado Mission School, a Presbyterian mission school at the time. He liked it there, he said. While there he met Keith Little. Both worked at the school to help pay their tuition and were roasting wild rabbits the day Pearl Harbor was attacked. Eight months after that my father's parents signed their permission for him to enlist, because he was only sixteen and underage. It was Saturday, November 13, 1943. My father must have been in the tenth or eleventh grade at the time. The military records record his age as seventeen.

After WWII ended and the young Navajo marines were discharged, many did not have a high school diploma, including my father. Riverside Indian School in Riverside, California, where my grandmother taught, accepted such students; among those were some of the Code Talkers. My father's records show that he took college courses in bookkeeping at the Western School for Private Secretary. I assume the G.I. Bill enabled his studies. Around that time, my grandfather, Benny Tohe's, coal mine business was growing at Coyote Canyon. He called my father home to help, so my father didn't complete his studies. At some point, my parents met again as young adults, married, and began raising our family. Coal was in demand as an energy source at many of the reservation schools. A number of *Diné* men were hired to work in the mine and to deliver coal to the schools. My mother said her charge, besides taking care of our family, was to drive to Gallup in the 2-ton truck to buy dynamite for the mine. She said she didn't know how dangerous it was for her to drive her friend and me, still a baby, into Gallup to buy and make the delivery. As my family's wealth increased, we owned a number of horses that Hollywood filmmakers sometimes rented when they made films in the local area. My *nalí* Glen used to have a color photo of a group of horses lined up with "Hollywood Indians" in full feather headdresses. My father bought a full-blood quarter horse for my mother named Nippy that he entered in the horse racing competition at the rodeos. The Cold War was in effect and energy companies sought cheap resources from the reservation. At some point, my father prospected in uranium, but my mother didn't say what became of that. Eventually the Tohe Coalmine business came to an end. Once I asked my father where it was and all he said was, "It's over there," with a wave of his hand to the east. I took that to mean he didn't want to talk about it.

Maybe it was around the time of the Tohe Coalmine business that my father began to enter extreme rodeo as a saddle-bronc rider. The family had horses and the means to enter into rodeo and racing competitions. My father was a true *Diné* cowboy. To win or place he had to stay on the wild bucking horse for the required amount of time. My mother said he won sometimes. Every year we attended the Flagstaff Pow-Wow, as it was called then, but without the colorful dancers and drum music that it is today. He wore his competition number flapping on his back and always his felt cowboy hat. My younger brother, Ben, took up bull riding in his youth, perhaps following in our father's extreme rodeo footsteps. Rodeo is big on the Navajo reservation. When my father was in his 50s, he was inducted into the All Indian Rodeo Cowboys Association (AIRCA) Hall of Fame.

After the Tohe Coalmine business closed my father became a welder. Sometimes when we drove through the reservation he would point out water tanks and buildings where he had worked, places where he suffered injuries to his hands and face. After he retired, he didn't travel far from home. He received news through the radio and the *Gallup Independent* that arrived daily in the white metal tube posted by the highway near his hogan. He enjoyed reading, and it seemed he always had subscriptions to *Western Horseman* and *Reader's Digest.*

During the summers my older brothers and I occasionally stayed with our father and extended family, who owned a herd of cattle and horses. Since the herd belonged to the entire family, everyone had to take responsibility for them. This meant riding on horseback to round up the cows for branding, vaccinations, and whatever else was needed in the summer months. I was happy to get out of doing domestic chores and to saddle up to look for our cattle. In the morning my *nalí* Glen packed our lunches, a tortilla sandwich with peanut butter and jelly or a tortilla and spam sandwich. My cousin and I made Kool-Aid and poured it into our thermos jug. It was an all-day trip in the hot summer and a hat was essential. On the wall of the hogan hung my father's welder caps, a navy blue one with white polka dots left over from his welder days. Since I didn't have a hat, my father said I should wear one of his. I chose the red one. I liked wearing it and what it represented. I was fourteen and happy with my adult responsibility to ride horseback all day to round up our family's cattle. My cousin Winifred, who had been groomed by her mother Ethel, my dad's sister, to care for the cattle, wore my father's navy blue hat. She was a few years younger than me and knew our family's brands and even some of the cows by their spots and markings. My father wore his gray felt everyday cowboy hat.

After loading our packs with lunch, Kool-Aid, and water, we rode away for the day. Some days we rode to the south, other days to the west and north. Once we rode west to the little community of Mexican Springs. My cousin and I were happy to come upon the trading post where we bought a candy bar. My father didn't liked sweets, so my cousin and I shared the treat before heading down the long hill eastward toward home.

By the time we crossed Highway 666, the afternoon sun was dropping into the western horizon. We had found a few of our cattle that we herded home slowly. My aunt would keep an eye out for us. When we neared the old windmill, and she saw the little dust cloud behind the horses, she told my girl cousins to begin the evening meal in time for our arrival. We were tired, hot, and happy to be almost home. My father rode a little farther behind us, like he was guarding our backs. The saddle creaked under me, as the horses stepped over sagebrush and the holes of the prairie dog homes. Then I heard my father singing. I glanced back at him. He wore his cowboy hat. He was singing in Navajo, singing us home with a riding song.

King Mike.

With a brave heart, you have fought.
—RONALD REAGAN

Diné Bizaad bee Nidasiibaa
With the Navajo Language We Fought a War

WE WERE SO YOUNG THEN; our youth was still unfolding behind desks in classrooms and within the red earth of our homeland. The earth held our birth stems in the cup of her hands as she held the stories of long ago, as she held the stories of our ancestors return from *Hwéeldi* just a few generations ago.

We carry those stories of long ago even as we offer prayers to greet the white light that brings the Dawn People, as we hold corn pollen on our tongues and on our heads. It has always been this way growing up *Diné*.

Elders' teachings taught us to be hearty people, to be grateful for this life, for the air and water that sustain us, for the strength of sacred mountains that surrounds and protects us in all directions. In winter as in all seasons, make prayers to the Dawn People and to *Nahasdzáán*, Our Mother. Let not sleep steal the day. Life should have difficulty so that we may know times of ease.

One day a voice on the radio entered our world while mothers prepared the afternoon meal and fathers tended the horses. The horses turned towards the wind. The sheep rustled uneasily in the corral. When the call came barely 16 year boys still without facial hair signed away the last of their boyhood and stepped into uncertain manhood for a country that had always taken, removed, and stolen Indian lives.

We left with tender blessings and prayers of protection. Dressed in the language of The People we headed toward a battle with the Slant-Eyed People. We moved further into danger on a floating metal ship that broke into unknown worlds. We gave ourselves over to the warrior way. Our bodies, our lives were not ours since the day we took the oath. For love, for The People, for the ones back home, for the love of our children, for *Nahasdzáán,* for the nation of America as it is called now.

At night we look out over the Pacific Ocean, the home of *Asdzą́ą́ Yołgai.* The air covered us with a thick skin of moisture before we went below. In the early morning light the voices from home return:

Shiyazhí, ch'éénídzííd. Heełkááhdą́ą́' tsodílzin.
Beloved one, wake up. Say your prayers at dawn.
With prayers the Holy People brought
the gift of hozho to begin each day.

Shiyazhí, ha'íí'ą́. Nídiilyeed áko nits'íís bidziil doo
Beloved one, the sun has risen
Nourish your body in the early morning with a run
I wiped away the sands of sleep and ran and ran until my lungs hurt.

Shiyazhí, áłtsé yidzaazígíí bii' nani'na' áko binhají hadíítxih
Beloved one, rub yourself with the first snow and you will have a long life.
I rubbed the first snow on my body so that I can endure hardship.

Shiyazhí, na'ashǫ́'ii dich'ízhii nicheii át'é dóó nich'ą́ą́h sizį́
Beloved one, the horned toad is your grandfather and protector.
I placed him over my heart to protect me.

O Mother, O Holy People, O Sacred Mountains protect me, O Four Directions I am your child. 'Mama Water take care of me.' Here is my corn pollen. I will put it in my chewing gum so the military men won't think I am violating their laws.

Back at boarding school teachers told us to forget our language. Don't speak Navajo. Speak only English. They want us to speak only the language of the enemy because they want us to forget who we are. Now, in this war that carries us across the big water we are armed with our language. Our tongues will form the shapes and sounds of Bougainville, Guadalcanal, Suribachi, Saipan. Iow Jima will teach us a new song.

With hardship a way of life at home, we survived military life.
With *Diné bizaad* we were armed.
With *Diné bizaad* we went into battle.

It was a good day to die.
It was a good day to return
to the arms of our beloved homeland
and the earth that holds our birth stems to this day.

It was a good day to return to America
with honor, with love, with gratitude.

—LAURA TOHE
*Written on the occasion of
honoring the Navajo Code Talkers*

Acknowledgments

THIS BOOK WAS MADE POSSIBLE with the support and help of many who came forth with maps, directions, hospitality, kindness, and hard work. With appreciation and gratitude to my son Dez Tillman and to Dr. Jennifer Wheeler for the many hours they worked to transcribe and translate. To Ronald Kinsel, Michael Smith, Winifred Devore, and Candace Martinez, who helped in locating the Code Talkers and to dear friend, Dr. Evangeline Parsons Yazzie, for her editorial work. To Delono Ashley and Rex Harvey for their interpretations.

With special thanks to the families and descendants of the Code Talkers who helped tell the stories of their fathers and grandfather: Michael Smith, Frank Brown, Francine Brown, Herbert Goodluck and sisters Clara and Joanne Goodluck, Richard Mike, and a special thanks to Larry P. Foster for sharing his Code Talker research. To the family members of the Code Talkers who helped make these conversations possible: George James Jr., Barbara Billey, Kurt Etsicitty, Shirley Barry, Perry Begay, Velma Anderson and daughter, Carm and Tommy Jones, and to my long-time friend, Juanita Lowe. To the daughters of Tom Jones, thank you for your generous hospitality and delicious "soul food."

Thank you Tony Abeyta, artist extraordinaire, for your inspiration; to the Chinle Holiday Inn for making interview space available; to Joe Rueda, former student who first brought passionate attention of the Code Talkers' importance to my class. Thank you to Albert Smith who gave me a blessing for this book. With much gratitude to my friend and collaborator, Deborah O'Grady, whose beautiful portraits grace this book. Finally, to Caroline Cook, my editor, thank you for your patience and support for the years it took to complete this project. If I have forgotten anyone, know that you are included too.

This book was also made possible with funds from the ASU Exemplar Funds and by Rio Nuevo Publishers.

And with deep gratitude to the spirits who protect and guide my creative work. May they always surround me.

Ahéhee' nitsaa everyone.

Index

Acoma Pueblo, NM, 132, 231
Akee, Dan, 13–15
Albuquerque, NM, 21, 25, 26,
    33, 42, 77, 94, 132, 147,
    174, 189, 199, 207
Alcatraz Island, 85, 207
alcoholism, 8, 168, 229
Alfred, Johnny, 200
All Indian Rodeo Cowboys
    Association Hall of Fame,
    246
Anderson, Edward, 17–19
Arizona State University, 65,
    205, 206
Augustine, John, 200
Beautyway philosophy, 35
Beech Aircraft, 66, 70
Begay, Jerry, 200
Begay, Jimmy, 21–27
Begay, Perry, 21
Begaye, Fleming, 86, 103, 200
Bellemont Depot (Flagstaff,
    AZ), 21
Benally, John, 31, 199, 206
BIA (Bureau of Indian Affairs),
    6, 36, 66, 71, 147, 206
Billey, Wilfred E., 29–33
Billison, Sam, 33, 202, 206
Billiman, Howard, 31, 200
Billy, Sam, 32
Black Rock, 23
Blessing Way ceremony, 8, 89,
    91, 97, 136, 192, 201
boarding schools, 5–6, 14, 17,
    24, 50, 57, 74, 93, 109,
    126, 141, 147, 199, 244,
    248
bodyguards, 27, 97, 104, 119,
    137, 153, 159, 202, 206
    Dooley, Raymond A., 202
Born for Water, 102, 106
Bosque Redondo. See Hwéeldi
Bougainville, Guam, 97, 153
Bread Springs, NM, 139
Brisbane, Australia, 76
Brown, Frank and Francine,
    187–195

Brown, John, 187–195, 200,
    206
Bureau of Indian Affairs. See
    BIA
Burke, Bobby, 200
Burr, Sandy, 32
Cadman, Bill, 95, 206
Camp Elliott, 7, 31, 32, 46, 86,
    94, 102–103, 154, 200
Camp Matthews, 67
Camp Pendleton, 36, 59, 69,
    86, 87, 113–114, 118, 126,
    133, 165, 180, 189, 202
Camp Tarawa, 30
Canyon de Chelly, 188
Cape Gloucester, New Britain,
    76, 78, 96
Carson, Colonel Kit, 4
Cattle Chaser, Dennis, 95
Chemawa, OR, 170–171
Chinle, AZ, 1, 4, 26, 35, 71,
    103, 106, 129, 155, 163,
    166, 167, 188, 189, 219
Church Rock, NM, 141
Chuska Mountains, 24, 65, 109
clans
    Big Water People, 22, 66,
    94, 211, 224
    Bitter Water People, 13,
    36, 66, 73, 110, 126, 148,
    178, 224, 231, 239, 243
    Black Sheep People, 211,
    212
    Black Streak Wood People,
    57, 94, 132, 143
    Charcoal Streak People,
    22, 148, 231
    Coyote Pass People, 66,
    188, 193, 224
    Folded Arms People, 57
    Late Salt, 36
    Many Goats People, 13,
    57, 110, 224
    Many Houses, 86
    Meadow People, 110
    Mexican People, 36, 94,
    154, 160, 178

    Mountain Ridge People,
    198, 199
    Mud People, 154
    Near the Water People, 66,
    96, 110, 198
    One Who Walks Around,
    22
    Red Cheek on Side of Face
    People, 30
    Red House People, 45,
    126, 198, 211
    Red Running into Water
    People, 22, 30, 45, 86, 148,
    160, 211, 231
    Reed People, 126
    Salt People, 13, 36, 86,
    132, 143
    Start of the Red Streak
    People, 73, 193
    Tangle People, 73, 178,
    188, 193
    Towering House People,
    13, 22, 45, 86, 110, 154,
    198, 208
    Within His Cover People,
    178
    Water Flows Together
    People, 73, 211, 239
    Water's Edge People, 45,
    73, 94, 126
Claw, Thomas, 75
Clifton, AZ, 178
Coal Mine, AZ, 13
College of Santa Fe, 33
Congressional Medal of Honor,
    7, 106, 194, 209, 240
Cornfield, AZ, 148
Coyote Canyon, NM, 1, 241,
    245
Crownpoint, NM, 21, 24, 103,
    104, 131, 155, 177, 178,
    183
Crystal, NM, 109, 162, 187,
    188, 193, 241
Cuba, NM, 38
Diné College, 66, 216, 217
Draper, Teddy, 4, 35–43, 60,

205, 206
Enemy Way ceremony, 1, 15, 63, 103, 135, 151, 227
Etsicitty, Kee, 45–47
Etsitty, Deswood, 200
Farmington, NM, 29, 65, 88, 89
First Provisional Brigade, 225
Flagstaff, AZ, 15, 21, 42, 52, 59, 71, 165, 199, 204, 205, 246
Fort Defiance, AZ, 24, 113, 127, 138, 155, 167, 189, 193, 197, 198, 199, 205, 206, 224, 241
Fort Sumner. *See* Hwéeldi
Fort Wingate, NM, 14, 40, 47, 141, 143, 189, 211, 216
Fort Wingate High School, 45, 66, 102, 138, 173, 199
Foster, Larry P., 197–209
Gallup, NM, 3, 45, 79, 86, 88, 94, 113, 131, 132, 137, 143, 165, 166, 167, 197, 199, 214, 244, 245
Gallup Veterans' Memorial Plaza, 45
Ganado, AZ, 1, 19, 110
Gatewood, Joe, 95
G.I. Bill, 33, 138, 160, 213, 216, 245
Gilbert Islands, 200, 201
Gishal, Milton, 200
Goodluck, Clara, Joanne, and John, 211–221
Gorman, Carl, 191, 193, 200, 203, 206
Guadalcanal, 9, 19, 31, 36, 46, 76, 94, 104, 105, 126, 155, 190, 203, 215
Guam, 37, 43, 86, 87, 115, 153, 155, 156, 160, 205, 223, 225, 228, 233, 235, 236
Haskell Institute [Indian University] Lawrence, KS, 169
Hayes, Ira, 39, 69, 70
Hilo, HI, 37, 67, 70
Hogan Station, NM, 137
Hogback, NM, 85
Holbrook, AZ, 23, 205
Holiday, Samuel, 49–63, 103, 226
Honolulu, HI, 68, 156
Houck, AZ, 223

Hunters Point Naval Hospital (San Francisco, CA), 77
Hwéeldi (Fort Sumner), 4, 47, 49, 50, 58, 80, 81
Iwo Jima, 9, 13, 35, 37, 38, 40, 62, 67, 85, 87, 104, 116, 117, 126, 147, 150, 153, 156, 160, 164, 182, 201, 202, 203, 205, 232, 233, 234
James, George, 65–71
Japan (islands of), 29, 30, 31, 32, 33, 37, 66, 68, 77, 116, 117, 126, 148, 155, 156, 160, 161, 162, 182, 202, 203, 218, 233
Johnson, Peter, 40, 200
Johnston, Philip, 6, 30, 103
Jones, Jack, 5, 9, 73–83
Jones, Tom, 8, 85–91
Kayenta, AZ, 14, 19, 49, 58, 126, 219, 223, 226, 229
Kellwood, Joe, 93–99, 103
King, Jimmy, 206
Kinlahcheeny, Paul, 40, 200
Kinsel, John, 6, 101–107, 156, 214
Kirk, George, 32, 206
Kontz, Rex, 32, 206, 215
Laguna Pueblo, NM, 131, 132, 153, 154
Las Vegas, NM, 33
Leupp, AZ, 154
Little, Keith, 5, 109–123, 206, 244, 245
Long Walk, 4, 9, 80
Lukachukai, AZ, 24, 65, 101, 159, 160, 211, 216
Lukachukai Community School, 175
Lupton, AZ, 147, 150
Manti, UT, 191
Manuelito, Ben, 78
Manuelito, John, 31
Many Farms, AZ, 166, 174
marine battalions and divisions
First Marine Division, 76, 94, 95, 97, 148, 155, 239
First Signal Battalion, 76, 78
Second Marine Division, 145, 200, 201, 203
Third Marine Division, 40, 155, 211

Third Recruit Training Battalion, 231
Fourth Marine Division, 37, 40, 115, 155, 133, 232, 234
Fifth Marine Division, 9, 37, 201
Thirty-second Battalion, Division Headquarters, 85
Marshall Islands, 13, 37, 115, 150
Martin, Matthew, 200
McCabe, Edward, 76
McDonald, Peter, 206
"Meat grinder" (Hill 382), 116
medicine man, 8, 42, 63, 71, 88, 103, 106, 126, 138, 184, 188, 204, 207, 208
Mike, King, 200, 223–229, 248
Mike, Richard, 219, 223–229
Monster Slayer, 102, 106
Montezuma Creek, UT, 74, 79, 80, 81, 83
Monument Valley, 57, 74
Morenci, AZ, 66, 179
Mount Suribachi, 38, 40, 67, 69, 70, 147, 155, 156, 201, 234
Mount Taylor, 154
Nagasaki, Japan, 32, 101, 105, 161, 162, 203
Nahkai, James, 206
National Biscuit Company, 167, 168
National Navajo Code Talkers Day, 1, 118
Native American Rights Fund, 81
Navajo Code Talker Association, 3, 4, 30, 101, 106, 131, 195, 232, 243
Navajo language, 3, 5, 6–7, 8, 9, 10, 17, 21, 30–31, 33, 36, 38, 42–43, 47, 49–50, 62, 74, 75, 77, 80, 83, 91, 93, 99, 104, 114, 119, 121–122, 133–134, 141, 148, 149, 154, 157, 175, 179, 183, 197–198, 201–202, 204, 211, 214, 218–219, 220, 225
sacred qualities of, 13, 26, 50, 63, 91, 122, 107, 119, 204

importance of maintaining, 13, 26, 33, 71, 91, 99, 103, 122, 157, 218
New Caledonia, 46, 75
New Guinea, 19, 95, 155
New Mexico State College, 33
New Zealand, 29, 31, 104, 200
Nez, Freeland, 200
Notah, Willie, 200
Oakland Hospital, CA, 19
Oceanside Naval Hospital, CA, 79
Okinawa, Japan, 9, 31, 32, 87, 97, 126, 181–182, 223, 225, 226, 227, 233, 235
Oliver, Willard, 200
Pawnee Nation College, OK, 129
Peaches, Alfred, 60, 125–129
Peking, China, 227, 243
Peleliu Island group, 96
Phoenix, AZ, 17, 18–19, 25, 41, 59, 74, 93, 99, 113, 126, 199, 219
Phoenix College, AZ, 129
Phoenix Indian Center, 206
Phoenix Veterans Hospital, 17
Post-traumatic Stress Disorder (PTSD), 8, 13, 41, 49, 102, 159, 225, 229
Provo, UT, 59
Pueblo Indian culture, 73, 224
Pueblo Pintado, NM, 177, 183
Purple Heart, 35, 41, 77, 105, 106, 203, 239, 243
radiomen, 3, 5, 6–7, 30, 46, 236
Red Lake, AZ, 24
Red Valley, AZ, 180
Roi-Namur Marshall Islands, 13, 115, 150, 232
Rough Rock, AZ, 1
Russell Island, 77, 78, 95
Saipan, 9, 13, 29, 30, 31, 32, 37, 42, 59, 115, 126, 150, 155, 160, 180–181, 182, 190, 205, 232, 233,
San Diego, 32, 52, 59, 75, 79, 86, 87, 102, 118, 119, 126, 133, 143, 155, 156, 164, 174, 179, 182
San Juan Pueblo, NM, 73
San Xavier Indian Sanitorium, Tucson, AZ, 138
Sanders, AZ, 23

Santa Fe, NM, 25, 88, 102, 132, 179, 208, 244
Sasebo, Japan, 68, 161
Sawmill, AZ, 21, 40, 125
schools
    Albuquerque Indian School, 147, 189, 207
    Chemawa Indian School, 170, 171
    Chilocco Indian School, 70, 213
    Fort Defiance Indian School, 24, 102, 138, 199
    Ganado Mission School, 110, 113, 244
    Intermountain School, 171, 174
    Navajo Mission School, 199
    Phoenix Indian School, 74, 223
    Presbyterian Mission School, 110, 244
    Rehoboth Christian School, 139, 244
    Riverside Indian School, 245
    Santa Fe Indian School, 31, 211, 213
    St. Catherine Indian School, 102, 244
    St. Michaels Indian School, 102, 211, 213
Shiprock, NM, 65, 70, 74, 95, 103, 155
Shiprock High School, 33, 86, 199
Shonto, AZ, 126
Smith, Albert, 9, 131–139, 141, 143, 204, 205
Smith, George, 141–145
Smith, Jessie, 206
Smith, Michael, 9, 231–237
Smith, Samuel Jesse, Sr., 9, 147–151, 231
Snider, Duke, 198, 205
Solomon Islands, 133, 155
St. George, UT, 49
St. Michaels, AZ, 18, 193, 211
Sugarloaf Hill, 223
Tarawa Atoll, 31, 104, 190, 200
Thompson, Frank, 200
Thorn, Husky, 225
Tinian, Mariana Islands, 13,

29, 32, 115, 150, 160, 180, 190, 232, 233
Todacheene, Carl, 208
Todachine, Paul, 40
Tohatchi, NM, 23
Tohe, Ben, 238
Tohe, Benson, vi, 1, 66, 112, 200, 239–247
Tohe, Laura, 239–247
Toledo, Andrew, 95
Toledo, Bill, 102, 103, 153–157, 183
Toledo, Frank, 38
Treaty of Guadalupe Hidalgo, 80, 82
Tsaile, AZ, 65, 66
Tso, Chester, 200
Tso, Samuel, 7, 75, 159–175, 206
Tsosie, David, 29, 30
Tsosie, Samuel Sr., 60
Tuba City, AZ, 13, 58, 95, 103, 114, 155, 226
Two Grey Hills, NM, 199
University of New Mexico, 33, 129
University of Wyoming, Laramie, 133
USS *Arthur Middleton*, 203
USS *Dashing Wave XAP*, 203
USS *Karnes*, 203
USS *Mount Vernon*, 46
USS *Sandoval*, 203
Wellington, New Zealand, 200
Wheaton College, IL, 33
Willeto, Frank Chee, 177–184
Wilson, William Dean (formerly Yazzie), 200
Window Rock, AZ, 7, 9, 30, 106, 107, 129, 137, 138, 155, 183, 187, 199, 206, 211, 212, 219, 231, 235, 240
Window Rock Veteran's Memorial, 210, 231, 235
Wingate Ordnance Depot. *See* Fort Wingate
Winslow, AZ, 125, 165, 205
Yosemite National Park, 19
Zuni Pueblo, NM, 132, 208

About the Author

LAURA TOHE is *Tsé Nahabiłnii,* Sleepy-Rock People clan, and born for the *Tódích'íinii,* Bitter Water People clan. *Jóhonaa'éí Tółání déé',* The Sun Clan People, from Laguna Pueblo, are her maternal grandfathers. *Ma'ii Deeshgiizhnii,* The Coyote-Pass People clan, are her paternal grandfathers. She is the daughter of Code Talker Benson Tohe, and grew up on the eastern border of the Diné (Navajo) homeland. A poet, writer, and librettist, Laura's work has been widely published. She is also a professor with Distinction in the Department of English at Arizona State University. She lives in Mesa, Arizona.

PHOTO BY JULIARE SCOTT

About the Photographer

DEBORAH O'GRADY is a fine art photographer whose work has been exhibited nationally and internationally, and as a video projection for live concert performance at the world premiere of *Enemy Slayer* at the Phoenix Symphony. She has been a regular presenter at the national Art & Psyche conferences and is the founding chairperson of the Friends of the (San Francisco Jung) Institute. Her work with Meyer Sound Labs in Berkeley, California, led to the creation of the patent-pending Libra System—passive acoustically absorbent images that meld art and science. Deborah's work may be seen at www.deborahogrady.com. She lives in Berkeley, California.